Music
PHYSICIAN
FOR TIMES TO COME

Other Books and Tapes by Don G. Campbell
Books
Music and Miracles, Quest Books, 1992
100 *Ways to Improve Teaching with Your Voice and Music*,
Zephyr Press, 1992
Rhythms of Learning, Zephyr Press, 1991
The Roar of Silence, Quest Books, 1989
Master Teacher, Nadia Boulanger, Pastoral Press, 1984
Introduction to the Musical Brain, Magna Music, 1983
Compact Disc
Essence, Spirit Music, 1993
Sound Cassettes
The Roar of Silence, cassette book, Quest Books, 1993
Accelerating Learning with Your Voice and Music, Zephyr Press, 1992
The Power of Overtone Singing, IMHE, 1992
Healing Powers of Tone & Chant, Quest Books, 1990
Healing Yourself with Your Own Voice, Sounds True, 1990
Cosmic Classics, Spirit Music, 1988
Crystal Rainbows, Spirit Music, 1986
Runes, Spirit Music, 1986
Angels, IMHE, 1985
Crystal Meditations, Spirit Music, 1985
Lightning on the Moon, IMHE, 1985
Video
The Roar of Silence, Quest Books, 1992

Music
PHYSICIAN
FOR TIMES TO COME

An anthology
by Don Campbell

*This publication made possible with
the assistance of the Kern Foundation*

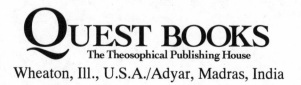

QUEST BOOKS
The Theosophical Publishing House
Wheaton, Ill., U.S.A./Adyar, Madras, India

The Theosophical Publishing House
P.O. Box 270
Wheaton, IL 60189-0270

A publication of the Theosophical Publishing House,
a department of The Theosophical Society in America

Library of Congress Cataloging-in Publication Data

Music : physician for times to come / Don Campbell, [editor].
      p. cm.
      "A Quest book."
      ISBN 0-8356-0668-6 (pbk.) :
      1. Music therapy.   2. Music, Influence of.
ML3920.M87 1991
615.8'5154 — dc20   90-50585
                                                                          CIP

Printed in the United States of America

♺ printed on recycled paper

For John, who reminded me that the vibratory principle of all knowing, healing and being is One Fundamental Essence.

We trust that the magic of sound, scientifically applied, will contribute in ever greater measure to the relief of human suffering, to a higher development and a richer integration of the human personality, to the harmonious synthesis of all human "notes" of all "group chords and melodies"—until there will be the greater symphony of the One Humanity.

Roberto Assagioli, M.D.

Contents

Contributing Authors

Roberto Assagioli, M.D., 1888-1974, was a psychiatrist in Italy who devoted himself to writing and training. He developed a comprehensive psychology he called "Psychosynthesis." His writings include the books *Psychosynthesis, The Act of Will,* and more than three hundred papers. His innovative psychoanalytic methods are still widely practiced, and have influenced many of the therapeutic modes being developed today.

Barry Brodie, Ph.D., an associate and friend of composer Kenneth Mills, received his doctorate from the University of California at Berkeley. He leads a drama group called The Earthstage Actors which works on the Dramatization of Spiritual Awareness.

Don Campbell is founder and director of the Institute for Music, Health, and Education in Boulder, Colorado. He also serves on the faculty of the Naropa Institute and is a leader in the emerging field of sonic healing, a therapeutic mode gaining increasing recognition in traditional medicine. *The Roar of Silence, Rhythms of Learning, Introduction to the Musical Brain,* and *Master Teacher, Nadia Boulanger* are books Campbell has written. His extensive discography as an artist and composer includes *Cosmic Classics, Crystal Meditations, Crystal Rainbows, and Runes* (Spirit Music, Boston/Boulder) and *Lightning on the Moon* and *Angels* (Greater Spiral Records, Portland, Oregon). His educational background includes studies with Nadia Boulanger and Robert Casadesus at the Fontainebleau Conservatory of Music. He taught music and humanities for seven years at St. Mary's International School in Tokyo. He was appointed to the Guggenheim Education Project in Chicago, which is developing an innovative curriculum for inner-city schools.

Swami Chetanananda is director of the Nityananda Institute in Cambridge, Massachusetts, a non-profit center for the study and practice of meditation and the spiritual life. He is an American master of the art of meditation, and an initiate of the ancient Saraswati order of monks. His book *Songs from the Center of the Well* describes life as a manifestation of the Divine.

Manfred Clynes, D.Sc., is an academic leader in the study of emotional responses to music. He holds a doctorate in neuroscience from the University of Melbourne, an M.S. in music from the Juilliard School of Music in New York, and an engineering degree. He also did graduate study in the psychology of music at Princeton University. His music teachers included Pablo Casals, Gorodnitzki, and Edwin Fischer, and he has toured Europe as a concert pianist. He is noted in physiology for his discovery of the biologic law of unidirectional rate sensitivity, and he invented the Computer of Average Transient (CAT), a standard tool used in laboratories for assessing brain function. He has published over 110 articles and 5 books, including *Sentics*.

Barbara Crowe, RMT, is director of music therapy at Arizona State University. She has a Masters degree in Music Therapy from Michigan State University, and an extensive background in many areas of psychotherapy, including music therapy for geriatric clients and work with chronically mentally ill patients, emotionally disturbed adolescents, and mentally retarded adolescents. She has published numerous articles on music therapy.

Gary Doore, Ph.D., received his Doctorate in Religion from Oxford University. He was formerly editor of *The American Theosophist* and associate editor of *Yoga Journal.*

He is the compiler of two anthologies, *Shaman's Path: Healing, Personal Growth and Empowerment,* and *What Survives?*

Jonathan S. Goldman, M.A., is a musician, researcher, writer, and teacher. He is founder and director of SHA (Sound Healers Associations, Inc.) and President of Spirit Music, Inc., which produces music for meditation, self-healing, and transformation. He is author of *Awakening the Lotus Chord: The Sacred Science of Sound Healing* and *Hermetic Harmonics: The Overtones of Ascent.*

Cathie E. Guzzetta, Ph.D., RN, received her doctorate in nursing from Texas Woman's University. Presently she is director of the Holistic Nursing Consultants, Bethesda, Maryland. She has written many articles on holistic nursing, and has collaborated on several books, including *Holistic Nursing: A Handbook for Practice,* by Dossey, Keegan and Guzzetta, and *Critical Care Nursing: Body-Mind Spirit,* by Dossey, Guzzetta and Kenner.

Arthur Harvey, Ph.D., is currently professor of music at Eastern Kentucky University, where he has studied the current and potential applications of music in health care. He is executive director of the Music for Health Services Foundation, has hosted the T.V. series *Music and The Brain,* has published articles and coordinated two national conferences, "Music and Health" and "Music with Handicapped Persons."

David Hykes, singer, composer, poet, writer, and researcher, is a pioneer of work with Harmonic Chant. In 1975 he founded the Harmonic Choir in New York, which gives concerts all over the world. Hykes began studying sacred chant in the early 1970s, researching music from Tibet, Tuva, and Mongolia. He has undertaken numerous collaborative projects with the Dalai Lama, the Gyuto and Gyume monks of Tibet, and raga singer Sheila Dhar. In addition, Hykes has composed music used in films, including Peter Weir's *Dead Poet's Society,* and Peter Brook's *Meetings with Remarkable Men* (on Gurdjieff).

He has an upcoming book, *Harmonic Chant,* which will be published in 1991.

Hazrat Inayat Khan, 1882-1927, founder of the Sufi Order of the West, was born in India, where he became a master of classical Indian music by the age of twenty. Khan relinquished his career as a performer to follow the spiritual path, and became one of the first teachers of the Sufi tradition in the West. He lectured widely throughout Europe and the United States.

Derrick de Kerckhove, Ph.D., is associate professor in the department of French and a director of the Board of the McLuhan Program in Culture and Technology at the University of Toronto. He worked with Marshall McLuhan for over ten years as translator, assistant, and co-author. His artistic endeavors bring together art, engineering, and communication technologies. He has written over 150 programs for Canadian television. His present focus is "neuro-cultural research," which investigates the impact of the communication media and culture on the human nervous system.

Gordon Limbrick, a Canadian, is retired from a military career. During the Vietnam War he served in the United Nations Peace Corps. He has been a practitioner of Shabda (or Nada) Yoga, also known as Yoga of the Sound Current. He has been a student of esoteric philosophy and theosophy for many years.

Kenneth G. Mills is a musician, poet, and philosopher whose work is devoted to the principle of Oneness through sound. After a twenty-five year career as a concert pianist, he began a series of spontaneous philosophical lectures called *Unfoldments.* A recording of one of these called *The Quickening Spirit of Radiance* (Sun-Scape Records, 1989) has recently been released. In 1976, Mills founded the Star-Scape Singers, a vocal ensemble which has performed concerts around the world. *The Fire Mass* (Sun-Scape Records, 1989) is a recent recording by the ensemble.

Joseph Moreno is director of the music therapy program at Maryville College in St. Louis, Missouri. He has studied shamanic music and healing traditions in Kenya and elsewhere, and has long maintained an interest in ethnomusicology. He has given workshops and lectures in fifteen countries.

Jill Purce explores the relationship of sound to healing and the transformation of consciousness. After earning a degree in fine art, she was awarded a research fellowship in the biophysics department at the University of London. Her interest in the magical properties of voice led her to study the spiritual dimension of music with Karlheinz Stockhausen in Germany, and later to study with the Tibetan Chantmaster of the Gyuto Tantric College. The author of *The Mystic Spiral: Journey of the Soul,* she has given lectures and workshops on "Inner Sound and Voice" around the world.

Dane Rudhyar was a composer of avant-garde music and a writer of musical and social criticism, poetry, and novels. He is best known for his work in reformulating astrology along contemporary psychospiritual lines. He is the author of over a thousand articles and more than thirty-five books, including *The Astrology of Personality* and *Astrological Mandala.*

Seung Sohn is the 78th Patriarch of the Korean Chogye Order of Buddhism. He founded the Providence Zen Center in 1972, which is now located in Cumberland, Rhode Island. His books include *Dropping Ashes on the Buddha* and *Only Don't Know,* which are collections of his teaching letters and Zen stories, and *Bones of Space,* a book of poetry. He has established over twenty-five Zen Centers in the Americas and Europe and travels worldwide teaching Buddhism.

Alfred A. Tomatis, M.D., is a French physician, psychologist, and ear specialist. After earning his medical degree from the Faculté de Paris, Tomatis specialized in diseases of the ear and throat. His clinical work with opera singers led him to observe that the human voice can produce only sounds the ear can hear. This discovery was recognized by the French Academy of Medicine in 1957 and named the "Tomatis Effect." Dr. Tomatis has pioneered sound therapy treatments for ear and throat disorders and has developed many innovative theories regarding hearing. He has treatment centers in Europe, Phoenix, Toronto, and Portland, Oregon.

Hilma Walter, M.D., was director of the Itawegman Rudolf Steiner Clinic in Arlesheim, Switzerland. She published books and articles in German between the 1920s and the 1960s.

Bradford S. Weeks, M.D., practices medicine and psychiatry in Vermont. His professional focus is psycho-neuro-immunology, the study of the mind-body relationship, especially as it affects the treatment of physical and emotional pain. Music therapy is an important aspect of Dr. Weeks' therapeutic method. A student of nutrition, macrobiotics, homeopathy, and sacred music, especially Gregorian and Tibetan chant, Dr. Weeks has published articles on audition, immunology, and the therapeutic use of sacred music.

Herbert Whone is a professional violinist, artist, writer, and teacher. He graduated from Manchester University and the Royal College of Music in England. His books on music include *The Simplicity of Playing the Violin* and *The Hidden Face of Music.* He also recently published a book of photographs called *Touch Wood.* Whone's writings demonstrate that mastery of an instrument depends not only on science but also on an awareness of the instrument's relationship with the inner development of the musician.

Tim Wilson is a writer and radio producer. His productions include "Voice in the Wilderness: the Creation Spirituality of Matthew Fox," "The Child in Men," with Robert Bly and James Hillman, and "Chant: the Healing Power of

Voice and Ear," which includes conversations with
Dr. Alfred Tomatis. Wilson's theme in these programs
is how sound can help people return to the sacred.

Miriam Therese Winter is a Medical Mission Sister and
currently professor of liturgy, worship, and spirituality
at Hartford Seminary in Connecticut. She is the author
of the book *WomanPrayer, WomanSong: Resources for
Ritual*, and has recorded twelve albums of biblically
based song, including *Joy is Like the Rain* and *WomanSong.*

Acknowledgments

The compiler wishes to thank Quest Book editors Shirley Nicholson and Pamela Kent for supporting the vision of this book with brilliant editorial skills. He also wishes to thank the following authors and publishers for permission to reprint their material:

Roberto Assagioli, "Music as Cause of Disease and Healing Agent," from *Psychosynthesis: A Manual of Principles and Techniques,* Hobbs, Dorman and Company, Inc., New York: 1965.

Barry T. Brodie, "From Tone to a Sound Principle." Thanks to Lex Hixon for permission to print an excerpt from his interview with Kenneth Mills on New York radio.

Swami Chetanananda, "The Symphony of Life," originally appeared in *The American Theosophist,* Spring Special Issue, May 1985, Vol. 73, Number 5, pp 152-158.

Manfred Clynes, "On Music and Healing," was originally published in *Music in Medicine,* R. Spingte & R. Droh, eds., Springer-Verlag, Berlin, 1987. "On Being in Order" was published in *Zygon, Journal of Religion and Science,* Vol 5, No. 1, 1970. Both articles reprinted by permission of the author.

Jonathan Goldman, "Sonic Entrainment," was presented at the IV International Musicmedicine Symposium at Annenberg Center for Health Sciences, Rancho Mirage, CA, 1989. Arranged and edited for this anthology.

Cathie E. Guzzetta, "Music Therapy: Nursing the Music of the Soul," reprinted from *Holistic Nursing: A Handbook for Practice,* by B. Dossey, L. Keegan, C. Guzzetta and L. Kolkmeier, pp 263-288, with permission of Aspen Publishers, Inc., © 1988.

Acknowledgments

David Hykes, "Harmonic Meeting," © 1990 David Hykes and the Harmonic Arts Society, all rights reserved, reprinted by permission. A version of this article first appeared in *Musicworks 35, The Canadian Journal of Sound Exploration,* Summer 1986.

Hazrat Inayat Khan, "Healing with Sound and Music," excerpted from chapters 37, 38 & 39 of *The Music of Life,* copyright 1983 Omega Publications Inc., RD 1 Box 1030E, New Lebanon, NY 12125. Reprinted with permission.

Gordon Limbrick, "The Hidden Significance of Sound," appeared in *Theosophy in Australia,* No. 680, Vol. 53, No. 5, December 1989.

Joseph Moreno, "The Music Therapist: Creative Arts Therapist and Contemporary Shaman," reprinted with permission from *The Arts in Psychotherapy,* Vol. 15, Winter 1988, pp 271-280, © Pergamon Press, 1988.

Jill Purce, "Sound in Mind and Body," adapted for this anthology from an article in *Resurgence,* No. 115, March/ April 1986.

Dane Rudhyar, "Dissonant Harmony, Pleromas of Sound and the Principle of Holistic Resonance," from *The Magic of Tone and the Art of Music,* © 1982, Shambhala Publications, Inc. Reprinted with permission of Leyla Rael Rudhyar Hill.

Seung Sahn, "Perceive Universal Sound," and interview *Theosophist,* Spring Special Issue, May 1985, Vol. 73, Number 5, pp 135-139.

H. Walter, "Music as a Means of Healing," is a chapter from *Music: Its Occult Basis and Healing Value,* by Lionel Stebbing, New Knowledge Books, 1974. Reprinted by permission of the Rudolph Steiner Press, London.

Bradford Weeks, M.D., "The Physician, the Ear and Sacred Music," © 1990, is adapted from "The Therapeutic Aspect of Sacred Music," in *About the Tomatis Method,* Gilmor, Madaule, Thompson, eds. The Listening Centre Press, Toronto, 1989. Excerpted by permission.

Tim Wilson, "Chant, the Healing Powers of Voice and Ear," an edited version of "A l'ecoute de l'univers: an interview with Dr. Alfred Tomatis," appeared originally in *Musicworks 35, The Canadian Journal of Sound Exploration,*

Summer 1986. Reprinted by permission of the author.

Sr. Miriam Therese Winter, "Music: The Way Home," © Medical Mission Sisters, 1990.

Introduction: The Curative Potential of Sound

Each illness is a musical problem—the healing, a musical
solution. The shorter and more complete the solution—the
greater the musical talent of the physician. Sickness
demands manifold solutions. The selection of the most
appropriate solution determines the talent of the physician.

Novalis, The Encyclopedia

As we approach a new century where the information, culture, languages and peoples of the earth merge, we can observe music from a dozen standpoints as influential and significant to our health and behavior. Sonic scanning for prenatal observation; music as an anesthetic and pain reducer; the effect of music on memory; tone and chant immediately synchronizing brain waves and modifying behavior; specific sounds, music or tones stimulating localized physical responses—these are some of the uses of sound in the past decades. The scope of the field can be seen as a rising sun, a new morning in the way the art of sound can be used for healing and in the marriage of science and art.

This book grew out of the dawning awareness from a variety of professional disciplines of the ways we listen, perform and observe the effects of music upon the human instrument. Its primary purpose is to explore the paradigms that are emerging around several areas of research: sonic entrainment; the uses of chant to alter physical conditions; use of music for imagery in education and psychotherapy; and the influences of sound reported by philosophers in the Eastern, Western, Christian and esoteric traditions. New questions, new frameworks, new sources of physical, emotional and spiritual renewal are arising, and they do not regard music as only entertainment and performance

1

or taste. We are just beginning to realize the deep and profound scientific, medical, psychological and spiritual questions involved in the power of music.

Star systems are born out of what seems dark. Sound is born out of what seems silent. These events in nature suggest that the new paradigms evolving around us demand a broader standpoint than only in the light of science and logic. Neither science nor intuitive emotion need be discarded or ridiculed. They can be seen as major viewpoints for observing the great tree of being. As the ancient view of music as medicine is placed in juxtaposition to science, the emerging paradigms are creating still another direction that includes myths and science. A new logic on which to explore concrete curative applications is forming. The same tree is being approached from a number of different directions.

As written in ancient records both East and West, sound and tone may be the heart-mother and fire-father of all being. According to the Indian *Mahabharata,* creation took place in the silent, unmoving womb of the mother universe. Out of a unitary whole came the symmetrical and numerical variations that underlie physical structures. With the first movement and cry, light was created and formation began. In the Beginning was the Word. Was the Word outside of time, or was it the very instant of the commencement of time? In Greek *logos* means not only "word" but also "sound." Light, word, sound, vibration and thought are linked to the beginning of all knowing, all naming. Each is sibling to the rest, whether we view it acoustically, philosophically, theologically or metaphorically. But our senses cannot perceive sound as the music of the spheres. To consider the source of the Logos, we are like Faust on his Easter morning walk, contemplating "Who is Logos?" We confront the incomprehensible.

Music is like a thousand different languages rolled into one, all using tone, rhythm, melody and harmony, but not all understandable, likable, intelligent or useful to all people. Without experience not everyone can understand Bach, Stockhausen, Palestrine or Wagner. Music's vocabulary is so vast that even the most educated musical minds

2

in the West may not have tools to grasp the sophisticated and refined classical music of South India or the sacred chants of Tibet. Yet it is significant that we can understand and feel so much music without having to learn it. Music has unfortunately been named a "universal language" without consideration of the many levels by which it communicates. For example, we now know that sound and frequency affect the body and that repetitive rhythmic patterns influence the breath and heartbeat of the listener. At times these elements have a stronger influence than the words and melodies used.

Anthropology, medicine and science have investigated music's effect on the physical body. As early as 1830 J. Dogiel published studies that describe experiments proving that music evokes definite physiological responses:

1. Music influences the circulation of blood in humans and animals.

2. Music causes blood pressure to rise and fall. The oscillations of pressure depend chiefly on the influence of auditory stimulation on the medulla oblongata and its relation to the auditory nerve.

3. Variations in circulation depend on pitch, intensity and timbre of the sound.

4. The idiosyncrasies of each individual are apparent in the variations of blood pressure. Even one's nationality has some effect.

By 1926 dozens of researchers in Europe and America were in agreement that music effectively increases metabolism; changes muscular energy; accelerates respiration; produces marked but variable effects on volume, pulse and blood pressure; creates the physiological basis for the genesis of emotional shifts. In the early 1940s Henry Clay Smith showed how productivity of employees differed during "music" and "non-music" days. Over the past thirty years the place of music in the health of society has been given greater importance, due to music therapists, physical therapists, speech pathologists, suggestopedic language teachers, church musicians, psychiatrists and physicians. Anthropologists and ethnomusicologists have provided fascinating documentation of physiological and physical

3

modifications that affect health through studying the use of rhythm and vocal tones in shamanic societies. The popularity of North Indian classical music, which arose in the 1960s in the West through Ravi Shankar, made listeners aware of the sophisticated intellectual and esthetic systems that evolved out of recognizing the spiritual importance of sound and its curative powers.

The new paradigms of musical and healing perspectives recognize music as a healing tool. This is backed up by the discovery that sound produces physical forms, as Hans Jenny demonstrated in his remarkable work on cymatics. He showed that figures can be formed by vibration, for instance by vibrating crystals with electric impulses and then transmitting the vibrations to a medium such as a plate, a diaphragm or a string. He also produced vibratory figures in liquids and gases. By changing the pitch, the harmonics of the tone and the material that is vibrating, a new form results. When harmonic ratios are added to the fundamental tone, the variants create either splendid beauty or chaotic stress. From perfect kaleidoscopic mandalas to fishlike figures with spinal cords, sound creates form. The breath of creation takes dead matter and lifts it to life.

Musical tones, words and sounds that sustain a pitch for a few seconds begin to make patterns and create fields of resonance and movement in the surrounding space. People present, absorb and reflect these sounds. Listeners shift their bodies as they respond with altered pulse, breath, blood pressure, muscle tension and skin temperature. Even the sounds not heard by the ear are received into the body by the skin and bones and move the listener, who is never completely immune to their powers.

Music is obviously powerful but also subtle. A sound that brings beauty and release from pain to one person can be discordant, boring or painful to another. The wise physician finds the proper harmonies, ratios and rhythms for each patient, not to cover up the pain or illness but to balance the body and renew it to fullness and health. Such a physician heals by bringing the patient into balance and unity and unfolding the layers that shroud the central core principle from which all levels grow. He or she is wise in the knowledge of nature and calls out the wisdom and natural healing of the body. Music can be the medicine, the healing agent, in this process.

Once people listened to the sacred lyre of David, Orpheus or Apollo. In the time of Plato or Pythagoras, music was easy to understand. The spectrum of sound ranged around a dozen or so instruments. Performances were always live, and the modes, keys, ensembles were limited in tonal color because of the combination of instruments and voices available in the ensemble. Music in the ancient world was a mysterious and powerful tool for the attunement of the psyche and body.

Today we are bombarded with sounds that alter our minds and bodies so that we are rarely able to really listen. The sounds of neon lights, heating systems, televisions, computers and automobiles influence the fields of energy around us in disturbing ways. We are overloaded by dozens of recordings of melodies. Our spectrum for music lies somewhere between an eternal Muzak and a fine concert of Mozart string quartets, between loud popular music with no artistic sense and ecstatic chanting. Our sonic environment, mentally and physically, is so loud that we would not recognize the powerful healing and harmonic powers of Orpheus if he were among us. If we could rest for a year by eliminating recorded music and electronic and mechanical sounds, our bodies might resume their natural responses to pure sound, and we could recover their instinctive powers.

The ancient doctrines spoke consistently of harmonics, the relationship between tones. Pythagoras' key to geometry, astronomy, ethics and music was the ratio of numbers. In his *Timaeus* Plato taught that tone and musical intervals created nothing less than the world soul. Iamblichus noted that:

Pythagoras considered that music contributed greatly to health if used in the right way. . . . He called his method musical medicine. In the spring he applied himself to the following melodic method: he would sit in the middle of his disciples who were able to sing melodies, and play his lyre. To the accompaniment of Pythagoras' lyre, his followers would sing in unison certain chants or paeans (usually to Apollo who was also 'Paian' or the 'healer') by which they appeared to be delighted and became melodious and rhythmical. At other times his disciples also employed music as medicine, with certain melodies composed to cure the passions of the psyche, as well as ones for despondency and mental anguish. In addition to these medical aids there were other melodies for anger and aggression and for all psychic disturbances.

De Vita Pythagorica,
ed. Deubner, Leipzig, 1937

There was no doubt to ancient healers and philosophers that music is the bridge between body, soul and the earth. Our vocabulary may have shifted during the past two thousand years, but the awareness of vibratory fields of energy as the life force of the body is an emerging realization in medicine.

The ancient musical scales represented the mathematical structure of the world and the essence of humanity within the orderly system of creation. Plato said of this:

The motions which are naturally akin to the divine principle within us are the thoughts and revolutions of the universe . . . by learning the harmonies and revolutions of the universe . . . [each man is] renewing his original nature, and . . . should attain to that perfect life which the gods have set before mankind, both for the present and the future.

The perspectives of ancient Greece are rooted in even older Egyptian and Chaldean epistemologies. The influence of vibration on creation was acknowledged through the time of Kepler. The modern world is coming to honor these visions of perfect number systems, music of the spheres and God's mystic nature revealed through number, pattern and proportion. An older part of the brain is in touch with the power of these principles, and newer research suggests that they are evolutive and creative.

To consider music as a tool of healing, it is evident that we must understand its three basic components: tone, rhythm and harmony. The initial sound is the tone; it is the utterance of a sound. Rhythm gives definition, pattern and boundary to the tone. It can be a consistent repetitious beat or completely spontaneous moving in and out of a beat pattern. With vocal sounds that are musical, gibberish or linguistic, rhythmic patterns can be constant, syncopated or completely chaotic. Harmony is the ratio and relationship between the tones and their rhythmic patterns. Rhythm structures tone and sound. It gives shape to speech, melody, dance, poetry and the human body. Rhythm defines the eternal principle of sound and tone. Without rhythm energy, sound, light and forms could not be differentiated from one another as it is their frequency or rhythmic wave forms that define them.

Aristoxenos, an Athenean who lived around 325 B.C., realized the nature of rhythm and distinguished it from the sounds in which it occurs. He used the word "rhythmizomena" to indicate the overall piece or pattern in which the rhythm is embedded. He said:

We must imagine two different natures, that of rhythm and that of the material to which rhythm is applied. . . . For as the body takes shape and form in different ways if its parts are placed in various positions and postures . . . so each individual *rhythmizomena* takes a number of forms depending not on its own formative power but on that of the rhythm.

Thus changing rhythm can alter and change the medium to which it is applied.

In the articles that follow, you will find a dozen different perspectives about the effect of sound and music on the physical, spiritual and mental aspects of ourselves. This book provides the reader with a large scope of possibilities. Among them are: research on the ear and the power of listening by Dr. Alfred Tomatis; the application of music in hospitals by Dr. Arthur Harvey and Cathie Guzzetta, R.N.; the pioneering perspectives of music therapists Barbara Crowe and Joe Moreno; the spiritually rooted writings of Pir Hazrat Inayat Khan and Swami Chetanananda; the academic medical writings of Bradford Weeks, M.D.; the spiritual attention of a performing musician/philosopher, Kenneth Mills.

An array of avenues is now available for treatment and healing. This book does not pretend to include everything that is happening in the field. Within a few years, research in the following areas will provide a firmer foundation in the use of sound as a healing tool: Fabian Mammon's work in France on elimination of cancer cells by means of sound; the network of chiropractic techniques of Donald Epstein which view the full physical body as a wave form; Laurie Rugenstein's work in Colorado on vocal toning for physical and mental alignment; the sound and frequency entrainment research of the Monroe Institute in Virginia; the innovative research of students at the Institute for Music, Health and Education in Boulder, Colorado, which includes the analysis and composition of music specifically for physical healing, the curative aspects of tone, breath and color, and the use of imagery with sound. Hopefully this variety will create more dialogue between the worlds of medicine, anthropology, psychology and spirituality.

Artist, musician, physicist, doctor—all are approaching the paradigm of the fundamental vibratory essence that underlies their work. The ancients knew it; our bodies know it. The emerging physician, the new doctor of balance, fullness and resonance, rests on a new understanding of the physics of harmonics and the powers in sound. The overture is sounding for the twenty-first century. The ancient healers are calling forth our deeper senses. Orpheus, Apollo, Tubal-cain, Aesclepius, David, St. Gregory, St. Francis, Saraswati and St. Cecilia are sounding their calls. How soon will we be able to use the beauty of musical sound to compose ourselves into perfect octaves of harmony in mind, body and spirit?

I
Listening: The Art of Sound Health

*The education of the ear is fifty years behind the
education of the eye. We are still hostile to sounds
that surprise us.*

Pierre Boulez

*We have long been overconcerned with what produces sounds:
the voice, instruments, environments and machines. Only in
the last few decades have we had the wisdom to ask questions
about how we hear, how we focus attention through the ear.
By understanding the psychology and physiology of sound's
effect on the body and mind, we are developing insight on why
music and spoken language evoke such a wide variety of responses.
Personal taste and attention span can now be observed as only
a small part of the full spectrum of mind/body engagement
with sound.*

*Radio journalist Tim Wilson begins this section with a
fascinating interview with one of the most dynamic thinkers
and medical researchers of our time, Dr. Alfred A. Tomatis.
Their dialogue about the effects of chanting on the body, mind
and spirit is an appropriate overture to this anthology.*

*The left brain is focused on refined selective attention by
theorist Derrick de Kerckhove's article about oral and literate
listening. Bradford Weeks, M.D., takes the theories of Dr. Tomatis
and shows how the ear becomes a vital bridge of communication
between the inner and outer worlds.*

*The interview with David Hykes, founder of the Harmonic
Choir, blends listening techniques with awareness of overtones
and shows why these new sounds may be essential in the education of consciousness and the ear. Finally, a revision of a chapter*

from my book The Roar of Silence *gives information about overtones and an exercise that can challenge your ability to listen to your own voice's spectrum.*

1

Chant: The Healing Power of Voice and Ear

An interview with ALFRED TOMATIS, M.D.
by TIM WILSON
with commentary

Listening, says the French physician, psychologist and ear specialist Dr. Alfred A. Tomatis, is nothing less than our "royal route" to the divine. It is also something very few of us do well. In the following interview, Tomatis blends clinical precision and theoretical élan into a profound and subtle meditation on this most vital of human faculties.

It is hard to believe how heretical, only a few decades ago, Alfred Tomatis must have appeared to the medical (and musical) establishment with the simple observation based on his clinical work with opera singers, that the voice can only produce what the ear hears. (The French Academies of Science and Medicine officially acknowledged the young ear specialist's illumination by naming it after him.) Tomatis showed that the two organs are part of the same neurological loop, such that changes in the response of one will show up immediately in the other.

Though most of us feel this to be intuitively sound, such unity of organic function has not impressed itself yet on, among others, audiologists and speech pathologists. In major hospitals, the two departments can still be found at opposite ends of the building. We have a lot invested in this sort of separation.

Tomatis is an unorthodox "nutritionist," too. A hidden but primary function of the ear, he says, is to charge the brain with electrical potential. Sounds, especially the ones we make ourselves as singers and speakers, are a fantastic energy food.

11

But the good doctor doesn't stop there. A pioneer in prenatal psychology, Tomatis was one of the first to demonstrate that listening, and consequently "dialogue" with the mother, begin in the womb long before we are born. "All our lives," he asserts, "we seek to recover the audition of the fetus." It is the ear which shapes our most intimate associations. More than that, it is our link with the Logos.

If they didn't seem to fit so coherently into his view of human potential, and to be born out in day-to-day clinical experience with everyone from dyslexic children to Benedictine monks, some of Tomatis' pronouncements might appear as if they could only be taken on faith. "The skin is really differentiated ear, not the other way around," or, "Gregorian is meant to train one to rise up out of the body." These are the sorts of things you'd have expected to hear from the communications philosopher Marshall McLuhan, who was, perhaps not co-incidentally, also a strong Catholic. Religious though the overtones may be, the probing of both men follows the same course, tracing ritual, belief, culture and dogma back to "effects" whose ground is in the body.

This may be what has made so many people ready to hear Alfred Tomatis: the growing realization that there might be a real, physical, perceivable basis to our "spiritual" sense. If we feel there is something "above," it is just possibly because our bones are telling us, through our ears. It is this circuit which is the "royal route" he speaks of.

Some points not crystal clear in the original interview (conducted in French), I have expanded on in the light of subsequent conversations. For any errors in this embellishment, I confess *mea culpa*, and trust that Dr. Tomatis' thought is reproduced here with the highest possible fidelity to all of its frequencies.

Tim Wilson: Is it possible to explain in reasonably precise, scientific terms, the effect of chanting on the well-being of an individual?
Alfred Tomatis: We can only ask why, for thousands of years, people have chanted, and why in our research on

ascetic matters we have discovered songs called "sacred." They are sacred only insofar as they render this service to the singer. They are not sacred in themselves. But it is true that they have considerable neurophysiological effects. And there can be no such effect outside of the nervous system.

These people, over a long period of time, have come to the intuitive realization that there is probably something in the ear that it is possible to awaken, or at least to excite. And modern research has proved to us that there are two kinds of sound. There are sounds which for some time now I have termed "discharge" sounds (those which tire, fatigue the listener) and "charge" sounds (those which give tone, health). We have proven over the last twenty years that in order for the brain to remain dynamic, to think and operate with vitality, it must have sensory stimuli. A group of Americans has been able to demonstrate the number of such stimuli that are necessary. We know now that the brain needs three billion stimuli per second for at least four and a half hours per day, in order for a person to remain conscious, that is wide awake.

Let me tell you of a personal experience. It goes back several years. I had visited a monastery in France which had just been taken over by a new abbot, a young man. He had changed the internal rule of the abbey by modifying everything a little after the Second Vatican Council, and he was therefore something of a revolutionary.

When I arrived, there were those who wanted to retain the Latin, others who were for the existing rule, and still others who wanted to change and revolutionize everything. Finally everything was changed. They even eliminated chanting from the daily schedule. You know that Benedictines chant from six to eight hours a day, but this abbot succeeded in demonstrating that chant served no useful purpose, and that without it they could recapture that time for other things.

Well, in fact, these people had been chanting in order to "charge" themselves, but they hadn't realized what they were doing. And gradually, as the days passed, they started to get bogged down; they became more and more tired. Finally they got so tired that they held a meeting and frankly

asked themselves what it was that was causing their fatigue.
They looked at their schedule and saw that their night vigil
and the rhythm of their work deviated excessively from the
norm for other men. They seemed to live too differently
from the rest of the world, and they seldom slept. They
decided that they should go to bed early and wake up, like
everybody else, only when they were no longer tired. Well,
everyone knows from physiology that the more you sleep,
the more tired you are, and so it was for the poor Benedictines
—they were more tired than ever—so much so that they
called in medical specialists to help them try to understand
what was happening. They finally gave up on this after a
procession of doctors had come through over a period of
several months, and the monks were more tired than ever.
Then they turned to specialists of the digestive system.
One of the great French doctors arrived at the conclusion
that they were in this state because they were undernourished.
In fact, they were practically vegetarian—they ate a little
fish from time to time—and he told them they were dying
of starvation. I think my colleague's error was in forgetting
that they had eaten as vegetarians ever since the 12th Century,
which one would think might have engendered some sort
of adaptation in them. Anyway, once they started eating
meat and potatoes like the rest of the world, things only
got worse.

I was called by the Abbot in February, and I found that
70 of the 90 monks were slumping in their cells like wet
dishrags. Over the next several months I examined them,
installed machines, and began the treatment of re-awakening
their ears. I put the machines in in June, 1967, and I re-
introduced their chanting immediately. By November, almost
all of them had gone back to their normal activities, that
is their prayer, their few hours of sleep, and the legendary
Benedictine work schedule.

T.W.: And how exactly were you treating these people?
A.T.: With sound only. We know what sounds are stimulating
and we also have the technology to be able, in fact, to re-
charge people with them. You have to realize that to
meditate, to reach the plane of prayer, demands extraordinary
cortical activity. Put yourself on your knees one day and

try to pray, or try to meditate and you'll see how parasitic thoughts assail you—your vacation coming up, the friend who's displeased you, the letter you just received, the taxes you have to pay—thousands of things flood into the mind, to your subconscious, and you need to have an enormous cortical charge to overcome them. In the case of these monks, in giving them back their sounds, their stimuli, we succeeded in re-awakening them.

T.W.: Do the sounds do all of this by themselves?

A.T.: Not quite. It's a little complicated, but the human auditory apparatus is poorly understood, and every time you read a study on it, it's stupefying to see how little is known about it. There are several levels of misconception that persist. First, at the physiological level, people see the ear as a sense organ just like the others, even a little less important than the others. In fact it is more complex, and its role is primary. Next, everyone thinks he listens, but in fact hearing is probably our most deficient sense. We're not aware of how much of life we are missing. We are creatures of sound. We live in it, and it lives in us. But this is a fact we have forgotten just as the fish forgets that he lives in water. And just like the fish, we have to leave the water to realize it.

[*Tomatis is speaking both literally and metaphorically here of birth—the crucial transition for the development of each human's audition from liquid-conducted to air-conducted sound. There is a pronounced idealization of the pre-natal environment in Tomatis' work, an image of the womb as an auditory paradise, a condition of "super hearing" to which we aspire throughout our lives to return.*]

The ear has presented us with a scientific problem (let alone an aesthetic and spiritual one) of enormous proportions. The human ear has functions that have been completely ignored. We have known that one of those is to assure balance, but we haven't followed through the implications of this. The ancients who were less rich in technology had more time to reflect, and came to a more acute understanding of sound than we've been able to. They discovered the following: first of all, they realized that certain sounds released certain postural phenomena. In India there is a whole yoga of sound, Mantra yoga. In Mantra yoga, the posture has to be perfect for the mantra to work, which explains why some people have destroyed themselves in doing the mantra without knowing the key to proper listening. A mantra can damage a person much faster than it can restore him. So there's definitely a danger. In order to do a mantra well one should know well all the practice and the theory, and especially the way to listen.

What the ancients knew was that once one reaches perfect auditory posture, the body reaches out and literally incorporates all the sound that comes from outside. The subject identifies with himself, knows himself, touches himself both from outside and from within. Secondly, he assumes a posture that stresses verticality. It is impossible to arrive at good language without verticality, or to stimulate the brain to full consciousness. If the posture isn't perfect, it is very difficult to enter truly into real consciousness.

[*Verticality, it could be argued, is the backbone of Tomatis' thinking. The image of upward ascension informs both his physiological researches and his metaphysical speculations. It is also a rich source of allusions, many of them biblical. For example, Tomatis terms the human struggle towards uprightness throughout eons of evolution "le combat de Jacob." It was not a casual observation that he found the aurally depleted monks "slumping" in their cells. Not only, he discovered, does a different posture change the way one hears, but the converse. When he altered the listening curve of certain subjects, their posture immediately changed. Tomatis is also a prodigious linguist. He observes that the word "malady" etymologically implies bad posture, and suggests that his listening "cure" is nothing more than the reversal of this.*]

If you listen to music, especially if you're trying to listen carefully to classical music, you take on a special kind of posture. The head tilts forward a little, which actually raises its top-most point. It's a little like the image of the Buddha who is listening to what is called "the sound of the universe."

Alright, how does the ear function in all of this? Well,

its real function is unconsciously to assure balance. But in saying balance we are saying a great deal, much more than just physical equilibrium. It also means the tonus of the body. And it means all the gestures, all of the non-verbal language the body has with its environment. It is the ear which first establishes in the brain a spatial dynamic, on which the visual system is later superimposed. So the first function of the ear is vestibular.

The ear's other role, the one we think we know well enough about, is its cochlear function, the analysis and de-coding of sounds from outside. We have largely overlooked, however, the sounds generated from inside the body, particularly the ear's relation to our own voice. This function I call self-listening, or auditory-vocal control.

There is a third function of the ear, the one involved in the story of the monks I told you about. Doctors totally ignore this function, but zoologists know it well, it being perhaps easier to see in the simplest of animals, particularly in the fish. This is that the ear, the vibration sensor, serves to charge the organism with electrical potential. It is thanks to the ear that external stimuli are able to charge the cortical battery. I say electrical because the only way we know of measuring the brain's activity is through an electro-encephalogram, which gives an electrical answer. But of course it's not electricity that's inside. All modification of internal metabolism is translated by electricity—that is all we know how to see. The internal mechanisms which we call the neurological field are illuminated, charged, by stimuli. These stimuli come, we know, via the skin, the joints, the muscles, a thousand things leading into our bodies from the outside. But it is the ear which translates their potential to the brain. And so we've come to realize that the skin is only a piece of differentiated ear, and not the other way around!

The joints, the muscles, in other words the body's posture —everything we use to fight against gravity—all this is tied to the labyrinth of the ear. It is the ear's vestibular labyrinth that keeps these all under control, which is balance. To this mechanism alone I believe we can credit 60% of the cortical charge. You also have, thanks to the energy of the sounds themselves, which is processed by the cochlea, a complementary charge of about 30%. Thus the ear accounts for from 90% to 95% of the body's total charge. The ancients, then, must have known all this. They had a whole technique, which we see in Indian yoga, or in Zen with its bells, or every time a Tibetan goes to meditate. There is always someone there who makes sounds, a sumptuous OM for example. But there is something very interesting in that. You will have noticed that the sacred chants which come from places of high altitude seem to us to contain little but bass tones. Actually, these chants are also rich in high frequencies, but in order to produce them the singer must add lows at the same time. Otherwise the highs don't come through. (I am terming "highs" those frequencies from 800 Hz up.) This phenomenon is directly related to atmospheric pressure. In high altitudes it is very hard to maintain a high-pitched fundamental tone that is rich in harmonics without slipping into falsetto. This is what one hears in Tyrolean and certain other folk musics. To counter this, the Tibetans actually change the position of the larynx to sound the lower-pitched fundamental you hear in the OM. It's on the consistency and control of this fundamental that the quality of the overtones depends.

T.W.: What sorts of sounds do you use in re-charging people?

A.T.: At various stages in the process I will use sounds such as a recording of one's own mother's voice, filtered to simulate the listening one has pre-natally. Also music, but not just any music, because each kind has different results. Two kinds in particular have given me results in every corner of the world: the music of Mozart, and Gregorian chant from the Abbey of Solemnes, particularly the dawn and midnight masses for Christmas. [Discs also recommended from Solemnes: the Epiphany and Easter masses, and those for St. Stephen and St. Peter.]

If you put an oscilloscope on the sounds of Gregorian chant, you see that they all come within the bandwidth for charging the ear. There is not a single sound which falls outside of this. Gregorian chant contains all of the frequencies of the voice spectrum, roughly from 70 cycles per second up to 9,000 cycles per second, but with a very different envelope curve from that of normal speech. There is a characteristic slope which increases from low to high frequencies by a minimum of 6 dB per octave, which is to say an increase of 100% for each octave you go up the scale. This increase can be as great as 18 dB for each octave.

The most important range for this activity is between 2,000 and 4,000 cycles per second, or the upper part of the speaking range. It is this range which gives timbre to the voice, whereas the lower frequencies are used simply for the semantic system.

If your voice has good timbre, is rich in overtones, you are charging yourself each time you use it, and of course you are providing a benefit to whomever hears you!

Sometimes it's easy to lose track of what someone is saying, not because he isn't interesting, but because his voice is of poor timbre—it's too "low." Instead of charging you, it discharges you. Thus the sounds of Gregorian are, uniquely, a fantastic energy food. And here's an interesting detail. All the monasteries that closed down are the ones where they didn't chant.

The second important thing about Gregorian is that there is no tempo, there is only rhythm. If you look closely at the Gregorian inflection, if you take an *Alleluia* for example, you have the impression that the subject never breathes. This slowest possible breathing is a sort of respiratory yoga, which means that the subject must be in a state of absolute tranquility in order to be able to do it. And by inducing the listener to enter into the same deep breathing, you lead him little by little to something of the same tranquility.

T.W.: The listener is not making a sound.

A.T.: That's right. At some point there will be a sort of slow breathing which means we are forced to breathe just as tranquilly, showing that the listener is in suspension at the same time.

[*Better still, you can try this out for yourself, as Dr. Tomatis recommends, by singing along with one of the many recordings of Gregorian chant that are available. You might also want to have, though it's not essential, a copy of the Liber Usualis, the daily "songbook" for Benedictines. Even if you read only enough*

19

music to discern that the melody rises or falls somewhat from note to note, you'll be surprised to find that it is as if you were singing in precisely the same time, at the same moment, as the voices you hear on the recording. A minor miracle of simultaneity, this—a manifestation of the losing track of time which Tomatis describes as characteristic of Gregorian.

Time, then, considered both in terms of rhythm in music and of microseconds in aural perception, is just as important a factor as the frequency content of a sound. Each person has a unique delay between the moment of uttering a sound and hearing it uttered, according to which feedback it is altered. A group of monks singing together will over time come to have, in the subtlest of their corporeal rhythms, the same delay characteristic of serenity. Tomatis has shown that the Electronic Ear can, in artificially superimposing a different, more relaxed time value for auditory feedback, speed up the process of slowing down.]

That is why one is so comfortable and at ease. It's the sensation you have when you are listening to a great singer. You mimic him because, first of all, he excites all of your higher proprioceptor responses, and then you dilate to breathe strongly with him. You become sure of the note that comes next. It is you who sings the note and not him. He invites you to do it in your own skin. Whereas with a bad singer you want to die. He ties you in knots, he blocks you in, you're afraid, and nothing happens.

T.W.: Do you know the line in Eliot's *Four Quartets,* about hearing music so deeply that "you are the music while the music lasts"?

A.T.: No, but he's right, that's exactly it—on condition that it's good music! But in any case the music rubs against you, it manipulates you, and therefore it's important that it be of good quality.

There's another element in the Gregorian, if you listen well, still thinking of the *Alleluia* as an example. You see that the antiphon has notes that are held, and then suddenly they modulate to what seems like an ending. That sort of ending is very interesting. If you listen carefully, you notice that it is the beat of a calm heart, the rhythm of a tranquil heartbeat . . . systole, diastole. In other words you take a subject, no matter whom, who comes to church because he has problems to straighten out inside. You lead him into a chant of serene and supple respiration, and at a given moment you'll see his whole cardiac pattern calming. And little by little a feeling of well-being comes over him.

It may not be incidental, by the way, that Gregorian was until recently always sung in Latin. The stress of the Latin words happens to follow precisely this serene physiological rhythm in us that is very pure. You don't get that when you superimpose many vernacular languages, particularly French with its articles, on the chant. There's a real reef in the water there. But in the Bantu language, for example, Gregorian works very well!

Before we had the technology of the Electronic Ear, to bring a young monk into the choir would take three or four years. You can appreciate how the training is a long and difficult process. And for a monk, not being able to chant is very frustrating.

Those who aren't integrated easily have to live on the sidelines. But asceticism is more than cutting your hair or even changing your heart. In Greek it means to change one's habitual ways. And it is precisely the habitual hearing which the Electronic Ear is going to change. We now know how to bring a subject into the choir within two or three months. We use auditory modification to change the way he listens, because we know the bandwidths which allow him to enter the zone of charge and serenity. It is the zone of alpha waves, to be precise, in contrast to the coarser rhythmic zones of the body, which are like the antics of an agitated monkey. We can play on both zones.

The Electronic Ear is a cybernetic device with two principal channels joined by a sort of "gate," or door from one channel to the other. When the subject speaks into the device, the first channel presents to him, on headphones, the sound as his own ear would hear it. The second channel is filtered so that it allows the subject an improved hearing, particularly of the high frequencies. When this second channel is engaged, the person hears as a well-trained monk would hear. The switching back and forth between channels is effected by the way the subject controls, consciously or unconsciously, the frequency and intensity of his own voice. This produces an exercising of the muscles of the middle ear, a kind of gymnastics of the ear. The work of a monk is, in a sense, to become an athlete of the muscles of the inner ear, to learn to strengthen and control them.

There is a positive, direct relationship between what one hears and the way in which one vocalizes. The mouth reacts immediately because it is in the same neurological field as the ear. When you give an opening of response to the ear, you have immediately the same opening in the ability of the mouth. In training the monks with the Electronic Ear, one prepares the muscles of the middle ear to function properly, thereby leading the mouth to react in the same way. One starts by vibrating the larynx, and the desired bone vibration results. This excites the inner ear which in turn immediately excites the brain. The impedance or resistance of the bones alone is around 2,000 cycles per second and upwards. The technique of listening is to achieve again this conduction which many of us lose, the conduction which is precisely that of the fetus. All our life we try to recreate this primal audition. The "inaudible sound" one strives to hear in the final stage of Raja yoga, for example, is no more than that produced by the filtering of bone conduction.

[*It was in trying to determine what we hear in the womb that led Tomatis to his most provocative discoveries. He was not alone in pointing out that the ear is the first perceptual organ to mature—in the fifth month of pregnancy—but no one else seems to have inquired as deeply into how the fetus listens. The object of this first attention, a faint and slightly strident solo in the symphony of bodily sounds, is the voice of the mother. It is a sound which comes to us filtered naturally by bone conduction so that precisely the same high frequencies are emphasized that are later replicated by the Electronic Ear.*]

T.W.: Can you say more about the low-frequency zone?
A.T.: Let's take the Tibetan OM again. When most of us in the West make an OM we make a flat sound that is without timbre, empty. It's a sound in the throat that doesn't lead

to anything, but on the contrary tires the subject. That's because it's in the band of sounds which tire, which demand enormous work of the vestibule that orders the whole body through the spinal system, which makes the body move. It's also the effect of the tam-tam. The tam-tam exhausts the subject and can put him into another state. These kinds of drumming sounds gradually induce a loss of all awareness of the body, through a game that goes on within the labyrinth of the ear. The low frequency, percussive sounds cause exaggerated movement of the endolymphatic liquid which begins to move, just as it would in an elevator starting up. If this movement is too continuous, the subject loses the image of his body, and enters into a kind of hypnosis. Very few are able to resist moving to the beat of a drum. It puts us at the mercy of the drummer, a magus who can then do with his listeners whatever he wants. Military marches, for example, have long known how to exploit this phenomenon. We can be out of breath, tired and all, and with a good military march we move like one man. The high frequencies in instruments like the trumpets and bagpipes provide all the charge you want, and the drums provide a regimenting rhythm that makes you pick yourself up even when you're tired. But with the low frequencies alone, you'd never be able to keep it up.

T.W.: Is chanting a kind of hypnotism too?

A.T.: No. On the contrary. It is an awakening of the field of consciousness. At the risk of oversimplifying, hypnotic effects are those of relatively lower frequency which play on the more primitive areas of the brain. With Gregorian chant you are directly affecting the cortex, which controls the monkey rather than being led by him.

In order to avoid the awkwardness of having some monks with trained ears and some without, it is best to put them all on the same wavelength immediately. This is the situation you find naturally when they have been singing together for many years. There is an identical rising auditory curve, one which has undoubtedly been conditioned by the sustained breathing they do, and which makes for a unity that is hard to find elsewhere in the world. If you take two monks and charge their ears with opposite curves they will immediately enter into conflict at the level of language. And Gregorian needs perfect blending. If you give this sort of auditory curve to someone who is not a monk, he or she will become extremely aware.

It is impossible to arrive at this state of permanent consciousness, though, without having the opportunity of always being charged. And of course the environment of the monastery is a very important factor. The Benedictines are lucky in that they are vowed to silence. This is a verbal silence which keeps one from uttering unconscious nonsense. But it is important, if you succeed in extricating yourself from this condition, that a strong stimulus be provided—for at least four and a half hours a day as I said—in order that one can meditate or work. This is what the chant is doing.

The church in which the Gregorian is sung is extremely important, because it must sing at the same time. Its own resonance makes it unimportant whether there are six monks singing or a whole choir. The walls of the church itself are excited, reverberating the sound. And the whole technique of building churches is to amplify the high frequencies, to give the sensation of another centre of gravity above the head. Here again the stress is on verticality.

[*Tomatis is not alone in recognizing the way in which a church's acoustics subtly contribute to spiritual sensation. The Canadian composer R. Murray Schafer in his* Tuning of the World *suggests that the builders of the great Gothic cathedrals consciously shaped stone surfaces so as to create multiple reflections of the higher frequencies. This was to give the feeling of omnipresence, a sense that the sound was coming not from a single identifiable point but from all around. Such a numinous experience also struck McLuhan (from whom Tomatis may have borrowed the analogy of a fish being unable to perceive its own medium). In a phrase worthy of Joyce, he deplored the way that modern public-address amplification in churches reduced the comforting ambiguity of the "blessed mutter."*]

The sound produced is not in the mouth, not in the body, but in fact in the bones. It is all the bones of the body which are singing, and it's like a vibrator exciting the walls of the church, which also sings. The voice essentially excites bone conduction, giving the impression the sound originates from "outside," from beyond the body. This corresponds to many ascetic ideals. The ascetic does not so much reject the body as demonstrate his dominion over it.

In the past, some monks believed Gregorian was to be sung like lyric songs. They pushed very hard and sang Gregorian as if they were singing *Othello*. But this is false, because Gregorian is meant to train one to rise up out of the body. To give a sense of interiority, yes, but an interiority in the cosmos itself.

T.W.: I have vaguely heard of a researcher named Fromonti, who looked into something of this phenomenon, and was particularly interested in the modes and progressions of notes, their key and relative pitch if you like, not their absolute frequency content. Do the tones of the chant, their progressions and combinations, affect the charge that one receives?

A.T.: The brain can be charged from several progressions. If they are rich in the higher frequencies, those lower ones which are the determinants of a musical key are not important. You simply choose the key that's suited to your voice. The most important thing is the rising curve in the sound you are making. So if you are a bass you attack the low frequencies, but you're still creating a rich harmonic response with bone conduction. All the Benedictines, in fact, sing in the medium range, the range of a baritone. But their voices are so rich in overtones that you have the impression they are not men, but angels, yes?

T.W.: What about healing bodily ailments? Does it follow that because the brain is charged the body stays healthy?

A.T.: Well, rarely are the monks in bad health if they are singing and eating well! But if the level of awareness is very high, the problems of existence are eliminated. You begin to see that all bodily illness results from psychological problems absorbed by the body, as a sort of defense or protection, perhaps.

[Tomatis does not seem worried about deterioration in the quality of the external sound environment, a process which

*has begun to be described by the new discipline of "acoustic
ecology." Good listening, Tomatis insists, involves the individual
ability to shut out "parasitic" sounds, and to focus only on
the ones we want to hear. He seems to have been particularly
reticent about how electro-acoustic technology, itself perhaps
the product of poor listening, threatens our paradise. I hope
in a future interview to hear his views on this.]*

T.W.: What happens when a monk's hearing is impaired
so that he doesn't hear the high frequencies clearly?
A.T.: It's difficult for him to understand, to follow what's
going on. He becomes tired, as do many people with Gregorian chant when their hearing is not good. They feel
then that Gregorian is sad, when in fact it is a glorious sound.
T.W.: Do you yourself chant?
A.T.: I am fortunate to be able to make a lot of sound and
when I can I do, because there are sounds which are as
good as two cups of coffee. I work an enormous amount
and since I am able to work day and night I sleep only
about four hours a day. For years now I've been an early
sleeper and an early riser. I usually get to bed at about nine
o'clock, am up by midnight, and work until five in the
morning. It's a rhythm I've acquired. But also, if I have a
long job to do I always put on Gregorian while I work,
because it enables me to remain charged without difficulty.
I don't put it on very loud, but it's always in the background.

Years ago, when I was about 20 or 25, and I began to
realize the efficacy of Gregorian, I used to have problems
in getting other people to listen to that music. They were
people who had something against the Church, or the
Mass, and when they heard my Gregorian they'd turn up
their noses and say they hadn't come to hear the Mass.
Well, I couldn't do anything but play something else. Now,
since the Church has suppressed Gregorian, in France at
least, people no longer know what it is and it has taken its
place again for therapy. So much so that people who are
completely opposed ideologically to anything that might
be the Church ask me, "What are those extraordinary
records that buoy you up so?"

There is a level where we realize that we are in suspension, suspended like marionettes by something, by some Being, and that Being is He who leads us. I believe that when we reach the field of consciousness we become the same Being. It's the same thing, the terms are the same. We only run into difficulty because the words are hard to express, but this breath of life which breathes in each one of us is what one basically calls freedom. In biology it's called Life, in affectivity it's called Love, in psychology it's called Consciousness and in theology it's called God. The difficulty is to bring these all together within everyone's understanding.

In fact I am sure that when you are speaking well, your brain is used essentially to capture all the information that the Logos—the Universe, God—has to give. And when you are singing, it is God singing with your body like an instrument. When a monk has a high awareness of the presence of God, it is God singing through him. In Indian asceticism there is the phenomenon of good listening because it is a stage of wisdom. The ascetic not only listens to other people but listens to the whole universe. The universe asks only that we listen, but we look down at our feet, never above our heads. "To reach out towards that to which one listens"—in Latin that's *ab audire,* which translates in French as *obéir,* to obey. Unfortunately, that is seen as a constraint; man does not want to. Obéir is to let oneself go completely in listening. Who is it that speaks? It is the Logos that speaks. It is the universe that speaks, and we are the machines to translate the universe. But in order to do that we must realize that we depend neither on our own creativity nor on our own thoughts, but on the universe itself.

T.W.: Have you found any modern sacred music that produces the effect that Gregorian does? Are people writing and performing such music today?

[It is not certain whether, at the time this question was asked in 1978, Dr. Tomatis had heard of the many contemporary musicians who are working with harmonic chant. In any event, his answer is an interesting contrast to his opening remarks on sounds being sacred "only insofar as they render . . . service to the singer." When I asked a Tibetan abbot about the technique

*of producing what some have called the "transcendent overtone"
in his chanting, he said that there was no such thing, only an
indefinable quality which may become audible when the degree
of the monks' devotion is appropriate. Do we sing for ourselves,
then? For something, or some One outside of ourselves? Is there
a difference?]*

A.T.: I have spoken to musicians for years of these discoveries. I show them the curve, but I haven't found a single
promising artist. Each seems to have the impression (it's
undoubtedly his ego defending itself) that he will create
everything, do everything. He forgets that to make music
is, like for Fra Angelico, to paint for others and not for oneself.

Man has a great desire to put himself into a special state
of consciousness. But in Hebrew, to be heard is already
to be answered. If God listens to our plea, he answers it.
So it's dynamic, to listen is *ipso facto* to obey. The work of
man is to do what God asks of him, and what God wants
most is for His own to obey Him. So there is a whole internal
dynamic which is basically the psychology of breaking
down our "me," which is colossal.

He who lets himself go to listen to the universe, who will
transcribe all that the universe has to say, he will be a Plato,
a Socrates, a Pythagoras, an Einstein, etc. A Mozart also
translates in music what the universe says to him. And
then we have the man in the street, who thinks he's doing
something but who listens to nothing and who obeys even
less. It is for a monk and his meditation to bring himself
to listening, to the point of absolute obedience. And the
psychological problem that I find most widespread today
is that we have forgotten the notion, not only of listening,
but of obeying. If you look in the scriptures, the word you
find most often is "listen." The Rule of St. Benedict begins
with the words, "Hear, O my son, the words of the Lord,
and incline thy heart's ear." And so everything begins with
obedience. That is perfect listening.

*Much of the material in this article, with examples of chanting, is on an
audio cassette released by the Theosophical Publishing House (P.O.
Box 270, Wheaton, IL 60189) under the title* Healing Powers of Tone
and Chant, *which accompanies a tape on chanting by Don Campbell.*

2
The Physician, the Ear and Sacred Music

BRADFORD S. WEEKS, M.D.

The following chapter is a simplified version of a scientific article written in 1986 detailing my work and experiences in high-frequency audition (hearing) research. For those who are interested in greater scientific and medical detail than is presented here, I refer you to the original article (Gilmor, et al, 1989). The descriptions of Phase 1 and Phase 2 of the work however still contain considerable medical and scientific terminology. An understanding of these terms and of orthodox thinking on audition is necessary to fully comprehend the elegance, unity, and usefulness of the unorthodox theories and applications presented below. This work is aimed at both scientists and nonscientists, as well as musicians and spiritual seekers, in the hope that each may gain some appreciation of the viewpoints of the others with regard to sound and hearing.

Before the physician in me leads you through research in high-frequency audition, the musician within wants to share his personal experiences with sound. I am writing both as a physician and a musician since a common ground is only now being established between these two healing modalities. We often speak of the artistic and the scientific nature of medicine. Thus the Art of Medicine and the Science of Medicine are both acknowledged. However, this dichotomy between science and art, or rather between qualifiable and quantifiable knowledge, is an artifact of poor perception. Everything that is real, either in the world

Bradford S. Weeks, M.D.

or in people's minds, has both a quality and a quantity. When people talk about the art in addition to the science of medicine, it is because they somehow recognize this to be appropriate for an activity where mortals toil at the threshold of the spiritual world. Science alone is too impotent in an environment where lives are lost on a daily basis. We must call Art, with all her intangibilities and mysterious powers, to our succor. Unfortunately, few people are talking about the science of music therapy. Instead, they delegate it to the qualifiable domain of art alone. However, there is a nascent science to music therapy. Indications along those lines will form the core of this paper.

Accordingly, I write for scientists and non-scientists. Both will have to stretch a bit to meet me on the bridge of ideas. Non-physicians might have to consult some medical texts, but where can scientists turn when ideas like "soul," "spirit" or any qualifiable entity are discussed? The language of feeling and personal experience can be as intimidating to my professional colleagues as Latin or Greek medical language can be to patients. So, I write as both a physician and scientist and as musician to the scientific and musical side of all my readers.

I was fortunate. My mother sang to me as a child. She also played music for me and even encouraged me to sing along (a supreme act of love!). I was comforted by the rhythm, the sounds and the familiarity of songs. They lulled me calmly to sleep at night, provided the entertainment now sadly offered to kids by television and guided me gently through many childhood traumas. Music was a comfort, a reliable support for me. Through most of childhood, like a guardian angel, I had Music on my side.

Then, sometime around fourth grade I suffered an injustice as tragic as it is universal. Gamely trying to sing in the school glee club, I was singled out by the choir master and informed in front of the entire group that, for the sake of the upcoming Christmas performance, I must stand in the back row, mouth the word "watermelon" and make no sound. Apparently he needed my body to fill space but had decided he could do without the voice and the soul that came with the body. As I think back on that psychic

30

trauma decades ago, the most remarkable point is how willingly I accepted this judgment. I can't quite remember, but I suppose I did as I was told. Perhaps I sang very quietly at some points in the performance, but probably I was a good boy and spent the two hours mouthing the word "watermelon."

How strange that so many of us stopped singing in childhood because of similar criticism. Why did we believe our respective choirmasters (or whoever it was that stopped our song) when they told us we should not sing out loud? One woman was told not to sing by her mother, another by her boyfriend. One elderly man, finally learning to sing at seventy-five, was asked by a minister never to sing out loud. We all know friends who today refuse to sing along years after being told they have a bad voice. Why does not our humanity rear up and defend its birthright to sing and dance and be joyful before our Maker and our loved ones? Why do we so easily stuff our voice, the herald of the soul?

Long before I thought of becoming a physician, the professional warned by Hippocrates to "heal thyself," I did just that by instinctively finding a way to resurrect my voice. Perhaps I couldn't have done it without the generous foundation laid by my musical parents, but in the summer of my sixteenth year, I taught myself how to sing. I had fallen into an intimate relationship with a two hundred year old pine tree that enjoyed the winds and weather halfway up a mountain behind our house. I would meander up that mountainside, climb high into her branches and listen to the wind strum her needles. Way above the houses and buffered by miles of thin air from the music critics below, I gradually found my voice. Free from embarrassment, I learned to sing wildly to the world from the treetop stage as the inhibitions that were choking my voice loosed their grasp. I learned to sing to my heart's content. In doing so, I feel I reclaimed an essential part of my humanity. This tryst lasted but a few summer months; however certainly that ancient pine has proven to be the most influential summer love I have ever known. Since then, those who know music say I have a superb (albeit unschooled) tenor voice. "Didn't you ever sing in a choir?" they ask.

I am no different from you. Unless you have had throat surgery or ear trauma, that is, assuming no anatomical handicaps, I know that you too have a superb voice stuffed somewhere between your soul and your lips. I know this because I have helped introduce many incredulous people to their long lost voices. Quite frankly, I know of no medical accomplishment that can compare with the gratification I feel after helping people listen to their own voices and then sing along with themselves (and eventually others).

A brief word about technique. Consider the wisdom of the bumper sticker I saw on a Los Angeles freeway that said, "Get out of your own way." (If I had been a more capable driver that day and had been able to maneuver through that traffic, I would have followed that driver home and sat at his or her feet to seek enlightenment.) So it is with singing; we must get out of our own way. Music is what the human frame and soul is designed to do; we need simply to learn to allow song to have its way with us. Next, we need to attend to breathing. The physics of voice involve air being forced past vocal chords which vibrate, thus making sound. The bellows must deliver an even and ample source of air in order to generate a pleasant voice. In Aikido and most of the traditional martial arts we are taught, "If you can control your opponent's breathing by making him breathe at your rate and depth, you have the critical advantage." So it is with song: if the singer within can encourage the criticized child within to breathe regularly and "soundly" then, quite naturally, the body does what it has craved all along—it sings! Later, fine tuning involves the art of listening (see below), for the best singers sing mostly with their ears.

After music and I became reacquainted and formed a happy partnership, I continued to discover how essential its presence is to health. For sheer power, magnificent in its splendor, observe what music does with the vitality and happiness of handicapped children. For a brief, thrilling period of my life I was charged with doing music therapy with severely physically and mentally handicapped children in a West German school. Seeing the richness of emotional experience in a child whose crippled hand I guided across a cello's strings was as intoxicating as it was awe-inspiring. The empowerment these mangled children seemed to attain by initiating, being able to sustain and then, whenever they choose, to arrest a tone from string, wind, percussion or vocal instruments was profound.

Different instruments seemed to have different effects on the children first on their moods and later on their personalities. I began to consider prescribing different sounds as a doctor would specific medicines. Quickly, however, I found that these kids knew best which instruments they needed to nourish depleted aspects of their souls or personalities. Intuitively, they sought out the right energy; one day the soothing cello vibrations, one day the bleat of a poorly played horn, next the crash of a drum, then back to the string instruments.

My interactions with them were blinding, as when one stumbles out of a dark room into daylight. In this case, the intensity of their relationship with music made other aspects of my life pale by comparison. The eyes of my soul were not accustomed to the brilliant power of music as therapy. I had taken the job thinking it would be fun; it would provide a distraction from their handicaps, a form of amusement. I did not realize how profound a source of nutrition and therapy the sounds would be for these handicapped children.

When I finally perceived what powerful therapy was happening around music, I felt a bit the intruder, somewhat unworthy to be witnessing such pure therapeutic power. I felt as must have Phaeton, the son of Apollo, who took Helios's sun chariot for the ultimate joy ride. Put yourself in the chariot as the wild horses surged across the sky pulling the mighty sun behind their thundering wings. Imagine the exhilaration young Phaeton felt riding that sun chariot. That is the feeling the music therapist feels in discovering and riding along with the extraordinary therapeutic power of sound. Phaeton's ride ended in tragedy when the steeds, sensing an unfamiliar hand on their reins, flew too near the earth. To save the parched earth from catching fire, Jupiter destroyed them with a

Bradford S. Weeks, M.D.

thunderbolt. The power of music in therapy is far more forgiving. I know of no toxic side effects from music therapy save unnecessary ear trauma related to excessive volume.

Working with those crippled children who grasped passionately for their musical birthright taught me to respect the power of music therapy. My belief in music therapy has been repeatedly reinforced in a myriad of ways as varied as the suffering people bring to my practice. Novalis, the German poet, wrote:

Every sickness is a musical problem. The healing, therefore, is a musical resolution. The shorter the resolution, the greater the musical talent of the doctor.

I think I understand what he recognized. One can never be certain with poets, but I think I have seen it too. And so I have come to believe that the part of us that sings is quite closely related, if not identical, to the part of us that grows and heals. The vitality released when the adult patient rediscovers his or her abandoned child-voice is miraculous to behold. It makes the practice of medicine rewarding and fun. Novalis wouldn't be surprised to learn that the medical literature is completely unambiguous in finding fewer intra- and post-operative problems with patients whose surgeons talked with them prior to the operation. He would perhaps wonder, as do I, how much better the operative results would be if surgeons sang with patients prior to their surgery!

When studying human anatomy and the intricacies of biochemistry in medical school, I discovered that background music of Gregorian and Tibetan chants facilitated my memorization ability. Once again, music revealed another aspect of her power to me. It was this experience of music somehow seeming to enhance my concentration ability which led me to the study of the therapeutic aspect of sacred music.

A Study of the Therapeutic Aspects of Sacred Music

In all matters of opinion, our adversaries are deranged.
                                        Mark Twain

A radical reinterpretation of current thinking about the

34

ear follows. It first caught my attention because of its clinical applicability as therapy, as well as its theoretical elegance. The characters involved in this report are varied. The cast includes otorhinolaryngologists, neurologists, audiologists, Tibetan and Christian monks, an extraordinarily varied patient population, and of course, the sources of original interpretations, the investigators without whose shoulders reinterpretations would not be possible.

The study I am reporting on was organized into four distinct phases in order to thoroughly evaluate on four separate levels the soundness of the following radical departures from orthodoxy: the mental (Phase 1, a literature search and review of theories); the physical (Phase 2, the actual therapeutic applications of the work); the emotional/ spiritual (Phase 3, immersion in the sacred rituals and acoustic environment of Christian and Buddhist monasteries); and the intuitive (Phase 4, the unification of the previous three phases towards a new synthesis of thought on audition).

Phase 1: The Role of the Human Ear

A man clings all his days to what he received in his youth.

Paracelsus

Searching the literature and taking degree of disagreement among specialists as my barometer, it quickly became apparent that the ear is a much studied, yet incompletely understood organ. What follows is a summary of orthodox and unorthodox views regarding anatomy, neurophysiology, and the potential of the ear as a therapeutic agent for illness throughout the body. This information was gathered from my medical school basic science curriculum, a literature search, and interviews with specialists in the field.

The human ear has two important functions: hearing with the cochlea (a snail-shaped canal in the inner ear) and balance with the vestibule (a central cavity of the labyrinth that makes up the inner ear). The ear is routinely given short shrift in gross anatomy classes where its tiny but important muscles are rarely seen. In anatomy textbooks, the 8th cranial nerve (the acoustic nerve) routinely gets the least print.

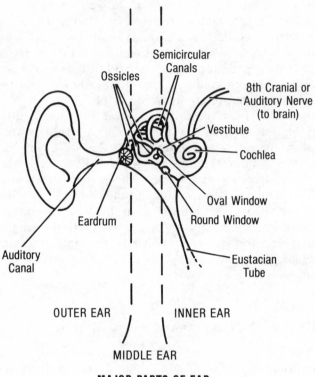

MAJOR PARTS OF EAR

Theoretically, the ear involves the transmission of energy from sound waves. Sound as vibrational energy moves from the eardrum to a membrane deep in the ear called the oval window, travelling through the tiny bones inside of the middle ear (ossicles). In addition, theory has it that this vibration is transmitted through the lymph or fluid in the upper portion of the spiral cochlea, up past the special high, middle, and low frequency vibrational receptor cells of the ear (cells of Corti), then descends again via the lower portion of the cochlea to the round window (another membrane of the middle ear lying just below the oval window).

According to the prevailing and orthodox ideas in the field, the only remaining questions about the function of the ear pertain to processes that transform vibrational or wave energy to electrical energy at special receptor cells (cells of Corti), and ultimately to an understanding of how the brain perceives the sounds that the ear transmits.

A comparison of the orthodox scientific views and more unorthodox ideas regarding the effect of sound and hearing on the human organism may lead to a fuller and more holistic understanding of this fascinating field.

1. Regarding the embryological origin of the human ear:

If you want to understand what something is, you must look to see where it came from.

Goethe

Orthodox: It is commonly understood that the ear is divided into three parts—the external ear (meatus and auditory canal), the middle ear (tympanic membrane or eardrum, ossicles, middle ear muscles, oval and round window), and the inner ear (vestibular canal and cochlea).

Unorthodox: An appreciation of embryology suggests that there are, practically speaking, only two parts to the ear— an external and an internal ear. My point here is that the ear is commonly functionally understood as having three parts while it actually comprises a duality. This distinction becomes therapeutically significant in terms of the perception of high-frequency sounds (see following).

2. Sound transmission:

We really ought to know by now how the ear works.
Ashmore in *Nature* 8/84

Orthodox: The external auditory canal is commonly considered to be a low-frequency filter of the sound transmitted through the ear. It is observed that bone vibrations of the skull can create sound waves in the external auditory canal, which cause the tympanic membrane or eardrum to vibrate (Tonndorf, 1972). The ossicles are understood as linking the sound vibrations which occur at the eardrum to the oval window. The middle ear muscles maintain the connection between the ossicles (according to Von Bekesy, 1960). However, this long standing interpretation is currently being challenged (Howell, 1984). The role of the lymph or fluid in the inner ear is thought to further conduct the sound waves of kinetic energy towards their destination, the sensory cells of Corti. An action potential, or electrical nerve message that travels along nerve cells, is generated by the sound waves received by the cells of Corti. It travels from these cells along the 8th cranial nerve to the cortex of the brain for final interpretation of the sound. The role of the cochlea is to maintain sound fidelity, and the round window dampens any excess kinetic energy generated by the sound waves—in other words it acts like a pressure release valve (Nuttall & Ross, 1986).

Unorthodox (Tomatis, 1974A):

A. The distance that separates the second and third ossicles or bones of the middle ear doesn't allow for conduction of sound with the fidelity commensurate with human hearing. Rather than transmitting the vibrational sound from external to internal ear, the function of the ossicles is thought to be a protective one. When there is intense sound travelling through the ear, the ossicles (and their corresponding muscles) respond to any excessive vibrational energy by pushing back from the middle to the outer ear. This outward pressure causes tenting of the tympanic membrane, whose edges then make a less tight contact with the tympanic sulcus (groove in the bone which is the contact between the eardrum and the bones of the skull). When the contact is less tight, the energy of the sound transmitted across this juncture is also lessened, and thus decreases the vibrational energy travelling via bone conduction to the delicate cells of Corti. In effect then, rather than solely transmitting sound, the ossicles serve a protective role by dampening excessive vibratory energy. (Although he was the first, Tomatis is no longer the only one assigning a protective role to the middle ear [Simmons 1964].)

B. The lymph or fluid in the ear is always moving (Juhn, 1983 [1986].) Therefore, it seems unreasonable to consider that it can carry and maintain specific sound waves amidst the turbulence. Additionally, it has been observed that sounds which are sequential in nature can be transmitted

virtually instantaneously through the ear, which is also
inconsistent with this idea (Fritze, 1985). The function of
the fluid in the ear, as in other parts of the body (joints,
brain), is to do what fluid does best: to absorb excess energy
and protect the surrounding structures from damage.

C. Removal of the ossicles does not diminish the conduction of sound waves through the other bones of the head.
However, some loss in the viability of sound transmission
through the ear may occur since contact between the eardrum
and the structures of the middle ear is lessened without
the ossicles.

D. Dr. Alfred A. Tomatis, an authority in auditory
neurophysiology, claims that hearing occurs primarily as
a result of sound conduction through the bones of the
head, and is not due to sound conduction through the
ossicles of the ear. He feels the primary site for sound
transmission and hearing is the portion of skull bone that
runs from the tympanic sulcus (a groove in this skull bone at
the point of attachment to the tympanic membrane) along
the petrous bone of the skull.* This theory proposes that
sound waves hit the tympanic membrane, causing it to
vibrate. The vibrational energy travels along the fibers that
radiate out from the center of the membrane to its attachment to the petrous bone in the skull at the tympanic sulcus.
The petrous bone then vibrates, thereby directly sending
the sound waves to the basilar membrane. Attached to
the basilar membrane are the cells of Corti, the sound
receptor cells that transmit sound wave messages to the
brain. If the sound is too loud or carries too much vibrational
energy for the delicate basilar membrane cells, the excess
vibrational energy splays out to the fluid in the cochlea
or inner ear,† which bulges out the oval window, in turn

---

*"Petrous" means rock-like; the petrous bone of the skull is the
temporal bone that surrounds and protects the inner ear. It is the
densest bone in the body and the only inert bone that remains
unchanged from the time of birth. Therefore, it is ideally suited
for sound conduction.

†Fluid traditionally plays a protective role in the body, as in
protection of our joints. The fluid in the cochlea of the inner ear is

pushing on the ossicles of the middle ear (the pressure release valve). This causes tenting of the tympanic membrane, with the resultant effects discussed earlier. Evidence for supporting this theory of audition comes from the well known fact of physics that sound travels with greater fidelity through a dense medium (such as bone) than through a less dense one (air, water, or cartilage).

Opponents of the bone conduction theories feel that the soft tissues found in the skull would lower the fidelity of the sounds traveling by this route. However, the bones adjacent to the eardrum receive vibrational energy directly from the eardrum. (Note that whales hear by conduction of sound through the skull bones.) Sound waves of intense force are required for our acute sense of hearing. These have impact on the delicate and sensitive cells of Corti, which are receptors of the sound wave energy. The cells of Corti then translate the energy of sound waves into electrical energy that the nerves and brain can interpret. The role of the middle ear in guarding the sensitive cells of Corti within the inner ear becomes very important.

E. Flock observed that the sensory cells of Corti, which are also hair cells, surprisingly contain molecules with functions not expected in sensory cells, e.g., actin, a protein whose function is to cause contraction! (Flock, 1983). The cells of Corti may have a different function from what was previously thought—they may be involved in the mechanics of sound transmission through the inner ear rather than having a purely sensory function. Tomatis suggests that the eddying currents found in the lymph fluid of the inner ear may be a direct result of the initial vibration of the membrane on which the cells of Corti rest, rather than the reverse or usual interpretation, which is that sound is transmitted through the eddying lymph and in turn stimulates the membrane and sensory cells of Corti (Tomatis, 1974 A).

F. A muscle (the stapedius muscle) which regulates one of the tiny bones of the middle ear is the only muscle in

---

more likely to have its conventional role of protecting the ear, for which it is well suited, than to be involved in sound transmission, for which it is a poor conductor.

the human body that never rests (even the heart pulsates and thereby rests between each beat) (Tomatis, 1974 A). This constant movement is significant with regard to Tomatis's theory of cortical charge (see below).

3. Ear Neurology:

The Nerves of the Terrible Pterygopalatine Traffic Circle: every anatomy student's nightmare

The ear is the Rome of the body. As a student of gross anatomy, I was struck by the fact that almost all cranial nerves lead to the ear. Cranial nerves 2-11 are either directly connected with other nerves or indirectly linked with them via branching. In order to appreciate fully the many varied roles of the acoustic or 8th cranial nerve, one must understand its link to the function of vision (Tomatis, 1974 A). It is customary when dealing with brain functions to link eye, head and neck mobility with the optic nerve. However, these functions are also under control of the acoustic nerve.

As if this wide scope of neurological involvement is not enough, the ear also has a fascinating tie into the 10th cranial nerve or the vagus nerve—"the path of the wandering soul." The vagus is literally responsible for our gut reactions, since it is the link between the automatic functions of the internal organs and the brain. It is surprising to realize that the eardrum and the vagus nerve are in contact with each other. What is the significance of this interaction? Let us track the path of the vagus throughout the body. The nerve wanders on from its liaison with the ear, next making contact with back muscles; it then sensitizes the larynx which allows us to speak, sing, or scream. The vagus then travels to the lungs and heart before diving through the diaphragm to innervate all of our internal organs (including the entire intestinal tract via communication with sacral nerves).

Hearing has substantial effects on the rest of the body, due to its contact with the vagus nerve. But this ought not surprise us. What would a scary movie be without the emotionally manipulative sound track? As the ear gains greater appreciation as our primary sensory organ—as well as having an extensive effect on many internal organs, due to its connection with the vagus nerve—a theoretical basis for audio-therapy's effectiveness in the many physical and emotional conditions it can treat comes into focus.

This is only a glimpse of some of the major reinterpretations of ear structure and function. The bibliography offers the reader these and other equally innovative assertions in greater detail than the scope of this report justifies.

Phase 2: The Work of Dr. Alfred A. Tomatis

Creative imagination is frequently associated with the interplay between two conceptual frameworks.

Koestler

Phase 2 of this study involved working with Dr. Alfred A. Tomatis in Paris (one of his forty-five therapeutic centers worldwide). I spent a week there interviewing patients, technicians, and staff, and also observing therapy.

Born in 1920, Dr. Tomatis earned his M.D. from the Faculte de Paris before specializing in otorhinolaryngology. En route to establishing the International Association of Audio-Psycho-Phonology, Dr. Tomatis was distinguished as follows: Chevalier de la Sante Publique (Knight of Public Health) 1951; Medaille d'Or de la Recherche Scientifique (Gold Medal for Scientific Research) 1958; Grande Medaille de Vermeil de la Ville de Paris 1962; Prix Clemence Isaure 1967; Medaille d'Or de la Societe Arts, Science et Lettres 1968; and Commandeur de Merite Culturel et Artistique 1970.

As a scientist, Tomatis is recognized for his experimental breakthroughs in the field of auditory neurophysiology. For example, while treating hearing impaired factory workers by day and opera singers suffering from spots before their eyes at night (scotomas), Tomatis noticed a similarity of symptoms between the two patient populations. After further investigation, he formulated the law describing the feedback loop between the larynx and the ear: "The larynx emits only the range that the ear controlled." In other words, one can reproduce vocally only those sounds that the human ear is capable of detecting. This discovery was recognized by the Academy of Sciences of Paris and the French Academy of Medicine who in 1957 named this theory about the ear and voice the Tomatis Effect.

As a clinician, Tomatis has achieved the reputation for successful and unorthodox therapies whose scope exceeds the range of ear, nose and throat disorders. The list of illnesses he has successfully treated with high-frequency sound therapy includes: ear, nose and throat disorders: hearing and voice loss (Tomatis, 1960 A), stuttering (Tomatis, 1954), ringing in the ears, inflammation of the middle ear (Tomatis, 1986); neurological disorders: spots before the eyes (Tomatis, 1974 B), drooling (Tomatis, 1974 B, 1986), eye-muscle imbalances (Tomatis, 1986); psychiatric disorders: depression, (Tomatis, 1974 C), attention deficit disorder, hyperactivity (Le Gall, A., 1961); learning disorders: dyslexia (Tomatis, 1967), inability to concentrate (Tomatis, 1986); and a variety of balance/coordination disorders related to problems with the inner ear (Tomatis, 1986). These therapeutic coups occur by retraining the ear muscles using another Tomatis invention, the electronic ear that utilizes filtered sound. The claims regarding the therapeutic value of this technique were what drew me to France to study with Tomatis.

Among Tomatis' innovative ideas is the notion that bass sounds are felt throughout the body in a manner similar to the sense of touch. His electronic ear is based on this proposition. It is a machine that contains a microphone, amplifiers, filters, and earphones. It is designed to help the ear acquire three functions: listening, monitoring of language, and laterality, or the ability to change from left to right ear dominance in hearing.

The electronic ear works by delivering to the listener's ear sounds which are progressively filtered along a continuum, from normal, non-filtered sound to sound in which all except frequencies greater than 8000 hz (hertz) have been filtered out. (Hertz is a measure of the frequency of a sound wave; 1 hertz is equal to one cycle of sound waves per second.) In addition, the sound delivered to the listener alternates between two channels which are set to produce maximum bass and maximum treble sounds. Consequently, the stapedius muscle (the muscle of the middle ear which regulates the stapes, one of the three tiny bones or ossicles) must exert control over the stapes in order for one to hear the ascending high-frequency sounds, as well as hear the

Bradford S. Weeks, M.D.

fluctuations between bass and treble at a given frequency. This challenge to the poorly toned middle ear muscles (especially the stapedius muscle which is primarily responsible for the ability to discriminate high-frequency sounds) works like micro-gymnastics; the exercise helps one reattain the ear's ability to focus sound (as opposed to the brain's focusing on sound).

The Tomatis test is a critical diagnostic tool for determining hearing disorders. This test determines the ability to detect sound at a predetermined intensity for frequencies ranging from 125 to 8000 hz. The results of this test allow evaluation of the patient's ability to recognize pitch differences in closely related sounds (auditory discrimination). The test also determines how well air conduction and bone conduction of sound are functioning in the patient. Finally, the ability to detect the direction of a sound (spatialization) and each ear's individual ability to detect sound (laterality) are tested.

Tomatis is given credit for being the first to appreciate the important distinction between hearing and listening. The former is non-selective and does not require focusing, while the latter does require focusing to pay specific attention to one of the many sounds which may be heard simultaneously. Hearing is less strenuous than listening. Listening involves will power. Tomatis's listening test differs from the hearing test of the audiologist in that the listening test measures not only the physical capabilities of the ear, but also the degree to which the ear's potential is being utilized by the patient. Audiologists frustratingly acknowledge that many people who come to them with hearing problems can hear perfectly well according to the results of their audiograms (standard hearing tests). In fact, the problem is not with hearing but with listening. A course of therapy with the electronic ear has been shown to improve these listening problems.

The electronic ear also trains the right ear to be dominant. This is beneficial because of the assymetry of the pathways over which sound travels through the body (Gacek, 1972). According to Tomatis right ear dominance has the effect of speeding up the processing of both sensory information and knowledge (Tomatis, 1974 A).

44

Perhaps the most provocative theory involves fetal audition (Tomatis, 1981). He suggests that the mother's voice can penetrate through her bones to the intrauterine world, and it is the child's first target of communication with the extrauterine world. Traumas during pregnancy can result in unpleasant associations with certain sound frequencies and have been associated with hearing loss. Tomatis has had success in treating this kind of hearing loss as well as neurosis by simulating sounds experienced during uterine life, including the mother's voice. These sounds are progressively filtered from 8000 hz to 100 hz. He calls this procedure "sonic rebirth." A fascinating spinoff involves learning a foreign language such as Arabic by undergoing sonic rebirth while listening to a course of filtered Arabic, thus sensitizing one's ears to its idiosyncratic sounds (Tomatis, 1960 B).

Other innovations Tomatis introduced include the idea that the brain receives more stimuli from the ears than from any other organ. He makes further startling assertions: the skin is derived from cells that become ear tissue rather than vice versa; the ear preceded the nervous system (Tomatis, 1974 A); the cells of the body which "sense" evolved from the tissue that produces the cells of Corti of the ear (see Flock et al, 1983). Tomatis successfully treats many problematic maladies by using his appreciation of the peculiarities of the human ear.

The most exciting theory of Tomatis's, and the one which led me to consider the role of sacred music as therapy, is the concept of cortical charge. Experience tells us that some sounds put us to sleep (lullabies) and some keep us awake (traffic); some calm us (surf on the beach) and some make us dance all night (rhythm). A hard driving beat practically forces us to tap our feet. The screech of chalk on a blackboard makes us scream and contract in discomfort. We are constantly bathed by sound.

Tomatis has devoted his career to analyzing the effect various components of sound have on our bodies. The claim that music exerts a profound effect on us is beyond question. What remains is only to establish how the components of sound affect our bodies. (Psychosomatically? Physiologically, due to the wandering path of the vagus nerve?) According to Tomatis, the primary function of the ear is to provide the cells of the body with electrical stimulation or cortical charge. The cells of Corti deep in the inner ear (the cochlear-vestibular area) transform sound waves into electrical input. According to Tomatis:

> The charge of energy obtained from the influx of nervous impulses reaches the cortex [of the brain], which then distributes it throughout the body toning up the whole system and imparting greater dynamism to the human being (Tomatis, 1978).

Tomatis has stated that not all sounds have an effect upon cortical charge. The cells of Corti respond much more intensely to high frequency sound than to low frequency sound. He calls sounds rich in high harmonics "charging sounds," in contrast to sounds rich in lower tones, which he calls "dis-charging sounds." Tomatis feels that low frequency sounds supply insufficient energy to the brain and may even exhaust the individual. This may help explain why a depressed person may listen more intently to the sounds of his or her own internal being (heartbeat, breathing, etc.) which fall in the low-frequency range. For the depressed person, hearing no longer is a route of communication, but the sense becomes directed inward (Tomatis, 1978).

Sonic training with high-frequency sound can be very useful therapeutically, according to Tomatis. A cortical charge generated during sonic therapy could be used to energize the individual. The effects of this treatment might manifest in increased motivation and competence in work, better concentration, increased memory skills, lower susceptibility to fatigue, and generally more dynamism and energy (Tomatis, 1978).

Application: Anecdotal evidence suggests that certain high-frequency sounds confer alertness and stamina to the listener and result in enhanced performance. For example, students report that listening to Gregorian chants or classical music increases their ability to concentrate. Or consider the time honored prescription, "whistle while you work." The fife, bugles and bagpipes (high frequency sound) traditionally were used to motivate soldiers going into

drums = low FREQ = ORder
Fife & bugles = high freq = motivation

battle. Perhaps these shrill high-frequency tones impart an enthusiasm by stimulating a cortical charge. Drums (a low frequency sound) simulating the heartbeat were used to give order to this enthusiasm (left—right—left—right).

Scientific method is the ultimate test for the reinterpretations of the time-honored theories of hearing. This requires that the new theories must agree with observations, be internally consistent and be comprehensive. The first criterion can be tested in labs or clinics that have the opportunity to reproduce Tomatis's studies. The internal consistency of new theories may be determined by the presence or absence of any logical contradictions. Simplicity and elegance of a theory are desirable as well. Lastly, the comprehensiveness of a theory is measured in terms of its ability to show the relationship of phenomena previously thought to be unrelated. Therapeutic usefulness is a marker that also serves to positively evaluate the work of Tomatis.

Phase 3: Sacred Music

Gregorian Chant
Listen, my Son, to the voice of your God
and open wide the ears of your heart.
> First rule of the
> Order of St. Benoit

What is Gregorian chant? How is it different from music? Why is it sacred? How does it promote listening? These questions must be answered before descriptions of my experiences can be understood.

Gregorian chant is a body of chant collected from many cultures by St. Gregory (Pope from 590-604 A.D.) in an effort to standardize the Catholic mass. Gregorian chant differs from music in a number of essential ways. Most importantly, this chant has no meter. Timing is based not on a rhythm noted on music sheets, but rather on the human breath. In fact, the chant master who trains novices (four years before they join the choir) and leads the chant, controls the group's respiration rate by drawing forth increasingly long phrases from the chanters. The extension of the controlled exhalation necessary to maintain a good

Bradford S. Weeks, M.D.

tone has the physiological consequence of slowing down
the rate of breathing and thereby slowing down the heart.
It follows that a reduction of blood pressure occurs during
the chanting. In addition, without their conscious knowledge,
those listening to the monks begin to alter their breathing
too. What occurs, then, eight times daily for traditional
Gregorian chanting monks, is a form of respiratory yoga.
The result is that physical and then emotional stress
evaporates permitting a profound feeling of peace to fill
one's being.

Over the past three decades, many Catholic monasteries
have closed down. Tomatis claims that of these closures,
none involved monasteries which practiced the traditional
Gregorian chant. It is a reasonable hypothesis that cortical
charge and its consequent boon to energy levels, concentration, alertness and general well-being of the monks is an
important factor in the health of the Catholic Church. In
fact, in works citing Dr. Tomatis and his "house-calls" to
failing monasteries, the Church has called for a return
to the traditional, Latin form of the chant.

When I originally read "open wide the ears of your heart"
in the first rule of the order of St. Benoit, founder of the
Gregorian chanting Benedictine Order, I thought of the
heart's auricles, flaps above each atria whose function is
unknown. It delighted me that, indeed, the heart does have
an ear of sorts. For the moment, therefore, unsatisfied
that it was so named solely due to resemblance, I wondered
what the heart has to do with listening. However, "to listen"
and "to obey" have common etymological roots. It should
come as no surprise to learn that each chant master whom
I interviewed explained that chanting is an exercise in
listening. Listening is an exercise in obedience. At best,
true listening is an approximation of selflessness whereby
one person opens not only their ears, but their heart to the
words, both spoken and non-spoken, of another.

Tibetan Chant
*The ear collects the spiraling energy from the cosmos, this energy gives
life to man and we see this vitality in the light which shines forth from
our eyes.*

Tibetan Medical Doctor

The Physician, the Ear and Sacred Music

In 1959, seeking strategic military positions as well as natural resources, China invaded the tiny mountain nation of Tibet. One of the world's last countries whose rulers were monks, Tibet's monasteries and ancient religious culture were quickly and brutally annihilated. Today, the Dalai Lama rules a government-in-exile based in Dharamsala, northern India. The world knows little about the holocaust which took place at the foot of Mt. Everest. Tibetan representatives, political, religious and medical, have slowly made their way to the West in order to demonstrate the importance of their cultural tradition and plead for justice before the world.

I first heard traditional Tibetan overtone chanting in 1985 when representatives of the Gyume College of Tantric Buddhism toured North America. The Gyume are part of the Galugpa Sect (Yellow Hat), a form of tantric Buddhism founded by the legendary Tsongkapa (1357-1419). The chant did not impress me at first. Its rumbling guttural sounds, deep mutterings from the throats of monks, sounded neither musical nor inviting to my ears. Not until the ritual was almost completed did I begin to listen to and appreciate the clear overtones which soared above their fundamental chanted tones. It was then that I experienced the ancient hooni or throat singing, whereby a single monk masters a technique enabling him to chant three notes simultaneously —one monk singing a three-note chord. This so-called "one voice chording" is a sound created by a deep chanted bass note which is the fundamental upon which a note two octaves higher and a note a fifth above that are produced simultaneously. It is an ancient form of chant which is at once bewildering and hauntingly familiar to my ears.

At their refugee monastery in Dharamsala, India, I learned that the overtone chant is performed only during special occasions. These include festivals or national emergencies requiring non-stop prayer, and fasting sessions which can last up to three days. These ritual chanting marathons are an ordeal which requires mastery of the overtone technique. Without this mastery, herniations, respiratory acid-base disturbances, esophageal lacerations and a variety of traumas to the throat have occurred.

49

Bradford S. Weeks, M.D.

Speaking technically, the goal for the monks is to make their bones sing, thus sparing their throats. A medical doctor familiar with this form of chant explained this apparently bizarre goal using the following analogy: "As the bow sets violin strings vibrating, but it is the violin body which sings, so with proper chanting posture, the larynx of the monks contacts the vertebral column thereby setting the axial bones to singing" (Tomatis, 1986).Theories aside, the most impressive aspect of these marathon chants is their very existence, which demands incredible stamina. Additionally, the lack of trauma to the body or throat of the master chanter suggests that the chant is in accordance with rather than contrary to physiological processes.

The greatest difference between the two forms of chant is the frequency at which their fundamental tones are delivered. The Gregorian is a high-frequency tenor chant while the Tibetan is a low-frequency guttural chant. For the investigator interested in high-frequency sounds, however, it is interesting to realize the Tibetans produce a series of harmonic overtones based on a sub-harmonic "undertone" of the guttural fundamental chanted note. These overtones of undertones are audible in the same frequencies as Gregorian chants. Given that high-frequencies, in that they are more difficult to listen to than low-frequencies, train listening (and therefore obedience), it seems that both Gregorian and Tibetan chants are sacred sounds.

What then is the role of musical accompaniment in sacred music? Perhaps it serves as a guide for pitch, perhaps as a guide for timing. While this may be the case, let us also consider the possibility that these instruments produce high-frequency overtones which impart a cortical charge necessary to keep the participants enthused (from *en theus*, "god within"). Tibetan horns and cymbals, massive Zen gongs, Christian church organs, and steeple bells—all these instruments produce, along with their deep rich fundamental notes, soaring resonant overtones—for "him that hath ears to hear." However, while the fundamental notes are obvious (palpable even to the deaf), the overtones are discernible only to those who can truly listen; only to those who can "get out of their own way" and obey.

In summary, despite their apparent differences, both chant forms with their respective instrumental accompaniments create for chanters and listeners alike an acoustic environment rich in those sound frequencies which Tomatis has determined charge the cortex. Therefore, cerebral stimulation as well as a form of respiratory yoga with profound autonomic repercussions ensues. The paradoxical term "excited relaxation" is often used to describe this post-chant state. For myself I felt refreshed.

Phase 4: Synthesis—Music as a Bridge between Medicine and Religion

Poetry is my way of taking life by the throat.
Robert Frost

Sacred music, the archetypal ordering of sound (more precisely, its domestication for human use), appears to be a form of health maintenance for monks across cultures. In singing, through alteration of breath rate, that is, through altering our body's sense of time, we participate in something far greater than our individuality. In order to sing, we must inspire deeply, and be inspired as well. The good doctor is one who can listen deeply, as must the priest.

Music, to the degree that it is sacred, trains this listening. Sacred music, cross-culturally, has resonant high frequencies which demand a certain effort (compared to lower frequencies) on the part of the listener. This strenuous listening stretches the listener and, in turn, imparts a selflessness, a patience and a stillness which clears the way for true perception of phenomenon. And is perception not the goal of the pure scientist, the clinical diagnostician and the theologian as well? For perception is primary. Only after clearly perceiving the phenomenon can a rational plan be formulated.

Tomatis has created an impressive therapy based on training one's true listening. His therapy suggests that the etiology for a varied list of medical problems is, of all things, faulty hearing. For upon retraining the ears via high-frequency audition, stuttering, dyslexia, attention deficit disorder, depression as well as a host of neurological disorders are ameliorated. Sacred chant comprises a similar high-frequency audition therapy and as such, has proven indispensable to the health of monasteries cross-culturally. Thus, further study of the human ear, perhaps our primary sensory and regulatory organ, appears as intriguing as it is therapeutically promising.

Music therapy can be very powerful but, because we barely understand the mechanism of its action, it may be ineffectively used. What constitutes an adequate training before one becomes a music therapist? What type of music is appropriate? More important, what type might be inappropriate and perhaps somehow damaging? "Primum non nocere" (First, do no harm). How to use melody, harmony, rhythm, counterpoint, frequency and tone? Should music therapists work on the soul or perhaps the mind as well? Can we get music into a patient's blood and treat leukemia? What are the risks? In the wrong hands can music destroy health, as Joshua's trumpets made the walls of Jericho "come-a-tumblin' down"? These questions will be answered in time. Much along these lines has already been learned and will be the subject of future books.

Let us not forget, however, that music therapy is in a long tradition of medical therapies whose mechanisms of action were not worked out prior to its widespread use. Even today, everything from aspirin to electroconvulsive therapy is commonly used without the doctor understanding how the benefit occurs. So, the music therapist need not feel interlopers at the feast of medical therapies simply because their gift is poorly understood.

Perhaps, in some future neurophysiological lab or experiential workshop the mechanism will be worked out. Much work has already been done. The new field of PNI or psychoneuroimmunology (scientific talk for "holistic health") suggests that the mind/body connection, the influence of thoughts and feelings on anatomical and physiological functions, is a real factor in healing. What had up until a decade ago been medical heresy (i.e., thoughts influence health), is now becoming accepted by the medical and scientific profession. Perhaps the M.D. of the future will refer patients with infections, depression or cancer to a music therapist for specific therapeutic tonal experiences. This is currently being done in some cultures to charge chakras—"energy centers" functionally related to the immune system.

Ultimately, we all are thrown back upon our own personal experiences. Mine have been compelling. I have seen the power of music free the breath of asthmatics, curb the distractibility of attention deficit disorder children, subdue the spasm of stuttering as well as bring peace to a dying cancer patient and his suffering family.

Eventually, board certification with its double-edged sword of awarding credentials will influence who will do music therapy. Until then, the effort will be made by those of us who can listen to what resonates between the worlds of sound and substance, of spirit and matter. It will be done best by those who understand that, truth be known, music uses us more than we her in doing therapy. (It takes a certain type of person who is pleased to be a servant of such a force in the name of healing. Most physicians and scientists prefer to master, not serve forces of nature.) Music therapy represents that human activity where we work closest with the angels. It demands the ability to listen; ear listening, heart listening, bone listening and blood listening. However, truly therapeutic listening requires a profound courage. Listeners are vulnerable. Their reality is perpetually uncertain. Their gesture is one of response and accommodation rather than insistence or inflexibility. Their reward is to look down on occasion from Helios's chariot upon the sunlit face of health and peace where once brooded clouds of dis-ease and turmoil. The music therapist is privileged to soar where Phaeton plummeted.

References

Flock, A. 1983. *Hearing—Physiological Bases and Psycho-physics*, Klinke, (ed). Berlin: Springer.

Fritze, W. & W. Kohler. 1985. "Frequency Composition of Spontaneous Cochlear Emissions," *Arch. Otol.*, 242, (1), pp 4-38.

Bradford S. Weeks, M.D.

Gacek, T. 1972. "Neuroanatomy of the Auditory System," in Tobias
JV (ed); *Foundations of Modern Auditory Theory,* Vol 2, p 239. New
York: Academic Press.

Gilmor, T., P. Madaule, B. Thompson, (eds). 1989. "The Therapeutic Aspect of Sacred Music," in *About the Tomatis Method.*
Toronto: The Listening Centre Press.

Howell, P. 1984. "Are Two Muscles Needed for the Normal
Functioning of the Mammalian Ear?" *Acta Otol* (Stockh), 98,
pp 204-7.

Juhn, S. 1986. "Biochemistry of the Inner and Middle Ear," in
G. M. English (ed), *Otolaryngology Loose Leaf Series.* Vol 1, Ch. 60.
Philadelphia: Harper & Row.

Le Gall, A. 1961. "Le redressement de Certains Deficiencies
Psychologiques et Psycol-Pedagogiques." *Inspecteur general de
L'Instruction Publique.* Paris. March.

Nuttall, A. & M. Ross. 1986. "Auditory Physiology," in G. M. English
(ed) *Otolaryngology Loose Leaf Series,* Vol 1, Ch. 60. Philadelphia:
Harper & Row.

Simmons, F. B. 1964. "Perceptual Theories of Middle Ear Muscle
Function," *Ann. Otol.,* 73, pp 724-739.

Tomatis, A. 1954. "Recherches sur la Pathologie de Begaiement,"
Journal Francais d'Oto-Rhino-Laryngologie, 3, no 4, pp 384.

———. 1960 A. "La Voix Chantee—sa Physiologie —sa Pathologie
—sa Reeducation," *Cours de L'Hopital Bichat.* March.

———. 1960 B. "L'Electronique au Service des Langues Vivantes,"
*Bulletin de L'Union des Ass. des Anciens Eleves des Lyces et Colleges
Francais.* March.

———. 1967. "Dyslexie," *Cours a L'Ecole d'Anthropologie.* Editions
Soditap.

———. 1972. "Education et Dyslexie." *Editions ESF.* Paris.

———. 1974 A. "Vers L'Ecoute Humaine." *Editions ESF.* Paris.

———. 1974 B. "La Reeducation de la Voix—Les different Methodes
de Traitment, *La Vie Medicale,* no 20, May.

———. 1974 C. "La Musicotherapie et les Depressiones Nerveuses,"
Rapport au IV Congres Int'l d'Audio-Psycho-Phonologie. Madrid.

———. 1978. Presented at International Kodaly Symposium in Paris.

———. 1981. *La Nuit Uterine,* Editions Stock, Paris.

———. 1986. Taped interview, Paris. August.

Tonndorf, J. 1972. "Bone Conduction," in J. V. Tobias (ed) *Foundations of Modern Auditory Theory,* Vol 2, p 20. New York: Academic
Press.

Von Bekesy, G., 1960. *Experiments in Hearing.* New York:
McGraw Hill.

3

Harmonic Chant—
Global Sacred Music

DAVID HYKES

(Based on an interview and workshops at the Listening Centre in Toronto*)

The Harmonic chant is a specific, independent discipline of contemplative music, like Gregorian chant, or North Indian *Khyal* singing. It is based on amplifying vocal "harmonics" or "overtones" as one chants, so that one person can sound whole chords and melodies at once, resonating these usually dormant higher sounds above the fundamental note, or "1," that is sung. These harmonics, universal in all musical sounds, whether sung or played, are to sound vibration what the color spectrum is to light: pure "tones" that, in music, blend to produce the range of auditory impressions perceptible to our consciousness.

As the founder, or perhaps I should say re-founder, of the Harmonic Chant, along with my colleagues of the Harmonic Choir, I will share my vision of it with you: I see it as a global sacred music for our time.

Harmonic Chant is something quite independent. At the

---

*In February, 1986, David Hykes gave a concert and a series of workshops in Toronto, produced by Tim Wilson and sponsored by the Listening Centre. The material for this article was taken from a transcription of the workshops, which concluded with an interview with David Hykes conducted by Tina Pearson and David Mott. Paul Madaule, a director of the Listening Centre, provided an introduction to the first workshop. A version of this material first appeared in *Musicworks 35*. © 1990 David Hykes and the Harmonic Arts Society. Use of the term "Harmonic Chant" is legally reserved by the Harmonic Arts Society.

David Hykes

same time, we had a lot of help, encouragement and inspiration from earlier cultures, and have "kept the contact" with them. In the beginning, we were inspired particularly by the Tibetan and Mongolian forms or work with vocal harmonics. That is a debt I feel I have repaid, for we have made certain discoveries unknown to those traditions, which of course, found marvels of their own.

Our own work is open to all, each at his or her own level, and we do work with beginners. There are "entry level," knock-off versions of our work being offered out there in "workshop land." Yet the authentic Harmonic Chant, such as Tim Hill and I and the Harmonic Choir try to teach it, particularly rewards long-term study of its musical principles, which cannot be separated from its contemplative side.

Harmonic Chant has much to offer throughout the music world, and its influence seems to be spreading even to the realm of music education. There are several projects for curricula development underway in different countries, from the elementary level up to the teaching of conservatory professors. Through our recordings, touring, teaching, we find growing awareness of our work in countries all over the world.

That music has a sacred or healing quality is one of the oldest ideas associated with the practice of music, and therefore with the practice of listening. My years of study of the Gurdjieff work seem to me particularly relevant in this regard. There are some key ideas in the Gurdjieff teaching which I have tried, as best as I can, to take to heart: that certain musical laws are an accurate model of both self and cosmos; that music is sacred and should serve the sacred; and that the practice of art is not to increase egotism and a false sense of mastery, but to permit an eventual change in one's level of being. Gurdjieff speaks of the existence of what he called "Objective Music," and that is what I am in search of.

The Art of Listening

In the Harmonic Chant, we study how our own production of natural high-frequency sounds, the harmonics in our

56

voices—especially in "live" acoustic spaces like cathedrals, chapels and domes—can produce results corresponding to the ancient ideals of sound and the sacred. We have found a way, through the Harmonic Chant, that sometimes leads people to demonstrably finer listening. We want to study the process through which listening is nourished by a more complex kind of vibratory signal, one that includes both what we ourselves are producing and the incoming perceptual tide. Listening is the sum total of our receptivity on every level.

There is a key concept here—you might call it a synonym for listening—and that is *attention,* paying attention, giving one's attention. There is a large amount of deafness in us. I do not mean physical deafness, though I might include that. We are all hearing things all the time, but they go in very superficially. Obviously we need to filter impressions, but in extreme cases, this means serious problems on other levels: problems related to the body, posture, self-image and, of course, all sorts of problems with hearing itself, of tuning out frequencies that are part of musical or vocal sound. There are more subtle problems too, having to do with attitude and levels of energy.

The deafness I feel Harmonic Chant addresses has more to do with the fact that some of the sounds that are coming into us—whether from the voice, from music, from nature— are carrier waves for certain kinds of energy. They are bringing us impressions. This energy has a different effect on us when we are more aware of its full range and its "harmonic nature." The same goes for all the "reverberations" in our inner nature.

So we have three main questions: 1) How can we open our listening to hear more of what these sounds are saying within and without? The harmonics are in everything we already hear in the inner scales of vibration—in our voices, the voices of others, musical instruments. 2) How, being more aware of this complete scale of vibrations, can we increase our level of nourishment? In other words, how can we get more energy from sound? 3) Above all, how can we hear better how to serve others? Hearing more of "the whole story," the many rich impressions reaching us in open moments, could perhaps help us really be *in our place* in this life, participating in what Gurdjieff called the "common 'cosmic' harmony."

There is a difference between taking in these sounds unconsciously—which we do all the time—and actually working to hear them. As I see it, the difference is in the kind of listening evoked by what I call "harmonic listening," working with and paying attention to the full spectrum of communicative vibrations. This kind of listening is a doorway into a vast world of musical and inner experience.

Our listening energy is deeply conditioned by the way we use the voice for speaking, which is mostly the slave of our habitual mental and emotional modes of expression. Although we have much more in our voices than we usually realize, on the whole both our voices and our listening have been reduced to something that goes just from head to head or emotion to emotion.

We have largely forgotten the traditional idea that the voice actually comes from the body as a whole. We are each a kind of musical composition of different levels of vibration; the organs, the mind, the heart, everything in us is alive and moving, producing vibrations. It all participates in this extraordinary symphony which takes place in the concert hall of the body.

You can take the voice's role in this as a kind of parabola, like the parabolic antenna used in radio astronomy. A parabolic antenna takes whatever vibrations come into it and sums them, so that what comes out is more focused in one "ray." The voice is a kind of summation wave of all the other waves produced by the organs in a state of vibration.

If you listen to native speakers of a traditional culture, you may sometimes feel they are not saying much. Big rain yesterday; going to town on Tuesday—they say this kind of thing. But you feel so much *space* in and around what they say. Some other kind of communication is going on, not just mental information. This is something we have lost, this sensitivity to harmonics of *meaning.*

If we were more sensitive to the idea of listening, our own voices might be very different. Perhaps we would communicate much better with others, much more than we usually do, because the voice is a picture of the state of the whole person. It is like astrophysics: when you know the relationships of the elements in the spectrum, the refracted light of a star tells you what it is made of.

This is true for a whole traditional culture in North India, where for a few special musicians sound can still bring the sacred to life. In the morning they sing songs with special sounds, scales and modes, morning *ragas*, and later in the day they sing different *ragas*. These musicians know about the voice and listening and what is necessary at a given moment. It is as if there were a science of how to sound, or how to be, that was informed by all kinds of environmental influences, such as who you are with, the time of day, the acoustical circumstances.

We need to know how to make the right sound or to manifest the right thing at the right time. This is true for our inner life too. What we are thinking or feeling now, how we are sitting, all these things have a bearing on the quality of the vibrations that our particular symphonies are producing. Understanding this better is very much a part of the art of listening, or as we call it, work on listening.

The Harmonics of Being

How can hearing the harmonics help us? What are those harmonics saying? What is the message of the harmonics? Is there a message? Is there something innate in them that communicates to us? Is there a meaning on the level of vibrations that goes beyond words? Affirmation to the first questions—to which one might like to say "yes"—depends entirely on the state of mind of the singer or the listener at the time.

Maybe there are harmonics of the mind as well as of sound. Maybe the mind—our lazy, noisy mind—can quiet down on the surface and have a deeper idea of what these sounds are saying. Do they speak in another language, with another orientation, another point of view? Our listening hears the language of words and the sounds of the known world. How can we listen in the unknown, which is so vast?

Generally either the mind interferes by its own noise, or we feel fear and tense up. How can we go beyond, unfold the wings of perception, as it has been called? And why?

We are a part of that unknown infinity, too. Sooner or later, we will merge with it. It is a question of spiritual honor, dignity—of respect for the infinite, so to speak. We need preparation and readiness in the now, since our awareness of the presence of the beyond helps "attune" us to the demands of this life, this chanting of the harmonics of being, as it were.

An idea that can help orient us is that everything is in a state of vibration and is *saying something*. The fact that anything exists—even things that seem quite silent, like stones—means that it has some vibrations. Maybe the stone is not saying, "Hello, how are you?" but there is something being expressed as vibration by its being there, in its place.

Further up the so-called evolutionary ladder (we have plenty to learn from stones), what is being said becomes more and more on our wavelength, so to speak. We are closer to animals than to stones. And there is a language, a music, that goes beyond us. What is the sun saying? The stars?

There are harmonics in the stone and the same laws that made the stone made you and me. The aim of better listening is to hear the teaching, the harmony, of this creation, to hear it in yourself as well as to recognize it in the world around you.

You are freer in your response than the stone is. You have other possibilities. You can bring to life the creation in you in a way that the stone never can. You are on a different road, higher, with greater possibilities and greater risks, greater responsibilities.

How can we keep this practice in listening from being just more "self improvement"? I think what is the most important for us, for our growth, is being able to take in the speech of "those who know." Our state of listening can be sensitized to a point where, when certain people speak, an understanding comes to life in us.

Developing this kind of sensitivity to the quality of vibration of a speaker and being able to *hear* what could actually change your life is one of my main (and lofty) wishes for you in studying the Chant or any sacred music. Work on listening may help you recognize your teacher and hear the call of a teaching, and there is nothing more precious in this life. As my own teacher said, not without a certain putting-things-in-their-place tonality, "Those sounds are *very* interesting, but what *I* am interested in are the harmonics of *consciousness!*"

The aim of better listening is not to hear *more*, but to hear more *clearly*, especially the call toward consciousness. The harmonics are in everything. That means that there is really nothing with which we could not practice this kind of listening, even with silence!

In fact, listening takes place above all in silence. It is only when I am truly quiet that I can hear. Experiences of really understanding something through music, whether the chanting of *Hearing Solar Winds* or late Beethoven or the crickets in the field, is testimony to the power of silent listening.

Inner silence and listening awareness form a kind of mystical marriage or union. We hear best in conditions of complete inner silence. And we can work for those conditions. The silence we seek is an aspect of our being, which in certain conditions can come to life much more strongly, as a vibration.

The Way Up Is the Way Down

How can we know if these conditions are being met? Those conditions have to do with the physical state of our body, our posture, the relationship among the organic energies or vibrations of which we are composed, like breathing and sensation. And other factors need to be present, especially a kind of unstated but implied urgency or sense of *the need to work.* Can we feel and respond whole-heartedly to that?

We prepare the terrain for sound to come to life by sensing the space of our body in silence. When the sound comes, we begin with "mmm," the grain or seed of sound, which becomes charged. Then the harmonics come, like the flowering of a tree. The harmonics become meaningful in relation to the vibrations as a whole. They can be understood as the flowering of a work that has roots deep in the body, and much more of our work than people realize is in the cultivation of these roots. That is the path we try to follow to the flowering, moment by moment, of a "harmonic consciousness." "The way up is the way down," as they said in alchemy. (All this is true only "then," that is, in actual practice.)

The fundamental tone or "1," the note you start from, needs to be as full a resonance as that of the harmonic, since what interests us is a complete copresence between the fundamental and the harmonic. Without this, the symbolic meaning of the Chant as the copresence of the above and the below, the sacred and the individual, is incomplete and unrealized.

We are making these harmonics with the voice because they bring us "closer" than any other harmonics. We are doing our part "for the greater glory of this Creation," in a way, to symbolize what heaven on earth would be. Maybe it is just a dream we cannot wake up from, but we cannot stop feeling that our work here on earth is to make it like heaven. We have to sing our own songs, give of ourselves, make our own "joyful noise," not so that the Creator can hear us, but so that we can hear the Creator.

Obviously, *here* is our level, *here* is where we need to exercise, *here* is where we can help harmony come more to life. We could not do these things on the moon or on the sun; we have to do them on earth, as people. Chant locally, listen globally, so to speak.

Levels of Harmonic Energy

The question remains: How can these harmonics help? What are they saying?

They are like a call, a reminder, of the presence of a higher level of being. They are *re-calling* in a wordless way the ideal at the heart of all religions, all spiritual traditions, the possibility of another level, of moving closer in awareness to the sacred through our listening. It is the idea of *different levels* of vibration.

Coming into contact with these levels is the whole inner aim of our work. People in the Harmonic Choir have generally always been active practitioners of some kind of art or discipline, and not necessarily the same one. To me that makes our work more meaningful, perhaps both combining different qualities and testifying to the fact that people on different paths can work together.

It is not a matter of only the external techniques of Harmonic Chant. The real questions come with the hard work to find harmony together, as much as with so-called "harmonic energy" and the contemplative aspects of the Chant. We have to ask questions about the behavior of energy in ourselves, even the tonalities and atonalities of conscience and ethical decisions. As we like to say, "The real price of better listening is that I will hear how I am."

On a practical level, our work is concerned with questions about listening awareness in relation to vital energies within the space of the body, like the breath. For most of us the sense of the body is only mental most of the time, not actual awareness.

Besides being aware of what is within, we need a special sense of what is outside us. It is as if instead of listening to the room, you feel that the room is listening to you. The listening merges with the space. That requires a very different, less mental way of taking it all in, one in which we are more free to absorb whatever happens. Our being is extended far more than we realize, and that makes our exchange with the room possible. Obviously, the more conscious we are of our surroundings, the better the things we choose to say, sing, write or do. The more aware we are of the atmosphere—how we are being heard by others, for example—the more we are likely to find the right tonality.

How we act, how we manifest, how the vibrations of our movements and speech and actions reverberate in our environments, obviously come back to us in many ways. Tibetans and Indians call that karma.

All the harmonics this side of the Self are just the "me." But our real measure is in the openness of our listening to the question, Who is this "me," this "I"? The scale at some moments seems infinite, the silence and energy seem

vast. Sometimes certain experiences silence one so completely that only "the sound of listening" is there, and
"there" seems to be everywhere. When our awareness opens
to the presence of harmonic vibrations in the Creation
as a whole, it is like hearing "the music of the spheres."

In addition to "the music of the spheres" there is the
equally vast other pole, the Harmonic Chant of the inner
life of our being. When we are in a more awakened state,
in which the vibratory life of the different chakras or energy
centers are brought into a kind of alignment, like lenses,
quite a different light can pass. Again, presence to the
Chant in this sense demands total silence.

With regard to sound, these so-called other octaves of
experience can be *approached* through work with the
Harmonic Chant. These finer "octaves of impressions," as
Gurdjieff called them, are like the harmonics of the
"symphony of vibrations" which is the normally functioning
human organism. "As above, so below," but what is our
actual experience?

One of Gurdjieff's many crucial ideas we need to hear
is that these harmonics of being or "higher centers" of
thought, feeling and sensation are calling to us, but our
deafness, our "sleep," prevents us from hearing them.
According to Gurdjieff, these "higher centers" are fully
functional; it is the "lower centers," our ordinary thinking,
feeling and sensing, that are out of tune.

It is very difficult, in fact exceptional, to be able to accept
that it is this self which I actually am that must change.
Merely adding "higher information"—new ideas, teachings,
etc.—is fake "harmonics," putting off the real work that I
so obviously need to do on myself. It is like fiddling as
Rome burns, instead of beginning again the work of
attunement.

Listening can be studied partly in terms of physical
points and of areas of resonance in the body, and more
especially of hearing and sensing, of coming to understand
the linking of these separated parts by inner currents or
movements of energy.

Changing Harmonics

This listening that is in us and these harmonic sounds

are constantly changing. That is why we should beware of overly systematic formulas. Suppose you find the ultimate sound for the heart chakra and are about to publish your book and give workshops. People are writing you long letters about their incredible experiences. You have really got your formula. But if you are honest, if you are really listening, if you are sincere, you will find that the next day it will not be quite the same sound that you feel touches your heart or feeling, or anybody else's. Maybe you will suddenly feel that the sound is just mental resonance, or perhaps it will be lower or somewhere out in front or behind you. We are in a desert where there *are* oases, but the fact is that the sands are constantly shifting. What worked today will not necessarily work tomorrow.

We may feel that the word "harmonics" has something eternal and unchanging about it. It is as if we are in an ocean of vibrations and our weight, the lightness or heaviness of our energy is constantly changing. We are constantly floating down into the old thoughts, and sometimes floating up a little nearer to the surface, the air, the light. The harmonics we make today will not be the same tomorrow, nor will they have the same meaning, nor ask the same question. Vibrations we are in touch with that form the world we live in are constantly changing. We are not being acted on the same way now as we were a moment ago. Our states constantly change, unfortunately among only a few "chords."

Likewise, we never finish learning a skill, and it should continue to evolve and change. We have to do something long enough so that we forget that it is a skill and start to have real vibrations. That is why one feels fascination in watching someone at a forge or blowing glass or working at any traditional craft demanding concentrated attention. Maybe that explains why elder craftsmen sometimes have such a wonderful atmosphere. It is as if they have forgotten their "certificate" and their knowledge has become second nature. The knowledge is clear, direct, part of their being, not separate from them. The work that appears is really their own; it is full of their own true vibration.

The only real harmonics are the harmonics of being.

Being takes time. It is not a technique that you learn today and then do tomorrow.

Perceiving the Harmonic Order

In the Harmonic Chant, where words are secondary, I feel something that is close to a universal language of sacred music. People with very different backgrounds can work together. So I have been careful to keep the approach nondenominational, accepting that all those who come to us will have their own particular background or non-background.

Paradoxically, as much as the harmonics touch upon something universal, they also have the strange property of revealing singers rather totally—their motivation, their tensions, their understanding or confusion. The voice is like a person's signature or pulse—it says a lot about that person. It is like that refracted starlight whose colors reveal its elemental nature.

I come back to the question, What are the harmonics saying? Now we are at the point where we can see that *potentially* they are saying something about different levels of vibration and symbolizing the fact that our listening also has this scale. But this potentiality depends on one's level, one's state, at the moment, for its realization.

Perceiving the Harmonic Order

Basically, there are only two "right" approaches: searching for the higher state of being, and its actual presence in oneself. Anything else tends to lack intensity. These have a yearning quality, a sincerity, which reminds me of what I am searching for, and can even invoke it.

The listening that goes along with these harmonics is like a pressure wave or force. It can be the intimate, mystic partner to the sound. Each harmonic has—or *calls out*, you could say—a different listening. The problem is that our listening is like that of a bottom fish, far from the light. Listening is so conditioned that it inhabits only the lower levels of the sound. We have to get it to rise and find a new, more balanced distribution.

The harmonic can be a messenger. This becomes magical, because our world, like music, is a vibratory world. Our picture of it has to do with the way our listening or consciousness has crystallized it in us. We see only a kind of frozen architecture of listening. That gives us a certain level of impressions. Our view of the building depends on which floor the elevator takes us to, and consciousness is the elevator (or should I say elevators, since we want to see the whole building at once?).

In ordinary harmony, it is as if we cut a pie into slices, a slice for each person. We bring the slices of the pie back together through Chant. The voices merge, and it is suddenly like one of those wonderful French cakes with many layers —*milles feuilles,* a thousand leaves. So, instead of the slices being quite separate, the pie re-merges, and you have different levels—these harmonic levels in the sound. And the wonderful thing is that you can get out of the boundaries of personality. Combining your sound with another creates a very different perspective. It is like a kaleidoscope given a twist.

This makes possible a freeing movement in the way we perceive. We go beyond our habits into the unknown. This is shamanism or esotericism or religion or magic, a different view of the frequency domain—call it what you like.

The unfolding of perception changes everything for you. Perception becomes reordered along the lines of what we call "the harmonic order." You can move around perceptually in a new way. To the extent this inner kind of listening is fused with the body and has a real presence in the body, you have a kind of space inside that comes alive. Sometimes the body breathes as if for the first time. You enter into service. You go to work.

There is another density in the body that is quite different from the heavy density dictated by the ordinary mind. There is quite another atmosphere, more of air than of earth. Movement of perception up into another level and down into the body is a real movement. We really go there; we really are there, but "there" is *here.* Our interest is *in*-the-body experience!

The Harmonic Chant is a kind of carrier wave for this.

David Hykes

The listening moves, rises with the harmonics, as if you are on a mountaintop and can see all the way around. I had this experience on mountain crests in the Alps, where there is no sound except birds' wings as they soar endlessly in the currents sweeping up the mountainsides. At the same time, you feel the mass of the mountain, through your body.

There is so much open space *between* these places, these harmonics. Many people just go from one to the next, like shopping, going from one store to the next, noticing nothing in between. The listening actually tries to find these other places and be there. We often speak of the vowel points along the spectrum of open sounds as being like radio stations. There is a continuous spectrum of possibilities but a limited number of stations. To find the harmonics, you have to listen to all spaces between the stations. We forget that the music of the spheres takes place *between* the spheres. Probably the spheres themselves have their hands full just with turning!

The voice is the harmonics, plus all that space. It is like the color spectrum: a few colors like red, orange, and yellow make all the marvelous, unique things we see. The same is true for sounds. There is only the harmonic series, and the whole sonic universe—if not Creation as a whole—comes out of that.

The sonic universe is constantly reforming itself from a limited number of elements. The marvelous world of possibilities is in how these sounds, these laws, these proportions combine. I may chant every day at sunrise, but it is never the same twice, even if it is the same chant. The music, the harmony, is between the notes in the sense of space, and what passes between the notes. The music is in the connections that join things together.

The world that we make is formed, for better or worse, out of the notes and harmonics of our being. The world we have is a direct reflection of our intentions, or lack of them, and to make "Earth as it is in Heaven."

Building Together

Harmony is working together, whether to create a universe,

a cathedral, bread or a teaching. Our ability to work together is an absolute measure of the intensity of our wish for being. Gurdjieff said, "Laws are everywhere the same. God and microbe, it is the same system. The only thing that changes is the number of centers."

Concentrating on something together gives a different feeling, like trying to lift something very heavy together, or to push a car. An instant spark of coordination comes between people. There is a different rhythm; everyone is in touch with the basic pulsation that is going to make it work. People find their places.

It is the same when we are chanting. The more sensitive our listening to these levels of sound, the finer the structure we raise; the finer the space we create, the finer the vibrations we come in contact with. That is what the work of chanting together means to me. We are actually building something together. And this is real.

It is one thing to create or build something; it is another to take care of it. Chant bears on both the creation and the maintenance. Maintaining means doing our homework so that the Chant lives forever, or for a long time. We have to take care of this precious material. It is like maintaining a sacred site.

How shall we keep harmonics alive? It is a work. If the sounds are not sung, they cannot do any good. In a real ceremony or a real meditation, you give yourself totally to the work that needs to take place in you. There is no halfway. The real power of a ceremony is as a reminder to find the sacred again. That can only be through finding a silence inside, where I am silence and can work and be worked upon.

The greatest gift in this amazing life for me is that I can awaken anew. I can listen again *now*. I can serve again and again and each time feel the life force here, in my place, where I am. I can again be free to give thanks, to praise, to love, and to be grateful. These are the real harmonics, the harmonics of the heart. These are the vibrations that are really alive. The rest is just show.

David Hykes

Discography

David Hykes and the Harmonic Choir
  Hearing Solar Winds (Ocora Radio France/distributed by
  Harmonia Mundi)
  Current Circulation
  Harmonic Meetings
  (both Celestial Harmonies)
David Hykes
  Windhorse Riders (New Albion)
  Let the Lover Be (Auvidis, distributed by Harmonia Mundi)

For information contact:
  International Center of Harmonic Chant
  Harmonic Arts Society
  Pommereau
  41240 Autainville, France

4

Oral versus Literate Listening

DERRICK DE KERCKHOVE

Today our sight has dimmed; it no longer sees our future, having constructed a present made of abstraction, nonsense, and silence. Now we must learn to judge a society more by its sounds, by its arts, by its festivals, than by its statistics. By listening to noise, we can better understand where the folly of men and their calculations is leading us, and what hopes it is still possible to have.

Jacques Attali
Noise: The Political Economy of Music

Introduction

Attali's 1977 book on *Noise* describes how the economy of music has taken control over our sensibility and thus modulated significant aspects of our culture. It is an extremely perceptive enquiry into our cultural ground and into the predictive power we can derive from analyzing the music of our own time. In the excerpt quoted above, the author shows much perception in opposing vision to hearing as an aspect of our present cultural and social predicament. Surprisingly however, apart from a few observations about the impact of written music on the restructuring of musical genres and forms, there is no mention of the profound effect literacy has had upon our culture and especially upon our attitudes toward hearing. I say that it is surprising because the issue of written scores is a prime example of the kind of control literacy has taken over the psychodynamics of the western people. From the Renaissance onward until the recent reversal provoked by electronic technologies, the writing down of music has amounted to mastering sound and reducing to second class

71

status all the spontaneous popular forms or traditional folkloric rhythms. The opposition between writing and music is almost a biological one, as writing takes control of the brain while organized sound takes control of the whole body.

Generally, in dealing with our so-called "higher" senses, vision and hearing, we have the attitudes of producers, not consumers. We are perfectly content to use our nose and taste buds for fun, but we look and listen for profit. Most hearing and listening in our urban environment is functional. Even recreative listening tends towards the functional end, as we go to jazz, classical, pop concerts "to relax," to tell ourselves and to others that this is the time to stop and listen. Most of us go to concerts as we practice sports, dutifully, (when we are not doing it professionally). Our use of touch is also a rational, puritanical affair, except in rather specialized and almost driven circumstances. Yet, even in the context of public aesthetics, a difference must be drawn between looking and listening. We design things to look nice but we usually do not bother to make them sound nice. When it isn't given to whirring and purring and producing comical beeps, high technology's best compliment to the ear is to make its products silent, acoustically unobstrusive, which is the mark of efficiency. But our culture would sooner deafen us to undesirable sounds, than make such sounds less undesirable, or turn them into pleasurable experiences. Kids who grow up in the urban industrial cacophony have to create loud music to bring some coherence to all these sounds and smoothen the hard, shrill, broken edges of glass, brick and steel.

The soundscape of the urban culture is a rich wasteland. Huge amounts of human energy get sucked in the black hole of the city, which regurgitates it as white noise. We get back raw energy from this white noise, but we lose our sensitivity to sound in the bargain. Of course, we do not realize that we have lost anything because we have become accustomed long ago to give an ancillary role to hearing. When a whole society suffers from hearing loss, there's nobody left to tell about the damage done. In the world of the deaf, the one who can hear is Joan of Arc, a madwoman.

Our neglect of the ear may be one of the prices we have paid for literacy.

1. Can Media Affect Our Sensory Modes?

Close your eyes and imagine the world around you right now. If you are highly literate, the chances are that what rules your representation of this environment is a visual model. A box (the room) with things and people inside. The people and the things make sounds, which are only negligible noises unless you are required to interpret them. The words that are spoken now for you are read to you (a fact for which I am indebted to Mark Muldoon, but also a fact I deplore in this context because, even when read aloud, a paper is always a paper not a human communication). Nothing can be more absurdly literate than speech read from a text. Your listening is rigorously specialized. It is conditioned by the circumstances attending this event, by the position and role of the speaker, by the title of the paper, by the tone of the reader, and ultimately by the verbal or semantic content of the paper. Your only recourse to escape the constraints of this kind of listening is to walk out or to fall asleep.

Now, if you are not so taken by the powers of literacy, you are hearing sounds that others do not attend. You can achieve a perfectly useful and manageable representation of this room by layering many levels of sounds: the shuffling of feet, the ambient room sound, coughs and sneezes, plumbing gurgles and birds songs, if any. You would be able, by leaning your attention a little more closely, to hear the condition of your neighbour's mood or health. You can hear sounds as layered sculptures containing textures and designs, all bearing some kind of pressure upon you. But you may not need to hear the meaning of the words spoken from the chair. One experiment which I recommend to test the difference between oral and literate listening is to duck your head discreetly and close your eyes at your next crowded cocktail party. You will be surprised at the number of different conversations you will be able to follow simultaneously. Then open your eyes

and try to keep it up. You will find it difficult, if not impossible.
The reason for that effect is twofold: first, your eyes take
up a great deal of mental energy. Our sensory functions
are selective. There is only so much energy that can go
into a given situation for an efficient response. Survival
is the prompter. Certain senses require more energy than
others, such as vision, for instance, which requires 18 times
more energy than hearing. On the other hand, vision is
both faster and more comprehensive than hearing, especially
under our visuo-cultural conditions.

Because of their intuitive grasp of the tyranny of the
eye, many symbolist poets from Verlaine to Claudel have
recommended to shut one's eyes to become "a seer." But
the main reason, probably is that vision is obsessive and
exclusive. The frontal view afforded by the eyes supports
and encourages a specialization of attention which tends
to eliminate any other perception. As Canadian composer
Murray Shafer has suggested, with our eyes we are always
at the edge of the world looking in, while with our ears,
the world comes to us and we are always at the centre of it.
Of course, this effect is the same for everybody from the
jungle to the urban headhunter. But the frontal experience
of visual concentration is also what is acquired, sometimes
at the cost of great efforts, as one becomes literate. Thus
literate people, who need to make and control sense of
everything, first trust their eyes before they even consider
their ears, and second, tend to concentrate their attention
on the linear unfolding of events, conversations and situations. However there may be a hidden neurobiological
ground to our favoring one sensory ratio over another.

According to neurobiology, we grow into our environment
not only anatomically following genetic programming, but
also neurologically, following cultural programming.
Our brain, though initially geared to develop according
to common programs cross-culturally, is gradually exposed
to more and more cultural amplifiers and conditioners
which require selective responses and define the ratio of
our sensory inputs in daily life. It is obvious that we hardly
use our ears to find our way in an urban environment,
while this is not true for those who have to live in the bush
or the jungle.

It may be that, as babies, even as neonates, we can all perceive a great variety of sounds. This much is borne out by the research of Toronto psychologist Sandra Trehub and others which indicates that babies for a few hours and even days after birth can differentiate between different languages, but that this faculty seems to disappear quite soon, as the baby begins to settle in his or her maternal linguistic environment. Alfred Tomatis' theory that certain languages concentrate in preferred bandwidths may be given some relevance here as neonates begin to specialize their attention for airborne linguistic sounds which reflect the frequency range of the language and the voice of their mother. The interesting feature of Trehub's work, however, is not that the babies' ears become attuned in a specialized way, but rather, that they lose very quickly the ability to accommodate for other, non relevant sounds.

French neurobiologist Jean-Pierre Changeux has developed a theory of "selective stabilization of synapses" to explain why we lose rather than gain sensory flexibility after exposure to consistent environmental stimulants. The suggestion is that the growth and development as well as fixation of neural connections in the brain and the central nervous system is conditional upon preferred use of certain patterns over others. We train our nervous system by habituation, just as an athlete trains his or her muscles. Another way of looking at this process is to say with French linguist Jacques Mehler that, as we specialize "we learn by unlearning" other less appropriate responses. It is as if we were carving our nervous system as well as our destiny while we were growing up.

Beyond our biologically and neurologically determined selection of listening and hearing patterns, there are cultural conditions which restrict the scope of one's hearing to what is relevant to the specific social and psychological environment of the person. If we are to give credit to Benjamin Lee Whorf's theories about the impact of our vocabulary in defining and limiting our psychological experience, there is a possibility that we only hear, or pay attention to those sounds which are described by the vocabulary, (verbs, nouns, adjectives) and by the grammar (relationships) of our particular language. To wit, there are only two words, whether in French or in English, to describe the actions of listening and hearing, while there are dozens of verbs describing manners of looking (seeing, looking, perceiving, admiring, gazing at, glancing at, spying, etc.).

Even the way we use our own language can help to direct our psychological, and maybe our sensory experience. NLP, Neurolinguistic Programming, Bandler and Grinder's celebrated method of therapy, is partly based on the recognition that, as individuals, we privilege certain senses over others in our daily use of metaphors. There are those who insist on saying: "I see what you mean," as opposed to those who are content to acknowledge: "I hear you." NLP practitioners claim that those among us who evidence a statistical consistency in choosing our sensory metaphors are likely, not only to behave according to our privileged sensory modes, but even to show a better skill in the privileged sense than in the others.

Listening is a product of selective attention, as opposed to hearing, which is not inner but outer-controlled. As a selective process listening is "switched on" or "off." We switch to the listening mode for information and for taking stock of our environment. Even so, there are different kinds of listening: listening for words, for overt meaning, for hidden meaning, for emotions, for entertainment, for the self, for a global situation, for God, for meditating, etc. Each one of these listening functions requires a different set of attitudes, postures, expectations, judgments, storing and discarding measures. Each one can be called "a mode." We switch on one mode or another depending upon our circumstances and our need. As I suggested above, our cultural environment may prompt us to select one mode preferentially. I want here to emphasize the differences between two opposite modes, which for the convenience of this paper, I will call the "oral" and the "literate" modes of listening.

The basic difference between the two modes is that oral listening tends to be global and comprehensive, while literate listening is specialized and selective. One is attending to concrete situations and to persons, while the other is interested in words and verbal meanings. One is context-bound, while the other is relatively context-free. The first is cosmo-centric and spatial, while the other is linear, temporal and logocentric.

The ancient Greeks were acutely aware of the problems of perception and of their cultural consequences. Greek tragedy is nothing but the literary and dramatic response to new sensory conditions introduced by alphabetic literacy. However, the dramatists themselves did not know the real source of their predicament. When Tiresias tells Oedipus that he is blind to the truth of his position, what he is really implying is that Oedipus' excessive reliance upon his eyes and visual logic has made him blind—or more accurately, deaf—to anything beyond the evidence. The fact is that, as western people, we have become gradually deaf through no fault of our own, but through the rewiring of our nervous system by literacy.

2. How Literacy Takes over the Nervous System

We do not make sense by words alone. Images, multisensory mental stimulations, evoke complex patterns of stored information which enable us to recreate people, places, sensations in our mind. Changeux' work on mental objects may help us here to understand how we store images and experiences, how we process and reprocess them, and how the experience of a literate person differs profoundly from the experience of an oral one.

According to Changeux, there are three principal categories of mental images—or representations—which we use for steering our actions, our speech and our thoughts. They are **percepts, icons** and **concepts. Percepts** are mental images which come from being exposed directly to external and internal sensory stimulations. They create grooves in our nervous system which reacts to them as a photo-electric emulsion reacts to patterns of light and shade. Over the first years of our lives, we accumulate enough sensations with sufficient regularity to acquire a specific blend of preferred perceptions.

Derrick de Kerckhove

The important thing to note about **percepts** is that however culturally conditioned they may be, they are grounded in direct, immediate sensory stimulations. A **percept** is not a memory, it is a mental experience happening in time. We turn **percepts** on simply by directing our attention outward or inward to sensory stimulations, or off by attending to other, deferred mental images, such as concepts or icons, or a combination thereof.

Icons are stored mental images. They are evoked by memory. They are even more selective than percepts, even more conditioned by the specific events of a person's life. You bring up an icon by remembering. The word to "remember" is itself indicative both of the way an icon is made, and of the cultural content of the representations, i.e., it is a "made-up" image, made of bits and pieces from "the rag-and-bone shop of the heart" (W. B. Yeats). Imagination is the power to build icons and put them together in meaningful sequences. Icons differ from percepts in many ways, but the most important to keep in mind is that whatever sensory content icons have, it is always coming from memory, not from direct evidence. An icon is a stored percept, not a "live" one. This suggests that the amount of sensory stimulation contained in an icon is not as great as in a live situation. It is maybe something like comparing a live situation to a televised or videotaped one: the content is still there, but it is selected and edited for a specific purpose, and its sensory content is much reduced.

With respect to understanding the impact of literacy on our sensory lives, the whole issue of mental images really takes off when we consider **concepts.** A concept is hardly an image, rather it is a kind of abstraction, a structure which supports a notion or an idea, before it has been fleshed out in sensory inputs. Although there is a content in verbs such as **to be** or **to have,** there are no sensory modes to turn them into images. They can only help to build images, such as when they are used in sentences: "I have a paper in my hand" or "You are sitting in front of me." You can easily reconstruct a representation from a combination of icons—the memory of my face and posture, and concepts —the relationships established by **I—have—in front of—me.**

78

Such words only evoke images if they have things to relate to. The word **paper** is an interesting case. Since you do not see the paper I am talking about, you have to take my word for it and trust that I am indeed reading from a paper. What is the status of the notion of paper in your minds? It is precisely that of a **concept,** that is not quite a recollection, nor a direct perception. The word "paper" is a general category which you know simply because you speak English. The specific use of the word I am making here comes from the context of a public lecture. Thus the image you evoke rapidly in your mind when I say "paper" in this context, need not be very detailed or precise. You are not really bringing up an icon, but an abstract notion which will support the relationships both of the sentence, and of the situation.

In the beginning of his otherwise rather fanciful book on *The Rise of Consciousness in the Breakdown of the Bi-Cameral Mind,* Julian Jaynes gives a perfect example of our tendency to conceptualize our own experience: he suggests that if you think back and reflect on the last time you were sitting in a bath tub, you almost automatically create a fiction: you imagine yourself, hardly defined, seen from a short distance in a bath. But, of course, Jaynes points out that you have never experienced a bath in such a way, except maybe on a home movie made about you by someone else. You do not evoke the sensation of water around your waist—that would be an icon—, you merely throw together the **concept** of yourself in the **concept** of a situation involving somebody taking a bath in a bath tub that you recognize as that very one you did take your last bath in (that part of your mental reconstruction is a bona fide icon).

This is what a concept is, a mental representation, hardly an "image" at all, which contains little or no sensory information, but which has a great deal of adaptability to combine rapidly with other concepts or with icons, and even percepts to make sense. Now there is no reason to believe that any culture of the world is devoid of any of these categories of mental images. It would be silly to suggest that oral cultures are not capable of forming concepts, if only because concepts are the building blocks of language.

Alison Gopnik, one of the cognitive scientists doing research at the McLuhan Program, is studying the formation of concepts in early childhood, and from her work, there is little doubt that children begin to develop concepts long before they begin to read.

However it is not silly to suggest that learning to read and write emphasizes the use of concepts over any other mental category. Why? Spoken words are nothing but concepts once they are written down and separated from their context. While spoken words in live situations always perforce bring up percepts and icons, written words are concepts in isolation until they are combined into images by the reader. Literacy favours the use of concepts, merely by presenting speech in little units strung together. This makes for a conceptual use of language, even in live speech. David Olson's work on children's approach to meaning before and after they learn to read shows that literacy is the critical factor in their shifting attention from a person to what the person is saying in conversation about something specific. As people whose attitudes are ruled by literacy, we tend to listen for the meaning of words, rather than for the substance of an argument or for the intention of the speaker. This may not necessarily be the case for the oral listener.

3. Oral Listening

On the other hand, as McLuhan has pointed out in *The Gutenberg Galaxy,* the split between the eye and the ear, which is consequent to the diffusion of alphabetic literacy, can create strange difficulties in cultures which remain oral. There is this true and delightful observation about a Turkish scribe who was the only person who could read in a small coastal village. Whenever he had to read private letters for his illiterate co-villagers, he would cover his ears with his hands, to show that he wasn't listening.

The western movie cliché "White man speaks with forked tongue" bears witness to the predictable diffidence of Indian chiefs towards white settlers as they battled not only against their bodies at war, but against their papers in courts upholding worthless treaties and landright claims. As a direct effect of the growth of literacy, the development of drama in classical Greece introduced a new social role and a new attitude: the hypocrit. **Upokritos** originally meant "the answerer," in fact, the "actor," but etymologically the word signifies "the one who judges from beneath." The "hypocrits and the Pharisees" of the new testament may be associated by the oral man with the values of the learned people, i.e. literate. Pharisees were rich and therefore educated. Not only did they use their learning to interpret and turn the meanings of the sacred texts to their advantage, but they were known not to come up front on any issue, especially in confrontation with Christ. Everybody uses .language for communication and control, but oral people may use it more for communication than control.

In his recent *Orality and Literacy,* summing up many years of research into the comparison between the oral and the literate minds, Walter Ong suggests several features of what he calls "the psychodynamics of orality." Each feature may correspond to a characteristic attitude in listening, namely what to listen for, how to listen, who to listen to, and how to store or remember what has been heard.

Words Weigh What the Speaker Weighs

First of all, in a truly oral culture, words are not cheap: the fool is the one who talks too much. Everything that is said carries weight either for you or against you, so you have to choose your words. This feature corresponds to what Ong recognizes as "the power of the oral word." In an oral culture, words are supported by the presence, the energy and the reputation of the speaker, they are the extension of his or her power and they exact attention from the listeners as measured against the eminence of the speaker. On the other hand, French anthropologist Marcel Mauss reminds us that the power of the speaker is really granted by the listeners, just as it is the audience, well primed by promotion, P.R. and the reputation of the performer, which gives power to the TV actor, the concert hall musician, or the politician.

But oral words in a literate culture have little value. Even on paper, they can be cheap. It takes a great deal of procedural ritual to give weight to written words, such as in contracts, legal papers, decrees etc. While much of the power of oral words is given by their non-verbal markers, by itself the printed word does not yield any nonverbal information. Some years ago, *Psychology Today* assembled several research papers to indicte that, on the average, the total information content of ordinary human conversations went 7% to verbal material, and 93% to nonverbal cues. The oral word is never unaccompanied. Intention and forcefulness are largely given to intonation, volume, scansion and other oral and tonal values. Print and billboard advertising are nothing if not attempts to recover the power and nuances of oral delivery in visual form.

In this regard we are presently witnessing a reversal whereby the words of a statesman on television are given weight not by their content, but by the image of the person who pronounces them. Another reversal is the tendency of the law today to pay attention to oral contract, for hiring, firing, promise of marriages etc. These changes are sure signs that we are returning to an oral culture, or more precisely to what Ong calls a "secondary," i.e. electronic oral culture.

Associative Listening

The second feature proposed by Ong is that in an oral culture, "you only know what you can recall." Thus there is a heavy emphasis on memory, not merely the private memory of the speaker, but the collective memory of the audience. This kind of memory is contained, not outside the rememberer, but in the words, rhythms, gestures and performances of enacted recollections. In such a context, people are not terribly interested in new ideas or concepts, they listen for what they already know, much in the way we tend to look for recognizable features in new faces or new situations: "This reminds me of such an event" or "This face reminds me of so and so."

Oral people are in a condition of permanent associative thinking, not in speculative or specific idea processing. Such a cognitive set-up is very conducive to analogies and myth formation. A myth can only work if it lends itself to many human situations and many interpretations without losing its basic structure. Another corollary to the psychodynamics of oral memory is that information tends to be shared collectively, rather than held in private. Even the power associations of church and state in early medieval cultures were oligarchies of shared information. Private information ownership and control is one of the distinguishing features of a fully literate culture.

Difference and Repetition

Ong then goes on to describe the characteristics of orally based thought and expression. They are not all directly relevant to listening, but it is reasonable to assume that the shape of oral thinking will affect the shape of oral listening. Ong notes that oral thinking shuns subordination and favors repetition and additives, connectives such as **and,** rather than causal or temporal conjunctions such as **then, thus, therefore** etc. Because oral words fly, they have to be repeated and emphasized in ritualized forms so that the audience can hear them without complex mental deductions. There is joy in redundancy. Expectations are created by serial repetition in expressions and formulaes. Preschool children also like to hear repetitive characters and situations for their bedtime stories. Innovation bores the oral person while repetition bores the literate one. In musical forms, invention for invention's sake reached its highest degree in the 18th and 19th centuries, at the time when literacy reigned unchallenged in the western world.

Listening with One's Body

By noting with Ong that oral thought remains close to the human lifeworld and shuns abstractions, we can propose that oral listening searches for images rather than concepts, persons rather than names. Sense is made and organized around vivid images acting in context. The oral discourse

Derrick de Kerckhove

is built around narratives and, as Havelock demonstrates in his analysis of early Greek literature, prefers verbs of action over predicates. These figures, according to Ong—and, incidentally to Northrop Frye—are defined and opposed in agonistical tensions. Just as newscasters promote drama even when they have to report on unexciting budget decisions in the Commons, the oral listener will favor dynamic drama over static descriptions. Again, this tendency corroborates the suggestion that we first learn and make sense by body imitation. TV makes sense to the youngest child because it talks to the body, just as the mind works in its representations of reality, directly with images stored and borrowed from multisensory inputs in the total human nervous system.

The Space Between: Men and Women Hearing

A final selection among Ong's many relevant observations is his notion that oral thought is "empathetic and participatory rather than objectively distanced." The focus of oral listening is not so much the source of the voice as the space created between the interlocutors. The ego of oral people, though not unexistant, and sometimes highly expressive in case of loss of face, is generally much less personalized, and therefore weaker than the ego of literate people. Without undue irreverance to the women in the audience, the listening attitudes of oral people are participatory in the way women can listen. There is the fascinating research of Stanford psychologist Diane McGuinness, who suggests that women are genetically conditioned across all cultures to respond better to hearing than to vision. Men see twice as well as women, conversely women hear twice as well as men. This physical difference, adding itself to other more obvious ones, brings upon a radically different attitude to language in men and women. Men tend to consider language instrumentally, while women are more accustomed to speak relationally. The space between the speaker and the listener is where the oral culture's action is.

4. Literate Listening

Literate listening is a highly trained kind of **thinking**. In fact, I believe that as children we learn to think not only by reading and doing mental exercises and working a primer of logic, but by listening to the kind of formal, trained and structured talk of the classroom teacher. Thinking itself, for the literate person, is primarily structuring speech in the silence of one's mind. And of course we find most models of structured speech in books, but it is found there as a static succession of statements. It is only when we are required to put together the words and sentences of a complex delivery from a teacher that we turn the static into dynamic forms.

A trained mind is a mind whose principal task is to eliminate noise, i.e. unnecessary information, so as to make room for specialized responses. A mind trained by literacy is led to process information in thought rather than in action, and within thinking, in words rather than images, and within words and sentences, in concepts rather than metaphors.

The school itself is ruled by alphabetic literacy. Speech must yield information not sensations, knowledge, not emotions, structure, not rhythms. The effect of the alphabet is to dry up human dialogue, to decontextualize it so as to make it available for re-use in other contexts. It is quite fitting that Plato's "Dialogues" have been turned into the highest tribute to the literate mind. What began as an oral experience in Socrates' encounters with his friends and entourage, was laid down and mastered by writing that is decontextualized. One wonders what would come out of a tape recording of Socrates.

Sylvia Scribner and Michael Cole did a ground breaking study in the early eighties to demonstrate that the role played by the school was essential to distinguish between a so-called literate and an oral culture. They suggested that the forms of formal instruction are what children, and even late learning adults, take home from the school situation. Indeed, formal literate speech is not merely a succession of words, it is also presented by a posture, a

Derrick de Kerckhove

position and attitudes which are easy for a child to recognize and to adopt. In "real" life, nobody speaks like a professor, except, possibly, the newscaster on the radio. Still the influence of the classroom teacher on our manner of listening is such that most of us go on to interpret the meanings of daily life speech with much of the legalistic, pedantic way we were trained to use when we were analyzing sentences in our grammar classes.

However, we do not gain instant access to the abstractions of our literate condition. We must first learn things in the context of the situation we are in. The great Japanese actor ZEAMI says that, in Japanese, "learning" really means to imitate with one's body. We all begin that way. A child learns by gestures and imitation. It may be that it is easier for our nervous system to integrate information all-at-once by seeing, hearing and doing simultaneously, than by separating, sorting and storing specialized bits of information. It may even be more pleasurable: neurobiologists tell us that one of the most exciting tasks of the newborn is to coordinate sensations of different senses coming simultaneously. Even the two-year-old's fun of banging one's toy against the bars of one's crib may come from the recognition that touching, hearing and seeing all come from the same gesture.

Now compare the situation of learning, listening with one's body to that of reading. While reading the body is stilled, almost as that of someone asleep. The reader is either in silence, or has made sufficient reservations in his or her mind to turn the ambient noise into silence. That kind of control, by the way, bears witness to the power of literacy over our hearing. When we read, we literally "shut our ears" just as if we had "earlids."

Education expert Richard Sinatra suggests that, in order to interpret the content of the reading, the reader must arrange meanings in his or her mind in understandable images. He calls it "internal rehearsing." I have done enough research into the history and the effect of theatre, from Ancient Greece till today, to know that universal literacy must go through a stage where most people learn not to read but to observe actions on a stage. It is another

86

kind of transitional literacy such as the school teacher's structured speech. Theatre—and internal rehearsing throws back to the early experience of "learning with one's body."

At first, turning written words into images is fairly hard work. I will never forget my father leaning over my shoulder to make sure that I was reading Alphonse Daudet's short story for children, "La chêvre de Monsieur Seguin." The sun was shining outside, and I could hear my friends playing with my brother in the garden. I was quite frustrated. "It's so easy," my father said, "all you have to do is to imagine a little white goat, going up a flowery mountain, running and munching all day, and, at night, meeting a dark, fierce wolf, and fighting for her life." That was easy for him. He had seen plenty of goats, mountains, wolves maybe, and he had read the story before, many times. I had seen goats too, and mountains, and I had seen pictures of wolves, but somehow I had to make a real effort to put it all together, because the images didn't seem to fit. They were wooden and flat, and all I wanted to do was to run outside with my friends. It is quite obvious to me that most kids like cartoons, comics and TV because they don't have to provide the images from their own minds.

Conclusion

I used to play improvisations on the recorder. I sometimes had the urge to let out miles of melodies stored in my body by prolonged exposure to classical music by my parents. Music must store in the body in the way long and short term memory store in the brain. Some kinds of music dissipate in seconds. Other kinds remain a lifetime, stored in the limbs, or maybe the brain, or even the heart. When I played something that really worked, a strange thing would happen to my ears: right after I stopped playing, I would hear a buzzing sound echoing the size of the room, as if my ears had suddenly become a kind of sonar probing all my surroundings at once. Normally, my access to ambient noise is selective, not global. If I don't have a need for a sound, I don't hear it, unless it is very intrusive. But in this case, it is as if my playing had turned my body into a monitoring system designed for the fullness of being. I would hear more, and deeper than usual. It must be the reward of the musician. Needless to say, it was a great joy. I can't tell whether my improvisations worked because of the sound, or whether the sound only came because I played well. But one thing I know for sure is that playing like that would help me to move completely from the literate to the oral mode. We all need that more than ever. It should be part of the Lord's Day Act. . . .

5

*The Overtones of Health**

DON G. CAMPBELL

Western music today makes use of more overtones than
were used in earlier eras of history. Overtones are subtle
secondary tones at a higher pitch that resound when a
primary note is sung or played. They are important in all
choral singing. They are intuitively developed to blend
different types of voices singing together. Barbershop
quartets, Swiss yodelers and many Eastern European
folk traditions mix harmonic colors or overtones to create
unique blends of sound.

Nadia Boulanger, master teacher, has looked at the way
the use of overtones has evolved over time. According to
her, the changes in music over the past fourteen centuries
has been orderly and predictable ("Lecture on Modern
Music," Rice University Studies, 1925). She says that the
old adage, "The dissonances of today are the consonances
of tomorrow," has force as one experiences its truth personally. For example, it is hard for us to believe that
Monteverde (1568-1643) felt the interval of a third (such
as Do-Mi or Re-Sol) was harsh. Boulanger states that "the
history of harmony is the history of development of the
human ear, which has gradually assimilated, in their natural
order, the successive intervals of the harmonic series."
The chief diatonic chords in use in successive periods of

---

*Condensed from Chapter 6 of *The Roar of Silence* by Don G.
Campbell, Quest Books, 1989.

musical history became increasingly complex. The following table (which is only approximate) shows this:

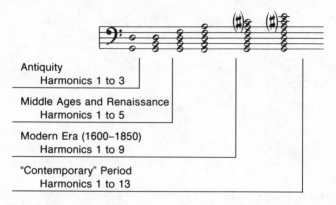

The early Gregorian scales, based on the sacred Greek modes, were notated in the seventh century. Their Greek names were kept, as were most of their sonic sequences. Dorian, Phrygian, Lydian, and Mixolydian were the most common modes. It was not until many centuries later that the Ionian mode came into popular use. It is known today as the major scale (the common Do, Re, Mi, Fa, Sol, La, Ti, Do progression). In India there are over 4,000 scales or *ragas*, each designated for a certain time of day, mood, or ritual. These are accompanied by *talas*, rhythmic modes that also have multi-purpose emotional ranges.

Our Western modes slowly fell into disuse after the year 1600 when the didactic major scale (inappropriately labeled "happy" by music teachers) and minor scale (similarly misnamed "sad") became the usual standard for musical expression. We seemed to lose some of the range and subtlety of emotions available to the ancients by the very strange idea that there is "happy" music and "sad" music. Fortunately, through the educational innovation and intuitive awareness of Hungarian composer Zoltan Kodaly and German composer Carl Orff, American and British children are again being richly taught the pentatonic (five note) scales and ancient modes.

After centuries of unison singing in the Gregorian modes, the interval of the fifth was introduced in a style called

Organum. Soon thereafter, intervals of fourths and thirds were used in melodic counterpoint to the old Gregorian melodies. As the centuries progressed, more chromatic music (half-steps, twelve tones per octave) introduced the intervals of seconds, using whole and half steps. Rules and laws about which notes could be sounded together developed. Compositions that broke these rules were considered diabolic and fictitious music. Those "evil" sounds of the fourteenth and sixteenth centuries are now quite acceptable to the liturgical ear, but Debussy and Ravel would have been burned in the Inquisition if they had been judged in that era by musical standards of the times.

It is of interest how our common scale—Do, Re, Mi, Fa, Sol, La, Si (modern Ti), Do—evolved. It was generally believed that sounds came down from heaven. Thus starting at the top of the scale:

Do   *Dominus*, God, Creator
Si (Ti) Siderial, Stars, Galaxies, Cosmos
La   *Voie Lacte*, the Milky Way
Sol   *Sol*, the Sun
Fa   *Fatus*, Destiny, the Planets
Mi   Microcosmos, the Earth
Re   *Regina Caeli*, Queen of Heaven, the Moon
Do   *Dominus*, God in Humanity

Chinese, Indian, Balinese and numerous other musical systems have sacred strategies for the powers and evolution of tones as they are used harmonically. Quartertones and microtones are found in many traditions and have been coming into Western music for the last few decades.

With the introduction of electronic sounds, our tonal sensitivity is evolving. We are learning not to judge new sounds as evil and uncharged. We are living in a period where technology is creating new standards. As with all evolving forms of life, what is needed will be kept. What is of no use will atrophy. Truly, new spatial and ambient sounds are being produced that could not have been imagined at the turn of the century. It will take the masters of the age to perfect and explore these sounds with the dignity and ethics necessary for human development.

The great overtones yet to be discovered are those within the mind. The exploration we have yet to make is inward. Personally, I take a mesoteric view of the physical and spiritual development of humanity. Mesoteric philosophy is grounded in both the esoteric and the exoteric. It is the middle pillar view for the Kabbalist, the moderate stand, with full curiosity and respect for the diverse. It is an inclusive standpoint where diverse elements in a system can be equally honored without criticism. The tarot card *Temperance* exemplifies the balanced nature of standing within two worlds with dignity.

When I began exploring overtones in my own voice, my listening abilities changed. At the same time, my speaking voice became richer, fuller and healthier. I began working with students with reading disabilities, dyslexic tendencies, stuttering and physical handicaps. Suddenly, my knowledge of the ear and the brain clicked into place with what I knew of tone and breath. Great physical and emotional powers can become balanced and reemerge, much like Dr. Tomatis's description in a previous chapter. What at first seemed like regression in sound and music skills turned out to be just the opposite, the nurturing basics for development and superlative growth.

These sounds in full array come not only from the throat, but also from the solar plexus, the base of the spine and the crown of the head. The whole body is a vibrating string and an air column at the same time.

By making elongated vowel tones and feeling the vibration in the body and the mind rather than attending to the outer sound, the brain waves synchronize and balance within minutes. The making of vowel and overtone sounds for three to five minutes brings a sense of well-being and balance to the body. When this is done with no stress or tension in the jaw, skin temperature generally rises and the mind calms. As the specific epicenters of sound and pitch are studied and determined for each individual, it will become possible to stimulate the body internally through toning.

It is possible to enhance the overtones made by singing, as described in Chapter 1 (Tibetan overtone chanting) and

Chapter 3 (David Hykes' Harmonic Chant). With practice, most ordinary people who are not necessarily musicians or singers can do it. The following exercise will begin to sensitize one to hearing and making overtones while chanting.

Exercise: Making Overtones

Although it takes a while to develop the clear overtones heard in Eastern chanting, it is not a completely foreign, mystical, and otherworldly art. We already produce overtones in our spoken vowel sounds.

This exercise will provide you with a few clues for discovering how to make a double sound with your voice. It's like trying to learn to whistle. It seems impossible until somehow it happens. Then you can't really tell anyone else exactly how to do it.

You may wish to be alone when you try this exercise. Unsuspecting neighbors or family members may think you have become strange and otherworldly as you make these sounds.

Sit comfortably with your eyes closed. Shape your lips as though you had a straw in your mouth. Stretch your lower jaw downward. Imagine the inside of your mouth becoming a very large cave.

Yawn and hold your chin down with one hand as you begin to make a low "Ooo" sound. Remember to keep only a small opening in your lips. Then, gently and very gradually, without changing the pitch of the "Ooo," begin to change the sound to "You" and then to "Eee."

As you fully exhale with a small opening in your lips and your chin down, make a sound something like this:

"oooooooooooooouououououououuuuuuuuuuuuuu
eueueueueueueeeeeeeeeeeeeeeee"

then

"eeeeeeeeeeeeeueueueueueuuuuuuuuuuuuuuuu
ouououououououoooooooooooooooooo"

Don G. Campbell

Do not be concerned about exactly how these vowel sounds are pronounced. If you begin with an "Oh" sound and move as slowly as possible to the "Eee" sound, you will naturally progress through all the other sounds. The key is to go very slowly and observe how your mouth and tongue change position as you modify the vowel sound ever so slightly.

Continue to go through this full sequence with each slow exhalation, with no break as you return to the darker sounding vowels. The slower you move your tongue between the vowel sounds, the more you will notice the overtones beginning to appear in your voice. This is not an authentic Tibetan technique, though it is somewhat similar to one of the Mongolian styles.

Making overtones is easier than you might suppose. Just start with these sounds, take your time, and know that you will discover a great power within your own voice. This exercise is very invigorating. But the greatest power of the tones occurs when the intention of the heart, the meaning of sacred texts, and vocal development are blended.

II
Music as Timeless Therapy

And yet this were surely again, to heal men's wounds
by music's spell . . .

Euripedes, Medea

I recall being in a large fundamentalist church in Texas in 1970 where therapists were considered "mind-manipulators" and unsaved souls. The same church now has two therapists on the staff. The power of a word like "therapy" changes with its familiarity, usage and adaptability. Since the late 1960s "therapy" has come to mean anything from clinical rehabilitation to an afternoon catnap for an executive under stress. It is now defined as: 1. the treatment of disease, as by some remedial or curative process; 2. a curative power or quality. (Gk.: m. therapeia, American College Dictionary).

For professionals who have devoted their lives to the study and practice of a specific therapy, it is distressing to see the overuse and seemingly unmindful application of "quick-fix" therapies that have suddenly emerged in popular books on every newsstand.

To the public, music therapy is generally an unknown field. Music holds a prominent position in our society and educational systems as a performing, entertaining art. It may be considered to have positive side effects of transformation, but these are not thought to be essential. Historically, music has been a primary tool for spiritual and physical alignment, used at political and social gatherings as well as for family, civic or educational ceremonies.

In this section, psychiatrist Roberto Assagioli, defines music therapy from the standpoint of a physician. Barbara Crowe, president of the National Association of Music Therapy, gives us insight as a professional using music as a healing tool in our society. Performing artist, scientist and renowned researcher Manfred Clynes brings our attention to the powers of music on the emotions. His instruments measure physiological responses to many kinds of music.

Registered nurse Cathie Guzzetta gives practical, clinical and visionary organization to the field of music as therapy in a hospital setting. Music therapist Joseph Moreno looks into the powerful shamanic musical tools and their relevance for current application. Arthur Harvey, Ph.D., explores the powers of music to transform attitudes in hospital settings.

6
Music: Cause of Disease and Healing Agent

ROBERTO ASSAGIOLI, M.D.

The healing properties of music were well known to the peoples of the past and they made considerable use of it. Among primitive peoples songs and musical instruments such as the drum and the rattle were used not only in order to increase the effect of herbs or drugs, but also as independent means of healing. Such practices have persisted until the present day among American Indians. Paul Radin, in his essay "Music and Medicine Among Primitive Peoples," reports that "among the Ojibwa, for example, the so-called *jessakid* practitioners are supposed to function simply by sitting near the patient and singing songs to the accompaniment of their gourd rattles. Similarly, among the Winnebago, those who have obtained their powers from the bear spirits can heal wounds by merely singing their songs." (Radin, 1948, p. 17)

It was known by the ancient civilizations that music has healing properties, and they deliberately used it for such purpose. In Finland's epic poem, the *Kalevala* (1958), we read of a sage who succeeded, by means of his music, not only in appeasing the fury of a mob, but actually in hypnotizing the people, sending them to sleep. In the Bible, it is reported that King Saul, being tormented by an evil spirit, called upon David, the skillful player on the harp; and "whenever the evil spirit . . . was upon Saul . . . David took a harp and played with his hand; so Saul was refreshed, and was well, and the evil spirit departed from him." (I Sam.

Roberto Assagioli, M.D.

16:23, King James version) According to the Arabs, music
has a beneficent effect on animals. They say that the singing
and playing of the shepherds make the flocks thrive. Among
the Greeks music had a special place as a curative agent.
Homer narrates that the flow of blood from the wound of
Ulysses was staunched by the melodious song of Autolycus.
(Andrew, 1953)

  We have more precise information on the use which
Pythagoras made of music. "Pythagoras," writes Porphyry,
"based musical education in the first place on certain
melodies and rhythms which exercised a healing, purifying
influence on human actions and passions, restoring the
pristine harmony of the soul's faculties. He applied the same
means to the curing of diseases of both body and mind.... In
the evening, when his disciples were about to retire, he
would set them free from all disturbances and agitations
of the day, steadying their somewhat wavering minds and
inducing peaceful sleep which brought with it propitious
and even prophetic dreams. And when they arose in the
morning he freed them from lingering sleepiness by means
of special songs and melodies." Porphyry also relates that
on one occasion, after Pythagoras had striven in vain to
calm and restrain a drunken man who was attempting, as
an act of revenge, to set fire to a house, he succeeded in
pacifying him by means of music. (Nauck, 1885).

  Plato accorded just as much importance to music as a
powerful means of psychotherapy and education, as is
shown by the following statement (among many others)
to be found in his *Republic*: "Rhythm and harmony sink
deep into the recesses of the soul and take the strongest
hold there, bringing that grace of body and mind which is
only to be found in one who is brought up in the right way."
(Cornford, 1942)

  Aristotle mentions among the various functions of music
that of emotional catharsis, which shows an interesting
similarity with the aim pursued by modern psychoanalysis.
(Warrington, 1959)

  We cannot deal here with the many other instances of the
appreciation and use of music for healing purposes by the
Greeks and the Romans and, later, from the Renaissance

on through the eighteenth century. Those interested in the history of musical therapy can find ample information in two essays, one by Bruno Meinecke, and the other by Armen Carapetyan, contained in the book, *Music and Medicine.* (Schullian, 1948)

In the nineteenth century, owing to the prevailing materialistic trend, this method of psychotherapy was comparatively neglected. One may even say that the tonic effect of music came to be more appreciated by the military than by the medical profession—every regiment with its own band and constant use made of martial music, of spirited marches to raise and keep up the morale of the soldiers. A few medical doctors, however, did make use of musical therapy. Among them was Hector Chomet. In his book, *The Influence of Music on Health and Life*, various cases of healing by means of music are mentioned. He reports the case of a woman subject to epileptic fits who one day happened to be listening to music when the symptoms of an approaching attack set in; the fit, however, did not occur. From that time on, at the first appearance of the symptoms, she arranged for music to be played, and in this way succeeded in entirely overcoming the attacks. (Chomet, 1875)

In the present century, and particularly in the last decades, there has been a renewed interest in musical therapy which has shown itself chiefly along three lines: as a means of soothing pain; through collective application in hospitals, especially in psychiatric clinics, with the general aim of producing calming or tonic effects on the patients; and as a means of occupational therapy.

A truly scientific musical therapy, and particularly its individual applications—namely those which aim at curing specific troubles in particular cases—should be based on a precise knowledge of the various elements of which music is composed and of the effect which each one of them has, both on physiological functions and on psychological conditions.

The principal musical elements are: *rhythm, tone, melody, harmony, timbre.*

Roberto Assagioli, M.D.

1. Rhythm

This is the primordial and fundamental element of music. The music of primitive peoples consists solely of rhythm. It is, indeed, what the poet d'Annunzio has called it, "the heart of music." Rhythm is the element which has the most intense and immediate influence on man, and it affects directly both the body and the emotions.

Organic life is based on various rhythms: the rhythm of respiration; the rhythm of the heart-beat; the rhythm of the various muscular movements; the rhythm of activity and rest; the rhythms of the various bodily functions, not to speak of the more subtle vibratory rhythms of every cell, every molecule and every atom. It is therefore not surprising that the rhythms of music exercise a powerful influence on those organic rhythms, either stimulating or calming them, harmonizing or creating discord and disruption.

The psychological life of the individual as well as that of his body has its various and complex rhythms: the rhythms of elation and depression; alternations of sorrow and joy, of fervour and lassitude, of strength and weakness, of extraversion and introversion. All these conditions are extremely sensitive to the influence of the rhythm of music. There are also certain activities wherein the rhythms of the body, the emotions and music interpenetrate and become fused in one integral rhythm. This happens in dancing, which one may truly call living music, expressed with one's whole being.

In rhythm itself we must distinguish various elements: chiefly *tempo* or speed (andante, moderato, allegro, etc.) and *meter* or grouping of beats. Each of them has its own specific influence; for instance, the more rapid the tempo, the greater is the emotional tension produced. A valuable analysis of the psychological effects of the various metric patterns or designs can be found in the chapter by Howard Hanson (1948) on "Emotional Expression in Music," of the book already cited, *Music and Medicine*. (Schullian, 1948)

2. Tone

Every note, while physically produced by a specific rate

of vibration, has at the same time both definite physical and psychological effects. As is well known, sound has great power over inorganic matter; by means of sound it is possible to cause geometric figures to form on sand and also to cause objects to be shattered. How much more powerful then must be the impact of this force on the vibrating, living substances of our sensitive bodies!

Each musical note has a specific *quality*, which cannot be expressed in words. This quality produces psychological effects, but one cannot ascribe a specific emotional quality to each note, and the various interesting attempts to relate each note to a corresponding color have not given any sure results, as the asserted correlations varied from individual to individual. More efficacious than isolated sounds are successions of tones in which the effect of each single note is increased by its combination with others of a different pitch.

3. Melody

The combination of rhythms, tones and accents produces those musical "units" or "wholes" which are called melodies. These are the results of the creative activity of the composer— an activity which is often spontaneous or inspired. Speaking in psychological terms, such musical creations as well as other kinds of creative artistic production are elaborated in the various levels of the unconscious, often in the superconscious. Melodies, being a synthesis of various musical factors, are a very apt means for the expression of emotions. They produce on the listener intense and manifold effects. They arouse not only emotions but also sensations, images and urges, and greatly influence the nervous system, respiration and circulation, in fact, all vital functions.

4. Harmony

While melody is produced by a succession of sounds, harmony is produced by the simultaneous sounding of several tones which blend with each other, forming chords. According to the respective rates of vibration of these sounds, the result will be either an harmonious blending or a jarring discord, both of which have definite physiological or psychological effects. Thus we may say that the prevalence of dissonances in modern music, being the expression of the discord, conflicts and crises that afflict modern man, tend with their suggestive influence to accentuate and exaggerate the evil.

5. Timbre [Tone Color]

The difference in the nature and structure of the various musical instruments, the human voice included, gives to sound a special quality which can hardly be defined in words, but which is easily recognizable, because it evokes special emotional responses. Everybody who has some musical sensitivity feels the specifically different *quality* of the impressions made by a violin or a flute, by a trumpet or by a harp, by a soprano or by a bass voice.

A composer, through the skillful combination of various instruments of an orchestra, can produce most powerful psychological effects.

*　*　*　*　*　*

Positive Effects of Music

Music can indeed be a powerful healing agent. There are many and diverse ways in which it can and does exercise a beneficent influence on both body and mind. First of all, its effect can be wonderfully restful and refreshing, and we need not emphasize how valuable this is in our times of physical exhaustion, nervous tension and emotional and mental excitement. The general and obvious prescription for the elimination of these conditions is a rest cure. But so many men and women of our day do not know how to rest, or even what real rest means. They are accustomed to constant movement and noise so that they are unable to keep still and endure silence. Here music comes to their rescue. As Father Gratry pithily says: "There is no agent so powerful in giving us real rest as true music. . . . It does for the heart and mind, and also for the body, what sleep does for the body alone." (Gratry, 1891) Indeed, many peaceful and solemn adagios, many soothing lullabies and barcarolles induce with their soft charm a beneficial relaxation in a more natural and healthy way than any chemical sedative.

More specific applications along these lines, with the purpose of inducing calm and soothing pain, have been made with patients undergoing dental treatment or surgical operations.

The following characteristic examples, which the New York Times reported a few years ago, will illustrate the kind and the results of such attempts: "The University of Chicago clinics experimentally introduced music to alleviate tensions of patients undergoing surgery. . . . So successful was the experiment that the University of Chicago medical research center will introduce music with anaesthesia in its six major operating rooms and its six preparation rooms, when it opens Chicago's first cancer research institution, the Nathan Goldblatt Memorial Hospital. . . . Music with anaesthesia is especially applicable to abdominal surgery, but it has been used in almost all types of operations. It has been found especially helpful to the peptic ulcer patients who are already so tense and nervous that the routine medical sedatives are not very effective. It is very important in cases where the patient is too old or ill to receive sedatives."

We have indicated how intensely music can work upon the feelings, and have pointed out the danger of this fact, but in many cases an emotional stimulus may be very opportune and helpful. For instance, there are a great many persons belonging to the practical or to the mental type who have an undeveloped or repressed emotional nature, and this is apt to make them arid, dissatisfied, shut-up within themselves. To them music may give the magic touch which reawakens and warms the heart and restores communion with nature, humanity, and God.

Then there is a kind of music, both instrumental and vocal, of a strong and virile nature, which arouses the will and incites to action. Such music has stimulated innumerable individuals to noble deeds, to heroic self-sacrifice for an ideal. Against all negative and depressive emotions, such as despondency, pessimism, bitterness, and even hate, music of a gay, vivacious and sparkling character, and also music that expresses true humor, acts as a true counter-poison. It cheers and gladdens, smoothing the wrinkled foreheads and softening into smiles the hard lines of tightly closed lips. Such effects are produced by many compositions of Haydn, Mozart, and Rossini.

What more efficacious, genial and acceptable means than music could a doctor devise for giving joy; that joy which the intuition of the ancients and the investigations of modern science alike declare to be a powerful tonic both for the mind and for the body?

The particular stimulating action which music exercises on the unconscious can have many good effects; for example, it can stimulate memory, a function that depends largely on the unconscious. In this connection the following statement by the accomplished musicologist, Mario Pilo, is of interest:

"For myself, music performs a special action in arousing my memory, which is capricious and undisciplined, subject to lapses and slips that are often very annoying. More than once music has enabled me to retrieve from its hiding place, quite suddenly, some reluctant and elusive memory: Several years ago, a Neapolitan melody of no special merit, which was being played on a mandolin by a neighbour, enabled me in a few minutes to remember the subject of a manuscript I had lost years ago, also the ideas contained in it which I had tried in vain, at intervals, to put together again." (Pilo, 1912)

Music can and does also quicken and facilitate intellectual activity and favour artistic and creative inspiration. There is, among others, the case of the Italian author Alfieri who relates that he conceived nearly all his tragedies either at the moment of listening to music or immediately afterwards.

Through its influence upon the unconscious, music can have a still more definite and specific healing effect of a psychoanalytic character. If of an appropriate kind, it can help in eliminating repressions and resistances and bring into the field of waking consciousness many drives, emotions and complexes which were creating difficulties in the unconscious.

Music can help also, through its charm and uplifting influence, to transmute and sublimate those impulses and emotional energies so as to render them not only harmless, but make them contribute to the deepening of experience and the broadening and enriching of the personality. We have the works of a great composer who, having lived through periods of intense stress and strain, was finally able to rise to some extent above his personal pain and to draw inspiration from it, expressing strength, joy and faith, and praising the goodness of life. I am referring to Beethoven. In some of his sonatas, particularly in the later ones, the releasing and sublimating process is easily discernible. The storms and alternations in the first parts of these sonatas are followed by a peaceful and triumphant conclusion.

The previously discussed process of integration into the conscious personality of unconscious contents, and their subsequent transmutation and harmonization, can in a certain respect be regarded as a process of synthesis. But there is a more specific process of psychosynthesis which is of three kinds, or rather, consists of three stages, each wider and more inclusive than the preceding one. They can be called respectively: spiritual psychosynthesis; inter-individual psychosynthesis; cosmic psychosynthesis.

The first—spiritual psychosynthesis—recognizes the inclusion and integration into the conscious personality of higher psychospiritual elements of which it is not consciously aware, because they reside in the highest sphere of the unconscious, the superconscious.

Truly religious music is very effective in producing or favouring such a synthesis. It awakens and stimulates the spiritual "germs" which exist in every one of us, waiting to come to life. It lifts us above the level of everyday consciousness, up into those higher realms where light, love and joy ever reign. There are many musical compositions which produce such effects. We can mention only a few of the most significant examples, omitting the consideration

of less accessible ancient and Oriental music: the Gregorian
Chant which still evokes the highest religious emotions;
then there is Palestrina, of whom it was said by Scott, in
his chapter on "Beethoven—Sympathy and Psychoanalysis,"
that he "was the first European composer to restore music
to its original function—that of constituting a definite
link between man and God." (Scott, 1928)

Next we must mention J. S. Bach whose music not only
arouses the deepest religious feelings, but has a still greater
synthesizing influence which we shall discuss later; nor
should we fail to mention Handel and his impressive
oratorios.

Among the later composers we find three who are markedly
different from each other, but whose music, in diverse
ways and with dissimilar techniques, produces powerfully
spiritual effects: César Franck, that pure and noble soul
who succeeded in giving adequate musical expression to
the *Evangelical Beatitudes;* Richard Wagner, who in *Lohengrin*
and *Parsifal* evokes with the magic of sound the flight of
an angelic host from heaven to earth, the feeling of spiritual
love and compassion, and the sacred rites of the Grail
Brotherhood; Aleksandr Scriabin who, through the use
of daring combinations of sounds, endeavors to lift the
consciousness to the heights of rapturous bliss and ecstasy.

The second kind or stage of psychosynthesis—inter-
individual psychosynthesis—is one which is established
between an individual and his fellowmen within a group
of which he forms a part—from the smallest combination
consisting of a man and a woman, to the family group
which includes the children, on to the various social groups,
the national groups and ever greater units, until his consciousness embraces in an harmonious relationship the
whole of humanity.

Such inter-individual psychosynthesis is promoted by
all music which expresses collective emotions and aspirations. It includes national anthems, marches and folk
songs belonging to particular occupations or group activities;
harvest songs, grape-gathering songs, etc., and many choruses
from the operas of Verdi and others. The highest and most
effective musical expression of the psychosynthesis of

humanity is Beethoven's Ninth Symphony, which reaches its climax with the intonation of Schiller's words *Seid umschlungen, Millionen.* (Be embraced, ye millions of men.)

The third stage—cosmic psychosynthesis—consists of an ever increasing recognition and acceptance by the individual of the laws, the relationships and the rhythms governing life itself, in its widest sense. It could be called the discovery of, and the tuning in with, "the harmony of the spheres," the conscious participation in the great life of the universe. This subject has been ably treated by Aleks Pontvik who expounded his views and has related some of the results of his musical experiments in a stimulating little book entitled *Grundgedanken zur Psychischen Heilwirkung der Musik* (1948) (Fundamental Thoughts on the Psychic Healing Effect of Music). In this book the author adopts the Pythagorean conception of the universe as an ordered whole. The cosmos is built according to harmonious—and that means musical—laws and proportions. And he quotes in this connection Brantzeg's summary of Kepler's development of this principle: "Before all things were created there was geometry. This, since eternity, is a reflection of God; it gave Him the original *pattern* for the artistic structure of this world in order that it may become similar to its Creator. The fundamental elements of geometry are the divisions of the circle. They produce harmonies, they create earthly forms through the harmonious consonance of music and they give to the constellations of the zodiac their cosmic pattern. In music, harmony is the result of the composer's intuition, but among the stars it is produced by the geometrical necessity of the heavenly mechanics. God has given to the human soul harmonious proportions." (Kepler, 1619)

According to Pontvik, the following conception gives the key to psychotherapy in general, and to musical therapy in particular: healing can be attained only by starting from the whole. "It means the establishing, or re-establishing, of an harmonious equilibrium through the reconciliation of opposing elements within the whole. Thus the healing process of psychoneuroses can be indicated in musical terms as a progressive development which brings about, or

107

restores, the fundamental harmonious chord." (Pontvik, 1948, p. 30)

The technique of this healing action consists, according to Pontvik, in the evocation or musical expression of primordial symbols corresponding to what Jung calls archetypes. The music which can especially produce this kind of healing influence is that of J. S. Bach. Pontvik found in his experience that Bach's music evokes religious symbols, particularly that of a temple, the harmonious proportions of which are in their structure analogous to those of the universe. He supports his contention by two interesting quotations; one from Albert Schweitzer, who not only has to his credit great humanitarian achievements but [was], besides, one of the most prominent authorities on Bach. Schweitzer (1915) calls a composition by Bach "an expression of the Primal Power which manifests itself in the infinite rotating worlds." The other quotation is from the writings of a Chinese sage: "Perfect music has its cause. It arises from balance. Balance arises from that which is right. That which is right arises from the world's significance. Therefore one can talk about music only with one who has become aware of the world's significance."

One of my students expressed in the following way the effect of Bach's music upon her: "When, last evening, in the light of the moon, I listened to the Second Suite, I became aware of all the grandeur of Bach's poise. His music is really a marvellous harmony of the three divine aspects; a song of love, unfolding itself in the light of intelligence, and impelled by will. That is why it enriches so much."

Musical therapy, in order to prove effective, should be applied according to certain rules which are based on psychophysiological, rather than on aesthetic or artistic principles. Here are some of the more important ones:

1. Prior to the performance, the patient or group of patients should receive *adequate information* about the piece to be executed. Its nature, structure and particularly the effect to be expected, should be explained. In this way the listeners can contribute intelligently to the influence of the music upon their unconscious, and consciously assimilate it. For

the same reason it is useful for the listeners to know before-hand the text of pieces which are to be sung, or to have the text right under their eyes. Often, also, in regular per-formances the strain to catch the words (which are not usually clearly pronounced, or which are submerged by the sound of the orchestra) interferes with the effect aimed at.

2. It is advisable for the patients to *relax* as much as possible before and also during the musical performance. This, too, helps them to "open the doors of the unconscious," so to speak, and to receive the full benefit of the musical influence. Such relaxation can be induced by a comfortable physical position, by subdued illumination, by verbal suggestions made by the doctor, and also by a short intro-ductory musical piece of a soothing nature, even if, subsequently, one wants to produce stimulation or joyous-ness through appropriate pieces.

3. The *right dosage* is of importance. In general, a musical treatment should be of *short duration*, in order to avoid fatigue and, therefore, possible defence reactions.

$$* \quad * \quad * \quad * \quad * \quad *$$

We trust that the magic of sound, scientifically applied, will contribute in ever greater measure to the relief of human suffering, to a higher development and a richer integration of the human personality, to the harmonious synthesis of all human "notes," of all "group chords and melodies"—until there will be the great symphony of the One Humanity.

References

Andrew, S. O., 1953. Homer: *Odyssey* XIX, New York: Dutton.

Capurso, A. & Others, 1952. *Music and your Emotions*, New York: Liveright (for Music Research Foundation, New York).

Chomet, H., 1874. *Effets et influence de la musique sur la santé et sur la maladie,* Paris: Germer-Bailliere.

Roberto Assagioli, M.D.

————1875. *The Influence of Music on Health and Life*, trans. Flint, Laura A., New York: Putnam.

Cornford, F. M., trans., 1942. Plato: *The Republic*, Book III, 401, Oxford: University Press.

Gratry, A. J. A., 1891, *Les Sources*, Paris: Doumol.

Hanson, H., 1948. "Emotional Expression in Music." In Dorothy M. Schullian & M. Schoen (Eds) *Music and Medicine*, New York: Schuman.

"Kalevala, The," 1958. Everyman's Series, Vol. I & II, New York: Dutton.

Kepler, J., 1619. *De Harmonice Mundi*, Book V, Augsburg.

Nauck, A., edit., 1885. Porphyry: *De Vita Pythagorae*, Leipzig.

Pilo, M., 1912. *Psicologia Musicale*, Milan: Hoepli.

Pontvik, A., 1948. *Grundgedanken zur Psychischen Heilwirkung der Musik* (Fundamental thoughts on the psychic healing effect of Music), Zurich: Rascher Verlag.

————. *Contributions aux Recherches sur les Effets Psychiques de la Musique*. Unpublished, privately circulated article.

Radin, P., 1948. "Music and Medicine Among Primitive Peoples." In Dorothy M. Schullian & M. Schoen (Eds) *Music and Medicine*, New York: Schuman.

Schullian, Dorothy M. and Schoen, M., 1948. *Music and Medicine*, New York: Schuman.

Schweitzer, A., 1915. *Johann Sebastian Bach*, Leipzig: Breitkopf & Hartel.

Scott, C., 1928. *The Influence of Music on History and Morals*, London: Theosophical Publishing House.

Warrington, J., trans., 1959. Aristotle: *Politics & Athenian Constitution*, New York: Dutton.

7
Music—the Ultimate Physician

BARBARA J. CROWE

As a professional music therapist, I hold certain beliefs and assumptions about music as a healing tool. I believe that music is an important tool for human health and well-being in a number of ways, many of which we are only now beginning to understand. I believe music is positively influential on people because of its unique ability simultaneously to be a structured experience and a transcendent event. I believe that the effects of music are not necessarily "provable" by the processes of scientific investigation but are "knowable" on several levels of human understanding.

Our forebears intuitively knew of the power of music to heal and used it for such. As the deep understanding of the non-verbal medulla oblongata and the limbic system which held this knowledge was replaced by the verbal, logical processing of our upper cortex, this understanding of the power of music to heal was lost. I believe music can be the ultimate physician and that we desperately need its full power back in our lives.

In order to examine the idea of music as a physician, we must know what a physician is and actually does. In our society today, we use the term to mean a doctor, a scientist, who cures diseases, eliminates our symptoms, and removes pathological states by carefully analyzing where our system has broken down and fixing the malfunction. A doctor is a technician, a mechanic for the body machine, but is the term synonomous with the term "physician"? Webster's Dictionary defines physician as "any person or thing that heals, relieves, or comforts." (Webster, p. 1353) The idea of healing in this definition implies much more than alleviation of symptoms or curing a body system. Our word "heal" comes from the Anglo-Saxon word *hal* meaning "whole" (Webster, p. 836). To be healed is to be made whole. Jeanne Achterberg defines healing as being released from a fear or grief that blocks our perception of being part of a greater whole. A healing occurs when one knows one's connection to the entire fabric of the universe (Achterberg, p. 19-20).

Ancient healing practices illustrate this restoration of a sense of wholeness as the essential component to healing. In the shamanic practices from many cultures, the healer was an individual who was able to leave normal consciousness and travel in the wider world of the spirits, usually with the help of repetitive drumming and rattling (Harner, 1980). On these journeys, the shaman learned how the patient was out of balance with the worldview of the community, and how the patient had lost power, the personal, protective shield. The shaman would bring back information, usually in symbolic form, to help the patient right the imbalance and come again into wholeness with the universe and, especially, the world of spirit. In another example the Wisada Balian, knowledgeable healers of the Indonesian island of Bali who are still active today, work closely within the mystical belief system of the Hindu religion. To the Balianese, illness is caused by evil spells and spirit possession. The Balian determines the source and cause of the evil spell and provides prayers and magic drawings to protect the victim. The patient is reassured that the natural order and balance in his or her life is restored. A healing occurs.

The two models of healing the sick—the Western medical approach of treating symptoms of pathology and the ancient practices of healing through transcendent awareness of wholeness and oneness with all in the universe—may seem to be opposite and irreconcilable. However, by accepting both approaches as part of a continuum of human development and therefore ultimate health, a new theory of healing may emerge. Ken Wilber (1989), Roger Walsh (1989), and others have postulated such a theory that sees human development as a continuum from a state of pathology through to a transpersonal transcendence of concerns with the self as separate and finite. On one end of this continuum is the state of pathology which can be characterized as the chaos and disorder that stems from our inability to cope with a complex universe. To move from this state, an individual must develop ways to structure his or her responses and behavior to make sense out of the chaos. Through sensory awareness, usage, and the development of perceptions meaningful to the establishment of ego-functioning and normal waking consciousness, order is established and some alleviation of pathology can occur.

From this state, our future development and health demands that we challenge and question the order that we have imposed on the chaos of our world and begin to explore the existential questions of life and death, of meaning and purpose. We search for more depth of understanding, more meaning than our habitual patterns of order can give us. It is at this point that experiences in heightened awareness or nonordinary states of consciousness are necessary to bring us to a point where we break through our ordinary state of consciousness, transcend these issues, and recognize our place as part of the whole universe. Healing, then, becomes a process of movement through these stages: from primal chaos, to structured order of sensory perceptions and ego-boundaries, through existential reaction to that established order, to emergence into a transcendent state of wholeness. Whether this is a lifelong process of maturity and growth or a shorter term healing of a physical or emotional illness, the passage is the same.

Within this model of human growth and development, experiences with music can be a primary force for healing, because music is simultaneously a structured and a transcendent event. Music as an activity is highly regular and rigidly structured, yet it affects our emotions and states of awareness and moves us beyond our needs for order and for the process of existential questioning. The structured nature of music derives from the rules and conventions of musical composition, tuning systems, and rhythmic patterns and meter groups. These organize the potential chaos of all the possible sound frequencies and durations into an ordered experience. Chords sound pleasing, melodies take shape, and music moves through time at a specific speed, with an obvious beginning and ending because of the structure imposed on sound. Music has a perceived spatial and temporal order (Sears, 1968). Yet this very structured auditory event has the ability to break through our ordinary levels of consciousness and perceptual conventions to open us for the transcendent awareness of oneness. The overwhelming emotional reaction to music that we describe as an aesthetic experience is evidence of this opening. We are "carried away" from the ordinary by the power of the music.

Throughout history, we have used music in all forms of worship to set a reverent mood and a mental state open to the influence of deity. Though highly organized and regular, music moves us into the transcendent, transpersonal state.

The theories and practices of the profession of music therapy as used today illustrate how music matches individuals' levels of functioning, helps them work through the problems and issues of that stage, and then models and drives them on into the next level on the continuum. An examination of music therapy techniques and practices with schizophrenic clients will serve as an example of the use of music to heal the first level of functioning, pathology stemming from chaos. Music therapy experiences for the schizophrenic client emphasize awareness of and response to the order and structure of music. Persons with this severe mental disorder are unable to distinguish real environmental events from their own internal processes. There is no imposition of structure, no ego functioning to differentiate self from surroundings. The world is chaos to them, and they have no consistent perceptual basis to interpret what they are experiencing. A music therapy activity for these individuals might be based on recognizing and responding to the auditory stimuli that is actually occurring in the environment. This might involve singing a song at the same tempo as others in a group, starting and stopping their musical performance at the same time as an accompaniment instrument, or recognizing and identifying what instrument is being played on a recording. The music models the imposition of order on the potential chaos of the sound and provides structure for response.

On the next level of the continuum of human development, music therapy activities can provide opportunities for exploration of existential questions and concerns. Individuals in this stage experience doubts, fears, depression, anxiety, stress, and other reactive behaviors. They need to explore their patterns of interpersonal relationships, their beliefs and value systems, their goals, and their concepts of self. One typical music therapy activity for these individuals involves musical improvisation, usually on rhythm instruments. In an improvisation such as this, there are few rules for the performance. The sounds produced mirror the group dynamics and issues and concerns of the individuals involved. The musical event makes these processes overt and obvious so that they can be explored and discussed.

Another common music therapy activity, lyric analysis, explores personal beliefs and values through the discussion of the lyrics of songs. The song provides the impetus for sharing ideas and opinions on topics expressed in the words. Similarly, musical activities that emphasize creativity can provide support for an individual's developing sense of self since creativity requires self-expression. What we create is a direct reflection of who we are. In such activities, the music therapist guides the client toward expanded self-expression by providing opportunities for song-writing, instrumental composition, and free vocal improvisation. In all these music therapy activities, clients are supported in questioning their beliefs and patterns of behavior.

Once an individual has reached a point where awareness of the transcendent is the necessary healing component, music can serve as an agent of change, providing a vehicle to reach beyond ordinary consciousness and ego-functioning to new awareness and new ways of viewing the self in the universe. As evidenced in shamanic practices, music can

Barbara J. Crowe

suppress our verbal, cognitive functioning and open the
symbolic, metaphorical subconscious which is our link
with the great cosmic oneness. As music therapist Grant
Rudolph expressed it:

The precise language of music directly communicates what cannot
be said with words. The experience at the moment of crossing a
threshold with music is one of surrender. Our controlling nature
gives up to a creative presence. Musically, some aspect of sound
becomes so complicated or boring that we cease to make it happen,
and we surrender control. Our ego opens for that moment and a
more complete awareness enters; attention focuses on a musical
event too fast or complicated for the thinking mind to encompass
(Rudolph, 1988, p. 68-70).

Many musical traditions, especially in Eastern societies,
emphasize this transcendent function of music, and they
identify four ways in which music can open the human mind
to a wider perception (Rudolph, 1988). The first musical
element that is used to create this "opening" effect is repetitive
and/or complex rhythms. These techniques, prominent in
shamanic practices, allow the healer to leave normal conscious awareness in order to journey in the realms of the
"spirits" (Harner, 1980). From a physiological perspective,
this seems to occur because of the action of the reticular
activating system (RAS) located in the brain stem. This
structure serves to alert the entire brain to incoming sensory
stimulation. Loud, repetitive sound such as drumming floods
the brain with input and successfully competes for attention
over other sensory channels. Normal verbal activity is
suppressed, and consciousness is freed to explore other
forms of perception and information processing (Achterberg, 1985).

Melodic subtlety is the second way in which sound has
been used to create an open, contemplative frame of mind.
The raga singing tradition of India is a prime example
with its emphasis on minute changes of pitch which fall
between the notes of our Western scale. Such small changes
of pitch are perceived in the lowest parts of our brain,
eliminating altogether the need for cognitive processing.

A third element, sound complexity or resonance, has

also been used as a gateway to the subconscious. The resonant quality of sounds is produced by the vibratory characteristics of an instrument. It is the pattern of frequencies produced, but not heard as separate pitches, that gives an instrument or voice its distinctive tone quality. The use of gongs, metal bowls, and overtone singing all come from contemplative traditions where sound complexity and the resonance of the human body are vital components in the production of a meditative mind state.

The fourth musical element found to serve an opening function is full-spectrum harmony, the patterns of consonant and dissonant note combinations. The use of harmony has been most fully explored in traditional Western music. This highly developed vertical structure envelops the listener in sound that is characterized by rapid movement from one tonal center to another. This shifting of center and perception of movement creates a mental state receptive to new awareness because the cognitive mind is flooded with complex sensory information that it cannot completely process.

The potential for the use of music as a healer in this last stage of human development is great. Human response to music is deep and profound and clearly can open the mind to new perceptions. Though musical experiences have been associated with mystical healing practices throughout human history (Rudolph, 1988), contemporary music therapy has only just begun to explore the awareness of the transcendent as a healing activity. Through such techniques as guided imagery with music (Bonny, 1973) these realms are being explored. In this practice, a client is given a relaxing verbal induction and then exposed to traditional Western classical music, which elicits images that are then explored and discussed with the therapist guiding the experience. But techniques such as this have only begun to tap the potential of music to heal on this level. If music is to become the physician for the new century, its full power must be rediscovered and utilized.

In studies I have recently conducted, the scope of the power of music to heal in the transpersonal stage of human development was expressed in unique ways. These studies involved the use of music to promote a wholistic form of problem-solving. Groups of music therapists were asked to answer the question, "What is music/music therapy?" while listening to a forty-five minute tape of music selected to promote a contemplative state of mind. Writing and drawing materials were provided for the subjects to record their answers to the questions. The responses elicited were quite extraordinary. They revealed a connection between music and our perception of a greater whole that went far beyond an experience of merely opening to new levels of awareness. The responses quoted below begin to reveal the depth of this connection between music and transcendent awareness.

Music is:
> *bonding with nature*
> *allowing creativity to express itself*
> *refreshment of the spirit*
> *a development of the spiritual within us*
> *getting in touch with eternal flow*
> *resurgence of self*
> *reconvening of life*
> *spiritual bonding*
> *involvement—an "at-oneness" with the rhythm of*
> *living.*

Music is a magical gift that reaches the whole universe.

Music is a never unfinished whole.

Music is getting in touch with the eternal flow, a language of all things.

Moisture from the drops of music nurtures and supplies vital nutrients to our physical and emotional well-being. We become healthy. We flourish as a species. We prosper. We grow. We laugh. We cry. We dance. We sing. We love. We live. We become one.

Music therapy seeks to connect human rift to uncover the universe in every soul.

Music therapy is being a complete being and celebrating joy and sorrow together, in expressing from the true wordless source of what we are.

Music therapy is personal power made manifest. It's a map to the place where strength and well-being and love lie buried deep inside us all. It is a force to create change from within, to find the healer in all of us.

Music—the Ultimate Physician

Music therapy is coming together to be washed in sound, to share this gift of highest expression, to become closer, cleaner, more whole in the sounds of ourselves. To feel and sensitize to truth in the moment of feeling. In being we know the source is here in the thoughtless now. . . .

Abandon to it.

From the results of this study, I have come to believe that the potential for music to heal comes not just from music's ability to break through normal consciousness and open us to transcendent awareness, but from the fact that music is the ultimate manifestation of this wholeness. Many philosophers and teachers throughout the centuries have expressed this idea including the Hazrat Inayat Khan (1983) who theorizes that sound, particularly beautiful sound, is the force of creation, the true whole. Music, then, becomes the voice of the great cosmic oneness and therefore the optimal way to reach this final state of healing.

As many ancient practices illustrate, the process of healing is one of becoming whole. For our society, this process involves movement along a continuum of personal development—from pathology born of chaos, through our reactive, existential questioning of order, to a point of transcendence of issues of ego and consciousness, to a perception of a whole greater than ourselves. Music becomes the ultimate healer, the physician for the next century, because it is simultaneously a structured ordering of chaos and a transcendent event—both a transpersonal opening and a direct manifestation of oneness. This dual nature allows music to match an individual's level of functioning whatever it may be and help the person move toward the wholeness of healing. And, because the process of growth and health is never linear but spiral, first moving forward, then back on itself, and forward again, music in all its aspects is available at whatever levels are needed at a given time, until the healing can occur.

References

Achterberg, J. (1985). *Imagery in healing.* Boston: New Science
Library.

Barbara J. Crowe

Bonny, H. L. and Savory, L. M. (1973). *Music and your mind: Listening with a new consciousness.* New York: Harper and Row.

Harner, M. (1980). *The way of the shaman.* New York: Harper and Row.

Khan, H. I. (1983). *The music of life.* Lebanon Spring, NY: The Sufi Order.

Rudolph, G. (1988). *Dreamsinging: Sounding the depths of psychic images.* Unpublished manuscript, Human Relations Institute, San Francisco.

Sears, W. (1968). "Processes in Music Therapy." In E. T. Gaston (Ed.), *Music in therapy* (pp. 30-46). New York: Macmillan and Company.

Walsh, R. (Speaker). (1989). *Clinical and spiritual aspects of psychotherapy.* Cassette recording NO. HEA 89. Los Angeles, CA: East West Foundation.

Webster's New Twentieth Century Dictionary, 2nd edition. (1979). New York: Simon and Schuster.

Wilber, K. (1989). *The spectrum of consciousness.* Wheaton, IL: Theosophical Publishing House.

8

On Music and Healing*

MANFRED CLYNES

The following challenging and significant article was
written by Dr. Manfred Clynes—academically the respected
leader in the study of emotional responses to music. His
pioneering work has helped to show how the conscious
mind dynamically affects the physical body through the
power of the emotions.

A primary focus of this article is to demonstrate how
music or music-like disciplines (*metamusic*) can assist in
the healing process. Specifically, Clyne's *Sentic Cycles* shows
emotional release during the listening or making of music.
However, Sentics does not require the high degree of
musical expertise needed to reach the same level of emotional expression through performance.

Clyne's premise is that music (or *metamusic*, such as in
the practice of *Sentic Cycles*) is a *link* between thought and
movement—"a direct crossing of the mind-body barrier."
Thus by voluntary response to musical (or metamusical)
expression, we can have simultaneous effects on the body
and the mind. Music becomes a profound and accessible

---

*Please see the article "On Being in Order," also by Manfred Clynes,
reprinted in the Appendix, prior to reading the following. In
addition, his book *Sentics: The Touch of the Emotions*, 1989, Prism
Press, Great Britain, distributed in the U.S. by Avery Publishing
Group, expands upon the material presented here. For an editor's
explanation of some of the more difficult terms and concepts
used in either of these articles (i.e., *Sentic Cycles, essentic form*) see
the introduction to this article.

route to one of the more elusive conundrums: Given that there is a connection between emotional and physical health,* how can we promote healing to affect both the emotions and the physical body? Music or *metamusic* can provide a vital key.

A brief preparatory explanation of some of the idiomatic terms used in this article follows:

Sentic state. The word *sentic* denotes the emotional state during our experience of emotional expression. It is not the emotional expression itself, however. It is a single channel of communication of emotional expression; at any one time in an individual there is only one sentic state being expressed. Each sentic state dictates the shape that its corresponding *E-acton* will assume.

Proto-sentic states. The correct, ideal or archetypal sentic state of a given emotion.

Essentic forms. The biologically innate forms of emotional expression, which in combination communicate emotion to others. They are comprised of *E-actons* that make up gestures, facial expressions, etc. *Essentic forms* "give movement its emotional meaning . . . a window across the mind-body barrier. . . . When we laugh, cry, sigh or yawn, we are driven to cross the barrier . . . but also, [one] can use essentic form at will to drive . . . body and . . . mind."

Ortho-essentic form. The correct, ideal, archetypal *essentic form* for a primary emotion. When we are expressing an *ortho-essentic form*, we are considered sincere; that is, the expression truly mirrors the *sentic state.*

Sentic Cycle. A *metamusic*; a form of active meditation; an emotional exercise. A person listens to a specifically timed, *sentic cycle tape.* The tape requests the subject to express either no emotion or the emotion of anger,

---

*Modern medicine has certainly demonstrated this, including the many studies on the profound effects that meditation-like practices can have on stress reduction, lowering of blood pressure and heart rate, increasing longevity of cancer patients, enhancing immune system function, etc.

hate, grief, love, sex, joy or reverence, to the rhythm or pulse of soft clicks with varying intervals of a few seconds. The subject expresses these emotions physically by tapping a finger rest with one finger. These movements are recorded on a *Sentogram.*

Sentogram. A record that shows shapes produced by emotions expressed during a *Sentic cycle.* It results from measuring muscle tension generated by finger pressure on a special finger rest while one is performing the cycle. The amount of pressure and the angle of the finger pressure are measured, and together they produce a characteristic curve or shape for each emotion expressed. (See Fig. 3-5 in "On Being in Order" in the appendix.)

Actons. Individual, simple components of movement that, when performed together, comprise a complete motion or action, such as raising a hand to one's mouth to eat. The nature of each individual movement is programmed in the nervous system before the motion actually begins. The individual *acton* includes both the decision to act and the execution of the action.

E-actons (Expressive-actons). The individual components of movement making up an expressive action that involves emotion and corresponds to an inner state, called *sentic state.* The "shape" of *E-actons* is defined by the sentic or emotional state that is seeking expression at any given time.

Expressive action (E-action). A class of movements made up of *E-actons* (in addition to simple actions which are comprised of *Actons*), programmed and directed by the brain, with the sole purpose to respond, express, or correspond to an inner state of feeling.

Musical pulse. The repetitive, automatic component of music or *metamusic.* The pulse has a distinctive form, and the character or nature of that form conveys a portion of the meaning of that music (or *metamusic*).

It would be helpful to read the article "On Being in Order," also by Manfred Clynes, reprinted in the Appendix, prior to reading the following "On Music and Healing." "On Being in Order" gives an expanded but decidedly more technical treatment of the material presented in this article.

—ED.

Music acts on both mind and body. To know how music works implies crossing the mind-body barrier, opening up a window on the mind-body problem. We shall, in the following, give some details of our work with the language of music that is, in fact, opening up such a window. (Clynes 1985 a, b, 1983, 1977, 1973, 1969.) This will permit us also to obtain a view of how healing can be helped by music (and by sentic cycles, a new metamusic that can release emotion, as music and musical improvisation can, without the need for musical skill and aptitude).

Music moves. Not only emotionally, but bodily: music dances inwardly and incites to gesture, to dance, outwardly. Song and gesture both contain movement generated by the musical thought and form. They are a transformation from thought to movement—a direct crossing of the mind-body barrier, as is a voluntary act of lifting a finger. Even thinking music, without sound, involves experience of movement in imagination.

But the movement of musical thought is not mere movement: it is expressive movement. The difference between movement and expressive movement is that expressive movement contains essentic form.

(Essentic form is the biologically given expressive dynamic form for a specific emotion [Clynes 1969, 1973, 1980, Clynes and Nettheim 1982].) Essentic form may be expressed in various sensory modalities and parameters, but cannot be divorced from its emotion state with which it forms an existential entity (principle of coherence, Clynes 1977, 1980). Thus, for example, it is not possible to re-train an individual to sincerely express love with the essentic form of anger, and vice versa. Essentic form also is the basis of the contagion of emotion: the production and recognition of essentic form are programmed biologically in concert. Essentic forms for a number of emotions have been experimentally measured and isolated, in studies which have covered some 15 years. It has also been shown that touch expressions of a particular essentic form can readily be transformed into sound expressions of like emotional expression, and that the emotional qualities of the sounds thus derived are easily recognized even by individuals from a different culture than those from whose touch they were created (Clynes and Nettheim 1982).

Essentic form gives movement its emotional meaning—a window across the mind-body barrier, provided to us directly by nature. When we laugh, cry, sigh or yawn, we are driven to cross this barrier—mercilessly, like a robber who flees across a bridge with his prey. We are not free. The expressive form commands our experience and our body. And by its contagion, other's experience and bodies. The commands are not always completely explicit, completely executed or completely followed, and they cannot be avoided without risk, nor sometimes without harm. Essentic form is also a form of biologic bondage. But it is a central part of our human heritage that relieves us from existential isolation. Essentic form is of Mother Nature, that permeates us all.

Understanding Mother may be more than man may try without unforeseeable consequences. Parting that curtain of mystery creates new freedom, and danger; a curtain also veils the next mystery.* In understanding essentic form, we consciously lift the veil from Mother Nature, not like the physicist studying the inorganic world—but even more radically: crossing the bridge between the conscious and the material—between the "heart" and mind, and the body. Not surprisingly, crossing this bridge opens up avenues of healing.

Essentic form and its specific feeling is there to be perceived by a human, who is largely defenceless against its power. His mind and body are driven by it. But also he, and only he, can use essentic form at will to drive his body and his mind. He has found the freedom to do this.

One of these ways is music. Music, in fact, is an organisation created to dictate feelings to the listener. The composer is an unrelenting dictator, and we choose to subject ourselves

---

*Goethe, in Faust II showed more than a glimpse of this problem, in the wondrous underground journey to the Mothers, and what follows.

to him when we listen to his music. This means, of course, that there are two kinds of musical experiences: music being thought and organised—the world of the composer—and music listened to, subjecting oneself to another's musical thought. That the two worlds have something in common is testimony to the universal qualities of human experience, the universality of essentic form. The most intimate is unmasked as the most universal.

Love, Joy, Anger, Grief—we carry these with us like a snail carries its house. The qualities and knowledge which they embody are not fortuitous. Consider the sweetness of sweet, the saltiness of salt. What creates their character—not the physical or chemical structure that characterises them and makes it possible for the receptors to identify them, but the very nature or quality of the experience, the sensation of sweetness or of saltiness? An answer to this question is not possible today. Likewise, the specific experience of Love, Joy, Anger, Grief and other "basic" emotions needs, at present, to be taken as datum—not something that can be understood in terms of other constructs alone. Tears may be a part of Grief, but Grief is not tears plus a number of other constituent parts. It is an entity.

An important part of the entity of Grief, or other pure emotion, is its cognitive embodiment, and the knowledge and attitude that is inherently linked to it, like a worldview. Thus love and trust go together, hate and the desire for destruction, grief and heaviness and separation. (An experimental study [Clynes et al., 1985] shows that even a small lie interferes with the feeling of love, but lying does not interfere with anger.)

Just as hunger tells us what to eat and how much, and thirst tells us how much to drink, so emotions have their own specific knowledge and action programs as part of their nature. When incorporated into music, the musical story they tell lets us partake of this knowledge and worldview in an organized way. Music of Beethoven, Mozart and Bach is not just a remarkable organization of sounds (Cooper and Meyer, 1960; Derek Cooke, 1959). It is capable of giving meaning to life, to place man in a hierarchy within which he can look up, and the energies associated with such a view.

Rock music too, implies its own worldview and associated energies. Being driven by music has some effect on brain chemistry, on the body, on attitude, and on decision making.

Links between the Language of Music and Neurobiologic System Properties

Now, let us look at the specific neurophysiologic and neurobiologic system properties of temporal patterns that allow this to happen. We shall be concerned with three functions of the language of music, and particularly with the first two of them: 1. The pulse and rhythm, 2. Melodic expression, and 3. Tone quality or timbre.

1. The Pulse and Rhythm

A basic neurophysiologic property used by the musical pulse (Clynes 1969, 1977; Clynes and Walker 1982; Clynes 1983, 1985) is the property of the central nervous system called Time Form Printing. This property allows a single initial command to determine both the rate and the shape in time of a repetitive movement pattern. It can do this either in thought or in overt movement. This property, initially described in Clynes 1977b, is an important function of the nervous system that needs to receive much more attention. Having initiated the repetitive pattern with a precise initial command, the pattern is then repeated without requiring further direct attention, leaving one free to act and think in other directed activity. The automatic repetition of the form and rate goes on until a separate command is given to stop. The musical pulse is an auditory example of Time Form Printing. It results in thinking of auditory patterns in accordance with the pulse form dictated by the initial command.

This repetitive voluntary motion, in thought and/or action, has two kinds of effect on the state and experience of the organism:

(I) It takes up a certain amount of space of the "computer register" involved in decision making. The person is doing something, and is thus relieved of having continually to

Manfred Clynes

make moment-to-moment decisions on what to do, and what to do next. A part of the decision making space is "occupied." Doing something and doing something continuously thus satisfies a requirement otherwise issued by anxiety. Anxiety, which does not know what to do next but issues commands that something needs to be done, is being shunted aside for a time. Something *is* being done. And that repetitive pattern required only one initial decision.* Thereafter, one has handed over the decision making process to a lower level, a subconscious mental agent, which keeps on printing out the same form over and over again. Thus the pulse is an abdication of responsibility and is enjoyed for that reason.

(II) The pulse is not only a repetitive function that distracts from responsibility of decision making, it also has a distinctive form. The character of that form has meaning. The repeated experience of that form reinforces this meaning and establishes a point of view and an emotional context by which other experience is colored. The nature of this context or state depends with high discrimination upon the form of the pulse. In the actual generation of sound, the pulse is realised through systematic deviations from the nominal values of the score in amplitude and duration of all the individual tones of the music. How this happens precisely has been determined (Clynes 1983, 1985a, b). A pulse matrix can be constructed that readily allows calculation of these systematic deviations. We identify the pulse from these deviations unconsciously, much as we recognise a person's particular gait. The pulse thus creates a point of view or a state on which a super-structure may be built and experienced. Of this superstructure, the melodic aspects are perhaps the most important.

Recent studies with the courting songs of the fruit fly Drosophila (Kyriacou and Hall, 1980), have shown that the pulsation rate contained in this song is modulated cyclically with a period of 44 seconds in the wild type males, but with a period of 40 seconds and 80 seconds in mutant flies that also have diurnal rhythms of 19 hours and 28 hours respectively, rather than the regular 24.5 hour rhythm.

*cf. compulsive or "nervous" tapping, autistic rhythmic behaviour patterns.

128

A gene for rhythmic behaviour (*per*) has been located in the X chromosome, which in fact is the gene for the diurnal clock (Konopka and Benzer 1971, and Bargiello and Young 1984), and it appears that the *same* functional gene also controls a clock relating to the courtship songs (Kyriacou and Hall, 1980). Von Schilcher (1976) had previously shown that the pulsation rate was an important factor in the mating choice. Findings of such a genetically controlled frequency modulation in a meaningful communication pattern leading to reproduction and locating the gene responsible for it and for a biologic clock are significant and encouraging steps towards obtaining a better understanding of the biologic basis of pulse in music.

2. Melodic Expression

Unlike the pulse, which is repetitive and automatic, melodic expression is continuously and subtly changing. Melodic expression consists of entities that are musical embodiments of essentic form (Clynes and Nettheim 1982, Clynes 1977). The melodic outlines are constructed so as to suggest essentic form. This suggestion, which can be ambiguous, is reinforced by amplitude relationships among the tones which resolve the ambiguity so that the combined gestalt clearly represents a particular essentic form. When the amplitudes are appropriately formed and the notes appropriately timed, we can get a clear and convincing embodiment of joy, of love, of grief and so on, and only then. Thus, to the degree that this form is well realised in performance, the possibility of moving a listener and transforming his state is given.

In this manner, music includes the repetitive motion of the pulse and also the inner gestures of essentic form, a varied superstructure in which one essentic form is chained to another, weaving a sentic story. In such a "story," essentic forms may follow one another with subtle changes or they may be strongly contrasted. In some compositions essentic forms of similar shades of feelings are enchained, thereby intensifying the mood in accordance with the sentic principle of a rhythmic repetition (Clynes 1977, 1980). Other music cherishes the heightened effect of the synthesis of opposites: different essentic forms are dramatically juxtaposed. In all these cases the listener becomes more deeply involved the better the expression—and that means the better the melodic forms correspond to the biologically given character of essentic form. We may understand, in this sense, the exhortations of Pablo Casals to students to play "naturally" (see also Blum, 1977).

When we thus experience the pure joy of a Mozartian theme, or the love of the D major theme of the 3rd movement in Beethoven's 9th symphony, something biological happens also. The first step of such a biological process is the involuntary recognition within the brain of the essentic form. Just as a yawn is contagious through an automatic recognition process of the nervous system, against which one is essentially defenceless, so a truly expressed essentic form is also automatically recognised. We see early manifestations in evolution of this phenomenon too in the mating dances and mating songs of insects, of fish and birds. In all this, the forms of expression act like keys that fit a particular lock—which opens the door that calls upon a specific program of that emotional quality. (In music, the musical language has to be understood for this to happen automatically.) The recognition process may cause a release of specific neurochemicals which may then activate further processes. It has been shown in recent years that neuro hormones (enkephalins and endorphins) directly affect states of experience; some of these are opiate analogues and react with opiate receptors (see also Stein 1985, Ader 1985, Palmblad 1985, Wybran 1985). It is suggested (Clynes 1977b, 1980) that the neurobiologic process of recognition of pure emotion essentic forms may release specific substances in the brain which then act to transmit and activate those specific emotional experiences. Depending on a choice of connectedness of the person (to be discussed in a later section), these may or may not be allowed to affect the body through autonomic nervous system and hormonal actions, through specific modes of inhibition.

3. Tone Color and Timbre

The nature of sound itself has a clear influence on the state of mind. We mostly regard noise as unpleasant, and are attracted by sounds like those of a celeste. Sounds of birds in the forest may give rise to an immediate sense of joy. The sound of wind and of the sea play their music on our sensibilities. The sheer loveliness of a sound, the diminuendo to infinity of the sound of a single bell stroke used in Buddhist meditation can captivate us in what seems a meaningful way. In the action of these on the brain, different sound spectra may exert different and specific influences on functions of the central nervous system, without organisation of the sounds into what we normally call music (as also colors alone can, without their being embedded in an artistic design).

Related to this is also that music of different composers gravitates to different kinds of tone qualities. Mozart often requires a sheer loveliness of sound, while Bach does not. The timbre of a Beethoven melody tends to be subtly and importantly different from that appropriate to a Brahms melody, and so on. These different sound qualities also have their counterpart in musical thought and qualities of feeling. But little is known yet about the chemical processes that may ensue in relation to specific tone qualities. This should become a fertile field for future investigation.

Neurochemical Processes in Relation to Music

The first step in the organism's responses to essentic form is its recognition. If we theorise that recognition of pure essentic form results in the release of a neurochemical specific to that emotion, then we may also expect that the better the realisation of the essentic form, the greater the production of the corresponding chemical substance.

In 1973, some years before the discovery of enkephalins and endorphins, the following was reported, based on findings with the repeated expression of essentic form with sentic cycles:

"That chemical processes are involved is highly probable from the observation of the increase in the intensity of the [emotion] with successive repetitions of [essentic forms] during the initial sequence generating a sentic state. It appears as if each acton adds an increment to a chemical concentration in the appropriate portions of the brain, until its own dissipation or metabolism would appear to match the rate of production, and no further increase in intensity occurs. After a sufficiently large number of [essentic forms] have been produced, it appears as if there is a degree of adaptation affecting the chemical that is being released and the level of intensity eventually falls off. This description parallels the rise and fall of sentic state intensity." Further,

". . . a chemical may be released as a result of the proper satisfaction of the conditions required by the [essentic form] and that this chemical becomes increased through the succession of [essentic forms] and is specific for that particular emotion. One could consider that there would be therefore, a link between the genetic program and the specific chemical produced.

". . . These specific chemicals involved in short-term memory, and in the satisfaction of [essentic form] production could then relate to the formation of long term memory which allows an individual [essentic form] to be remembered over a long period of time associated with its specific quality.

"These thoughts make it possible to consider that it may some day be feasible to isolate such specific chemicals, allowing emotion experience to be transmitted by direct chemical means, with a high degree of precision. The implications of such a possibility are difficult to estimate at present. The chemicals we are considering here are not hormones and the like, but rather the chemical representation of the emotion . . . as a short-term memory entity—an entity that then might control hormone and cardiovascular phenomena in turn through the appropriate brain processes." (Clynes, 1973)

We may further add that when adaptation occurs to a particular basic emotion through repeated expression, so that a person is saturated with that emotion (corresponding to receptor saturation), that person is generally quite fresh in terms of the ability to experience another, different emotion through the repeated expression of that new essentic form. This is additional evidence pointing to the probability of specific neurochemicals for each basic emotion (Clynes 1980).

Mixed emotions are consequently expected to be less

directly effective; and may also contain conflicting cognitive embodiments. Pure basic emotions should have clearer and more predictable effects on the brain, the central nervous system and the organism as a whole. Indeed, they are also most potent in the composer's hands, engendering music which we often consider most moving and beautiful.

A neurochemical substance released in the brain through the recognition process may act on other subsystems. But the way this can occur can be said to be conditioned by the mode of inner connectedness. In previous work (Clynes 1977, 1980), we distinguished between the Dionysian and Appollonian modes of emotion experience. The Dionysian mode, which we share with animals, implies possible responsiveness of the body according to specific and characteristic patterns for the emotion. The substance involved in the recognition acts on a subsystem which then may release a gestalt of bodily and experiential processes pertaining to that emotion. The behavioral accompaniments of the Dionysian mode are experienced as ego functions; the whole body tends to be involved.

In the Apollonian mode, which does not appear to be as possible for animals, the recognition process does not activate many of the bodily processes that are involved in the Dionysian pattern. The recognition process may be as intense, but the quality of experience is savoured, considered, or contemplated rather than responded to fully bodily and acted upon. This mode has importance in music and art, and in aesthetic experience. It is not experienced as an ego function, but somewhat like how one experiences a tree, for example, or a flower—with "otherness" inherently incorporated into the experience: the expression of such emotion becomes not "my emotion" but "the emotion" whether it be joy, love, grief or anger. Past the initial recognition stage, the chemical correlates in the brain of this kind of experience would be expected to be different from those of the Dionysian experience.

In general, the effect of music on the brain would be expected to be very different, depending on the quality of the expression, i.e. the purity of the essentic forms. We of course know this to be experientially so. And further, the enjoyment of music in the contemplative or Apollonian mode derived from listening to a late Beethoven quartet, say, is very different from Dionysian dancing to rock and roll. Yet in both modes the effectiveness of the music depends greatly on the proper realisation of the expression (essentic form) and the pulse.

Since we are now able to generate appropriate expression of the pulse in music at will, through computer synthesis (Clynes 1983, 1985a, b), we can use the theories we have established to make the music express a particular chosen basic emotion with rather high degree of faithfulness to essentic form. It then becomes possible to test experimentally biochemical effects produced on the organism by the same music played with and without such expression. Such a study relating to various specific emotions, in fact, is being carried out in collaboration with Drs. R. Spintge and R. Droh.

Concerning the Healing Powers of Music

A word of caution is appropriate when considering the possible healing powers of music. Mozart died at the age of 35, Schubert at 31 and Beethoven died before his 57th birthday. Obviously there are conditions that even the best music does not heal!

Such scepticism, however, should not prevent us from recognising the beneficial effects that music can have. Orpheus was no ordinary musician—and those of our time who have had the good fortune to hear Pablo Casals play know of the enormous power to change one's state that can be unlocked by surpassing musical realisation. This surpassing quality lies in the degree of livingness that imbues each phrase, as well as in the overall concept of the music. There does not appear to be a limit to this realisation of livingness—even for a Casals there remained always the possibility of further improvement, of greater perfection of form, of greater faithfulness to the quality which we call essentic form. It appears reasonable that the corresponding neurochemical changes, and thus the possible healing powers relating to music, should be enhanced by the quality of the performance, and probably even by the quality of the musical thought alone.

1. De-stressing

The possible healing powers of music relate to a number of aspects. There are de-stressing factors, such as:

(I) Pleasant and possibly social activity, as in ensemble playing and singing.

(II) Cathartic effects of releasing repressed emotion, and of contacting memories and associations.

(III) Generation of empathy, a feeling of belonging and connectedness with other life, or with the Universe.

The above aspects have in common the reducing of stress and anxiety through non-threatening activity. The removal of stress of course has many biochemical and physiological consequences, with which we shall not deal here.

2. Neurochemical and Immune System Reactions

But more directly, the release of specific neurochemicals in the brain associated with essentic forms of basic emotions may produce changes in the organism which depend on the context in which the essentic form is viewed. While it appears likely that the so-called positive emotions such as joy, love and, in the main, sex, have a more beneficial effect on the organism than negative emotions such as grief, anger and hate, nevertheless the function of music in releasing suppressed negative emotions may be of considerable benefit, as these repressions can cause much harm to the organism. Moreover, the experiences even of negative emotions in an Apollonian way serves in the main to increase empathy (as distinct from sympathy), rather than to cause bodily stress, discomfort and dysfunction.

Among the recently studied effects of emotion (and implicitly of music) on the ability of the organism to maintain itself is the effect of emotion on the level of functions of the immune system. A recent review of our present knowledge of these interactions is to be found in Guillemin, Cohn, and Melnechuk, 1985. Certain important aspects of the immune system appear to operate independently of environmental stimuli mediated through higher centers, but other aspects of immune activity are subject to both internal and external environment at various levels and

thus to emotion. Should specific neurochemicals be discovered for each of the basic emotions, it is quite likely
that their effect on immune system activity would also be
selective. Thus there may indeed be a biochemical basis
for the improvement of health brought about by the deliberate
cultivation of laughter, as noted anecdotally by Norman
Cousins.

In this connection mention should be made of the voiceless
laughter predicted by sentic theory (Clynes 1980, 1975)
substituting a different motor output such as finger pressure
(at the same repetition frequency) for the voice motor
output. This voiceless laughter can be readily cultivated
and is found to have the same dynamic and experiential
characteristics as the usual form of laughter (including
tears in the eyes and other physiologic concomitants).

3. Neuromotor and Exercise Effects—
Rebound Movement

Further beneficial aspects of musical performance on
health relate to the quality of physical exercise that it may
provide. This concerns in the first instance conductors,
whose rhythmic movements benefit from the effort-saving
property of the neuromuscular system manifested in what
one may call *rebound movement*. In a vertical rebound
movement, for example, beginning with a downward movement of the arm, the upward return is virtually effortless
compared with a similar up movement in a movement
which starts with this up movement, followed by a downward return. In each case the physical work done in the
upward movement may be the same, but the effort experienced when the upward movement is the rebound of
an initial downward movement is much less (Cavagna et al.
1981, 1979; Edman et al. 1978; Alexander et al. 1977; Thys
1972; Proske 1980). This may be called a quasi-elastic
rebound. (One cannot speak of actual elasticity properly
here since muscles can only pull but not push, and tendons
cannot transmit any substantial elastic force in a push
direction.)

Because of this the typical conducting movements provide

a greater stimulus to the circulation and metabolism of the body compared with other types of exertion of equivalent effort experience. This phenomenon is important in physical exercise in general, and may explain the ability of many conductors, at an advanced age, to conduct vigorously with what appears like a much younger man's movements, while their walking gait may well reflect their true age. Indeed, it is well known that many conductors retain their ability to conduct to a rather advanced old age. They may be aided in this by the effort-sparing exercise provided by conducting, in addition to other benefits that a life with music may provide.

Another benefit of exercise involved in musical performance on well-being may lie in the harmonious, well controlled and effortless movements that are involved in masterful playing of a musical instrument. Exercising the body in such a way can give the performer a sense of inner harmoniousness, of integration, quite apart from the musical content involved, and this is associated with a sense of well-being, of vigor without effort. (Such a sense may accompany mastery of playing scales and other "technical exercises" with complete ease and fluidity.) The possible beneficial effects also in this regard of some exercises with very slow movements may be mentioned in which the kinesthetic sense is trained of knowing where at any moment the body (or extremity) is in space—as also in Tai Chi. The overall effects of harmoniousness and integration often translate from specific mastery of the instrument to the motor behaviour of the entire organism. This emphasises also the appropriate mode of control of movement as being from the larger, proximal limbs toward the distinct extremities—not the other way around. In a harmonious movement one may feel the movement arising out of the central (lower) part of the torso, as Casals pointed out (this is also in accordance with teachings of ancient Indian sources).

Even in instrumental performance, a good measure of the effortlessness of masterful performance may be attributed to the effortlessness of rebound movement. This property of neuromuscular control has been rather inadequately studied and often falsely attributed to "muscular elasticity."

Music, Immune System Activity and Cancer

In relation to the possible increased (and more effective) immune system activity that can result from appropriate emotional exercise and emotional release (such as that provided by music) it may be observed (in a preliminary way) that it appears the death rate of musicians from cancer may be appreciably lower than the population average. A study examining the details of this is being initiated in collaboration with Ralph Spintge. This study will also compare the incidence of cancer among musicians to that of other groups of outstanding achievers such as doctors.

Healing Powers of Sentic Cycles

As we have seen, music may interact with the organism as musical thought, even as it is born in a composer; and also as it is being listened to. In each of these ways the whole experience is greater than the sum of its parts. We shall now describe a novel way of producing essentic form (first described in 1968) that combines the benefits of these functions—without sound, using touch as a mode of expression. Because it does combine these functions of music, it may be described as metamusic. But it also is an art form of touch. Like music, it involves expression in time, and the time forms it uses correspond to those of musical expression. As essentic form is common to more than one mode of sensory experience, the phenomena observed in producing essentic forms through touch have much in common with those involving sound. But producing essentic forms in touch is much easier to do than composing and playing music. It does not require knowledge of musical skills, notation or language. It is easily learned, yet it is as powerful as music in influencing our state. This new mode of expressive art has been called Sentic Cycles (Clynes 1970, 1973, 1977, 1979; French et al. 1972).

Sentic cycles is emotional exercise and expressive mediation in which a person sits upright on a chair and voluntarily expresses with the pressure of the middle finger of one hand on a finger rest, a sequence of emotions comprised of No Emotion, Anger, Hate, Grief, Love, Sex, Joy and Reverence, in timing co-ordinated by a sentic cycle tape. Each emotion is expressed about thirty to forty times (3-4 minutes) before proceeding to the next emotion, announced by the sentic cycle tape. The timing is given by a soft click played by the sentic cycle tape denoting the beginning of an expression. The person is required to do one expression beginning with each soft click, and to wait until the next click to do the next expression. The clicks occur at quasi-random times, at intervals from 4-10 seconds. This interval consists of the biologically required duration of the essentic form of that emotion plus a small and variable waiting period—providing a sort of dialog between the user and the tape. Each emotion has its own appropriate mean period between clicks, and one cannot predict when the next click occurs even after years of use.

The user is asked to let his breathing follow his expressive needs and to sit with eyes closed and feet firmly on the ground. The finger remains in contact with the finger rest throughout, except for the emotion of Joy where it is appropriate to let the arm rise up in a "jump for joy" manner, returning gently to the finger rest in a flowing, floating way towards the end of each expression. The entire sequence takes about twenty-seven minutes. At the end, one sits quietly for about one to two minutes. One is instructed to find the appropriate, different forms of expression for each emotion, and not to press indiscriminately.

The timing pattern of the tape constitutes the metamusic that ensures the effectiveness of the emotion generation. Without this biologically based timing program, sentic cycles are not effective. (The timing patterns, having been optimised on a very small number of subjects, appear to work well for subjects in general; as also a music performance—a particular expressive timing pattern—can be meaningfully shared by a larger audience or ensemble).

In music the expressive sound pattern touches us (in both senses of the word) through our ears; or is conceived in the mind. There are no spatial requirements for the expressive forms—they can come even through a telephone, for example. In effect, the source of essentic form in sound could be reduced to a point in space (although the effects of spatial distribution of sound may be further means of expressiveness). In expression with touch also it is possible to reduce the spatial aspect of expression almost to a point, as it were; and thus provide for the temporal essence of the expressive form. In sentic cycles this is accomplished by expressing with the pressure of a single finger. To receive the pressure a finger rest is used which when used successfully becomes integrated with the person as a single whole, in effect, like a musical instrument. The expressive forms, which are single voluntary acts having a clear beginning, middle and end, issue from the performer through the tip of his finger, through a single point ideally; and in doing so repeatedly the performer becomes fully attuned to the temporal form, both in production and perception. Like in music, the experienced intensity of the emotion is increased through repeated expression, up to a certain degree (but there is no pulse).

The emotional state is then deliberately changed by changing to a different essentic form. In this respect the art of sentic cycles parallels a precomposed piece of music: the time when a new essentic form replaces the previous one is governed by a preset program. (It is possible to do sentic cycles in such a way that the performer himself chooses when to switch to a new emotion and essentic form. In practice however, the performer tends to be so engrossed in the emotion that he is currently expressing that he tends to lose perspective and the desire for change, or at times he may be prematurely bored with that emotion.) Like a conductor, the sentic cycle tape reminds the performer to switch to the next emotion. Like a conductor also, the tape tells the performer when to initiate the next essentic form (it does so with the sound of a soft click). But with regard to each essentic form he is like a composer as well as a performer. He forms the shape spontaneously in accordance with his expressive thought. The quality of feeling is his own, like in a musical improvisation, not that of some composer who dictates to him, and of course, the associations, thoughts and memories that he may experience are his own. Yet these thoughts, associations and memories are induced by the emotional state which the expression generates. As in music, sentic cycles permit beneficial experience of generalised emotion—emotion that is experienced without a specific cause and is not directed towards any one individual. But the emotional state acts as a focus to draw memories, associations and thoughts into the consciousness of the performer of sentic cycles.

Thus, in addition to the neurochemical effect that the generation of emotion itself may have on the organism, as we described earlier in relation to musical essentic form, effects are also released which may relate to specific past memories, catharsis and spontaneously generated creative ideas.

One may reasonably expect that the immune system and other neurobiochemical functions that may be enhanced through music would respond likewise to the practice of sentic cycles. To test to what extent this may be so, a study shall be conducted parallel to that done with music representing different emotion, which will offer a comparison of these relative effects.

The third aspect of sentic cycles, that the experience of the whole is greater than the sum of its parts, arises from the particular sequence of the emotions that form it and the durations of each phase. Since each emotion produces its own neurochemical and hormonal reaction, and since the effect of these last beyond the end of the period assigned to that particular emotion, there is a cumulative effect both chemically and experientially that is a function of the particular sequence of emotions chosen in the design of the sentic cycle. In this respect also, the sentic cycle corresponds to a well designed composition in which there is a balance between its various sections or movements.

Thus sentic cycles combine aspects of the functions of composer and performer as well as the harmony of temporal proportion and sequence, through which the total experience achieves a perspective and cognitive realisation we associate with a moving aesthetic experience.

However, unlike in a musical performance, the body becomes very quiet. Thus the healing qualities that may be functioning in music are also tapped in sentic cycles. Experience (with several thousand cases, over more than a decade) has shown that they may be tapped even to a greater extent than through music for many since the composer's thought patterns—the feelings of a different individual—do not play a role. The sentic cycles experience is readily available to the unmusical as well as to the musical, to those without musical training and skill, and does not require familiarity with the language of music. The expressiveness of touch that it teaches is valuable in many aspects of life. In learning sentic cycles one learns about the nature of essentic form, or rather, one learns to rediscover essentic form as part of human nature one may have forgotten through the repressive influences of our civilisation and education.

At the end of doing sentic cycles, and for a goodly number of hours afterwards, one generally feels at peace. Both the body and the mind are often profoundly quiet, yet vital. This is the cumulative effect of the sentic cycle sequence. It may be that this sense of peace is the most healing element of all. Without this, the greatest music too—such as the music of Bach or late Beethoven—is a mockery of itself.

The author would like to thank the staff of the New South Wales State Conservatorium of Music, Music Research Center: Dr. Michael Rynn, Janice Walker, Dr. Nigel Nettheim, Darius Clynes and Dr. Ralph Spintge and Dr. Roland Droh of the Sportkrankenhaus Hellersen, Lüdenscheid for helpful suggestions and assistance to work related to this paper.

Sentic Cycle kits can be obtained from the American Sentic Association, Box XX, Sonoma, CA 95476, for $36.50 ($2.00 for mail and handling). They consist of a Finger Rest, Instruction Booklet, and the Sentic Cycle Cassette Tape. With these you can learn how to do Sentic Cycles in about 15 minutes, and then enjoy the benefits of Sentic Cycles whenever you wish for the rest of your life.

The book *Sentics, the Touch of Emotion* is now available in a newly reprinted edition, by Prism Press, $10.95 from booksellers.

References

Ader, R.: Behaviourally Conditioned Modulation of Immunity. In: Neural Modulation of Immunity, R. Guillemin, M. Cohn, T. Melnechuk (eds.), Raven Press, New York, pp. 258 (1985).

Alexander, R. McN., H. C. Bennet-Clark: Storage of elastic energy muscle and other tissues. Nature (Lond.) *265*, 114-117 (1977).

Bargiello, T., M. Young: Molecular genetics of a biological clock in Drosophila. Proc. Natl. Acad. Sci, (USA) *81*, 2142-2146 (1984).

Blum, D.: Casals and the Art of Interpretation, Heinemann, London, pp. 223 (1977).

Cavagna, G. A., G. Citterio, P. Jacini: Effects of Speed and Extent of Stretching on the Elastic Properties of Active Frog Muscle. J. exp. Biol. (Great Britain) *91*, 131-143 (1981).

Cavagna, G. A., G. Citterio, P. Jacini: Elastic storage: role of tendons and muscles. In: Comparative Physiology: Primitive Mammals, K. Schmidt-Nielsen (ed.) Cambridge University Press, New York (1979).

Clynes, M.: Music Beyond the Score. In: Symposium on Music, Reason and Emotion, Communication and Cognition, Vol. 18, Nr. 4 (1985a).

Clynes, M.: Secrets of Life in Music. In: Festschrift for Ingmar Bengtsson, Royal Swedish Academy of Music, Stockholm (1985b).

Clynes, M.: Music as Time's Measure. Journal of Music Perception, (in preparation) (1985c).

Clynes, M., S. Jurisevic, M. Rynn: (in preparation) (1985).

Clynes, M.: Expressive Microstructure in Music, Linked to Living Qualities. In: Studies of Music Performance, J. Sundberg (ed.), Publication of Royal Swedish Academy of Music. Stockholm. No. 39, pp. 76-181 (1983).

Clynes, M., N. Nettheim: The Living Quality of Music: Neurobiologic Basis of Communicating Feeling. In: Music, Mind and Brain: The Neuropsychology of Music, M. Clynes (ed.), Plenum Press, New York, pp. 47-82 (1982).

Clynes, M., J. Walker: Neurobiologic Functions of Rhythm, Time and Pulse in Music. In: Music, Mind and Brain: The Neuropsychology of Music, M. Clynes (ed.), Plenum Press, New York, pp. 171-216 (1982).

Clynes, M.: The Communication of Emotion: Theory of Sentics in Emotion, Theory, Research and Experience, Vol. 1, R. Plutchik, H. Kellerman (eds.) Academic Press, New York, pp. 271-300 (1980).

Clynes, M.: Sentics: Communication and Generation of Emotion Through Dynamic Expression in Nonverbal Communication: Readings With Commentary, S. weitz (ed.), Oxford University Press, New York, pp. 386-397 (1979).

Manfred Clynes

Clynes, M.: Sentics: The Touch of Emotions, Doubleday Anchor, New York, 250 pp. (1977a).

Clynes, M.: Space-Time Form Printing by the Human Central Nervous System, Society for Neuroscience, Los Angeles, abstract (1977b).

Clynes, M.: Sentics: Biocybernetics of Emotion Communication. Annals N.Y. Acad. Sci., *220 (3):* 55-131 (1973).

Clynes, M.: Toward a View of Man. In: Biomedical Engineering Systems, M. Clynes and J. H. Milsum (eds.) McGraw-Hill, New York, pp. 272-358 (1970).

Clynes, M.: Toward a Theory of Man: Precision of Essentic Form. In: Living Communication. In: Information Processing in the Nervous System, K. N. Leibovic and J. C. Eccles (eds.), Springer, New York (1969).

Cooke, D.: The Language of Music, Oxford University Press, London (1959).

Cooper, G. W., L. B. Meyer: The Rhythmic Structure of Music. University of Chicago Press, Chicago and London (1960).

Edman, K. A. P., G. Elzinga, M. I. M. Noble: Enhancement of mechanical performance by stretch during tetanic contractions of vertebrate skeletal muscle fibres. J. Physiol. (Lond.) *281*, 139-155 (1978).

French, A. P., P. L. Russell, J. P. Tupin: Subjective changes with the sentic cycles of Clynes. Dis. Nerv. Syst. *33*, 598-602 (1972).

Gruber, L. N., D. S. Janowsky, A. J. Mandell, S. C. Risch, L. Y. Huey: A Psychoacoustic Effect Upon Mood and its Relation to Affective Instability. In: Comprehensive Psychiatry *25*, 106-112 (1984).

Guillemin, R., M. Cohn, T. Melnechuk (eds.): Neural Modulation of Immunity. Raven Press, New York, pp. 258 (1985).

Kyriacou, C., J. Hall: Circadian rhythm mutations in Drosophila melanogaster affect short-term fluctuations in the male's courtship song. Proc. Natl. Acad. Sci. (USA) *77*, 6729-6733 (1980).

Konopka, R., S. Benzer: Clock Mutants of Drosophila melanogaster. Proc. Natl. Acad. Sci. (USA) *68*, 2112-2116 (1971).

Palmblad, J. E. W.: Stress and Human Immunologic Competence. In: Neural Modulation of Immunity, R. Guillemin, M. Cohn, T. Melnechuk (eds.) Raven Press, New York, pp. 258 (1985).

Proske, U.: Energy conservation by elastic storage in kangaroos. Endavour, New Series Vol. 4, Nr. 4, pp. 148-153 (1980).

Stein, M.: Bereavement, Depression, Stress, and Immunity. In: Neural Modulation of Immunity. R. Guillemin, M. Cohn, T. Melnechuk (eds.) Raven Press, New York, pp. 258 (1985).

Thys, H., T. Faraggiana, R. Margaria: Utilization of muscle elasticity in exercise. J. Appl. Physiol. *32*, 491-494 (1972).

Von Schilcher, F.: Anim. Behav. *24*, 622-625 (1976).

Wybran, J.: Enkephalins, Endorphins, Substance P, and the Immune System. In: Neural Modulation of Immunity, R. Guillemin, M. Cohn, T. Melnechuk (eds.) Raven Press, New York, pp. 258 (1985).

9

Music Therapy: Nursing the Music of the Soul*

CATHIE E. GUZZETTA

Grown-ups love figures. When you tell them that you have made a new friend, they never ask you any questions about essential matters. They never say to you, "What does his voice sound like? What game does he love best? Does he collect butterflies?"

Instead they demand: "How old is he? How many brothers has he? How much does he weigh? How much money does his father make?" Only from figures do they think they have learned anything about him.

St. Exupéry, *The Little Prince*[1]

And we must learn
that to know a man is not to know his name
but to know his melody
Unknown Oriental Philosopher

Music and medicine have been linked throughout history. According to Greek mythology, Orpheus was given a lyre by the god Apollo and was instructed in its use by the muses; hence the word "music." Apollo was the god of music, and his son Asclepius was the god of healing and medicine. The Greeks believed music had the power to help heal the body and soul. The shaman and medicine men provided patients with healing chants along with medicine.

Likewise, music has been a vital part of all societies and cultures, no matter how primitive or advanced. It is used in spiritual ceremonies and in celebrations. Armies march to battle with music, and mothers lull their infants

---

*Reprinted from *Holistic Nursing: A Handbook for Practice* by B. Dossey, L. Keegan, C. Guzzetta and L. Kolkmeier, pp. 263-288, with permission of Aspen Publishers, Inc. © 1988.

to sleep with song. Music is played during rites of initiation, during funeral ceremonies, and on harvest and feast days. There is something about the power of music that cannot be expressed in verbal language. It is of no surprise then that music is currently being applied as a therapeutic self-regulation modality.

NURSE HEALER OBJECTIVES

Theoretical

1. Discuss the definitions of terms associated with music therapy.
2. Discuss the principles of sound.
3. Discuss the psychophysiologic theories that explain why music therapy works as a self-regulation modality.

Clinical

1. List the factors involved in choosing music selections that are relaxing for clients.
2. Develop a music library for use with clients.
3. Choose several different music therapy techniques and use them in clinical practice.
4. Discuss with clients their internal responses when listening to music in a relaxed state.

Personal

1. Participate in "experimental listening."
2. Record your responses to various types of music in a music notebook.
3. In a music log, record your most intimate memories associated with music.
4. Participate in a music bath each day.
5. Participate in a toning and groaning exercise before listening to music.
6. Practice focused and conscious hearing each day to recognize subtle differences in sound.
7. Experience your internal responses when listening to music in a relaxed state.

DEFINITIONS

Cymatics: study of patterns of shape evoked by sound.

Frequencies: the number of vibrations or cycles per unit of time.

Music Therapy: systematic application of music to produce relaxation and desired changes in emotions, behavior, and physiology.

Oscillation: fluctuation or variation between minimum and maximum values.

Resonance: a structure that vibrates at a frequency that is natural to it and most easily sustained by it.

Resonant: increasing the intensity of sounds by sympathetic vibration.

Sonic: of or having to do with sound.

Sound: that which is produced when some object is vibrating in a random or periodic repeated motion.

Sympathetic Resonance: the reinforced vibration of an object exposed to the vibration at about the same frequency as another object.

THEORY AND RESEARCH

Origin of Sound

Sounds are used to create music. Sounds produce changes in our bodymind and are involved in modulating simultaneous changes in the autonomic, immune, endocrine, and neuropeptide systems. It is necessary to appreciate the principles and theories of sound to understand fully its tremendous capacity to achieve therapeutic psychophysiologic outcomes.

Sound is that which is produced when some object is vibrating in a random or periodic repeated motion. Sound can be heard by the human ear when it vibrates between 20 and 20,000 cycles per second. We also hear and perceive sound by skin and bone conduction. Our other senses, such as sight, smell, and touch, allow us to perceive an even wider range of vibrations than those sensed by hearing. We are sensitive to sounds in ways that most people do not even consider.

The interrelationship between wave forms and matter can be understood by rendering vibrations into physical forms. When scattered liquids, powders, metal filings, or sand are placed on a disk with a vibrating crystal, thereby causing the disk to vibrate, repeatable patterns form on the disk. As the pitch is changed, the harmonic pattern formed on the disk also changes. Thus, matter assumes certain shapes or patterns based on the vibrations or frequency of the sound to which it is exposed. The study of patterns of shapes evoked by sound is called *cymatics*.[2] The forms of snowflakes and faces of flowers may take on their shape because they are responding to some sounds in nature.[3] Likewise, it is possible that crystals, plants, and human beings may be, in some way, music that has taken on visible form.

The human body also vibrates. The ejection of blood from the left ventricle during systole causes the aorta to become distended with blood. The pressure produced by aortic distension causes a pressure wave to travel down the aorta to the arterial branches. The pressure wave travels faster than the flow of blood and creates a palpable pulse called the *pressure pulse wave*.[4]

Waves are a series of advancing impulses set up by a vibration or impulse. The pressure pulse wave is composed of a series of waves that have differing frequencies (number of vibrations per unit of time) and amplitude. In the arterial branches, there is one fundamental frequency and a number of harmonics that usually have a smaller amplitude than the fundamental frequency. The arterial vessels resonate at certain frequencies (fundamental frequency), thereby intensifying some waves while other waves are damped and disappear. This phenomenon is called *resonance*.[5]

The human body vibrates, from its large structures, such as the aorta and arterial system, down to the genetically preprogrammed vibrations coded into our molecular cells. Our atoms and molecules, cells, glands, and organs all have a characteristic vibrational frequency that absorbs and emits sound. Thus, the human body is a system of vibrating atomic particles, acting as a vibratory transformer that gives off and takes in sound.

Because our bodies absorb sound, this concept of the body as transformer is worthy of exploration. Sympathetic vibration or *sympathetic resonance* refers to the reinforced vibration of an object exposed to the vibration at about the same frequency as another object.[6] For example, consider two tuning forks that are designed to vibrate at approximately the same pitch. When one of the tuning forks is struck, it produces a sound that spontaneously causes the second tuning fork to vibrate and produce the same sound *as if* the second fork was physically struck. The sound wave from the first fork actually does physically strike the second fork, causing the second to resonate responsively to the tune of the first. This sympathetic resonance occurs because both forks contain similar vibratory characteristics, which allows energy transfer from one to the other. When two objects have similar vibratory characteristics that allow them to resonate at the same frequency, they form a resonant system.

The atomic structure of our molecular system is also a resonant system. Nuclei vibrate, and the electrons in their orbit vibrate in resonance with their nucleus. Moreover, as long as the atom, cell, or organ contains an appropriate vibrational pattern, it can be "played" by *outside* stimuli in harmony with its vibrational make-up.[7] The phenomenon of sympathetic vibration depends on pitch. Thus, environmental sounds, such as those emitted from a dishwasher or television, may be capable of stimulating or producing sympathetic vibrations in the molecules and cells of our body. Our entire body vibrates at a fundamental inaudible frequency of approximately 8 cycles per second when it is in a relaxed state. During relaxed meditation, the frequency of brain waves produced is also about 8 cycles per second. Moreover, the earth vibrates at this same fundamental frequency of 8 cycles per second. This phenomenon is called Schumann's Resonance and is a function of electromagnetic radiation and the earth's circumference. Thus, there is a sympathetic resonance between the electrically charged layers of the earth's atmosphere and the human body. Therefore, "being in harmony with oneself and the universe" may be more than a poetic concept.[8]

Music Therapy: What Is It?

Music therapy is defined as a behavioral science that is concerned with the use of specific kinds of music and its ability to affect changes in behavior, emotions, and physiology.[9] It complements traditional therapy, providing clients with integrated bodymind experiences and encouraging them to become active participants in their health care and recovery.

It is important to distinguish between *two* principal *schools* of *music therapy*. One school seeks to achieve a therapeutic effect by involving the client in communicative music-making; the other seeks to achieve its effects by listening to vibrational sound.[10] This chapter is primarily concerned with the latter school of music therapy and its application to nursing.

Goal of Music Therapy

Music therapy should not be confused with listening to music for entertainment, nor should it be confused with music education, which pursues the art of music. In Western society, we hear music for general entertainment purposes in department stores, restaurants, airports, and while waiting on the telephone. We turn on music in our homes, in our cars, and at work. The goal of music therapy, however, is not to provide entertainment.

Rather, the goal of music therapy, which is nonmusical in nature, is the reduction of psychophysiologic stress, pain, anxiety, and isolation. It helps clients achieve a state of deep relaxation, develop self-awareness and creativity, improve learning, clarify personal values, and cope with a variety of psychophysiologic dysfunctions.[11]

Appropriate music serves as an important vehicle in achieving the relaxation response by removing one's inner restlessness and quieting ceaseless thinking.. It can be used as a healing ritual to stop the mind from running away and enable thinking to become still so that one can achieve inner quietness. The healing capabilities of music are intimately bound to the personal experience of inner relaxation.[12]

Shifting States of Consciousness

When appropriately applied, music can be a way of reaching nonordinary levels of human consciousness.[13] One is able to pass from ordinary states of consciousness to an altered state of consciousness to achieve the mind's fullest potential. With music therapy, individuals are able to shift their perception of time. Individuals perceive two types of time: virtual and experiential.[14] *Virtual time* is perceived in a left-brain mode and is characterized by hours, minutes, and seconds. In contrast, *experiential time* is perceived through the memory.

Experiential time exists because we experience both a state of tension and resolution.[15] Tensions and resolutions are perceived by our memory in a linear sequence that is called a *disturbance* or an *event*. An emotion or a sound, for example, is a disturbance that can produce tension (producing psychophysiologic effects), which is followed by a return to equilibrium or resolution. Perception of time is influenced by the rate of these linear sequences or events. For example, slow-moving music lengthens our perception of time because our memory has more time to experience the events (tensions and resolutions) and the spaces between the events. Thus, clock time becomes distorted, and clients can actually lose track of time for extended periods, enabling them to reduce anxiety, fear, and pain.

In a relaxed state, abstract thinking is slowed. Music can assist the individual in moving through six states of consciousness: normal waking state, expanded sensory threshold, daydreaming, trance, meditative states, and rapture.[16] During relaxation, music is first perceived in a normal wakeful state. As relaxation continues, sensory thresholds are lowered, and expanded awareness states predominate. The individual can then continue to move to daydreaming, trance, and meditative states and progress to rapture, depending on the level of involvement with the music and relaxation.

Psychophysiologic Responses

Music produces alterations in *physiology*. The goal of music therapy and the type of music played (i.e., soothing or stimulating) determine the direction of the physiologic changes. Soothing music can produce a hypometabolic response characteristic of relaxation in which autonomic, immune, endocrine, and neuropeptide systems are altered. Likewise, music therapy produces desired *psychologic* responses, such as reductions in anxiety and fear. Some of these responses have been linked to the effects of music on the *hemispheric functioning* of the brain and the *limbic system*.

Effects of Music Therapy on Hemispheric Functioning. Left-brain functioning involves the rational, analytical, and logical way of processing information. Right-brain functioning, in contrast, is concerned with the intuitive, creative, and imaging way of processing information. Music may activate the flow of stored memory material across the corpus collosum so that the right and left hemispheres work in harmony, rather than conflict.

The right hemisphere is employed differently in the musical process than the left. The right "metaphoric" hemisphere is responsible for the major aspects of musical perception and music behavior, i.e., the recognition of pitch, a gestalt sense of melody, rhythm, style, and musical memory. The commonalities between the components of speech and music are a basis for the perceptual processes of the right hemisphere, which influence language functions and behavior. The left hemisphere is predominantly involved with analytic thinking, especially in verbal and mathematical functions.[17] It has been suggested that, when we ignore or do not listen to our right brain because we are busy, rushed, and stressed, the right brain probably sends foggy messages to the left brain. Such messages of imbalance may conflict with the logic of the moment in our left brain to produce physical illness.[18]

It appears that, as one's musical knowledge grows, the

brain's response to music shifts from a holistic to a more sequential and linear experience.[19] Music students and musicians tend to analyze the music to which they listen, classify the instruments, and critique the compositional techniques. Instead of integrating right and left brain functioning while listening to music in a relaxed state, such individuals tend to remain in or change to the left-brain mode. With practice, however, they can let go of these conditioned responses to achieve integration of both hemispheres.[20]

Because music is nonverbal in nature it appeals to the right hemisphere, whereas the traditional verbalization that the nurse uses in therapy with a client has its primary effect on the logical left brain. Music therapy therefore provides a means of communication between the right and left brain.[21] The more connections that can be made in the brain, the more integrated the experience is within memory.[22]

Music, even more than the spoken word, "lends itself as a therapy because it meets with little or no intellectual resistance, and does not need to appeal to logic to initiate its action . . . is more subtle and primitive, and therefore its appeal is wider and greater."[23] In a relaxed state, individuals can let go of preconceived ideas about listening to music and its patterns, instruments, and rhythm and shift their thinking to the right side of the brain to alter their states of consciousness.[24]

Effects of Music Therapy on the Limbic System. Music therapy evokes psychophysiologic responses because of its influence on the limbic system.[25] This system is influenced by musical pitch and rhythm, which in turn affect emotions and feelings. Our emotional reactions to music may occur because the limbic system is the seat of emotions, feelings, and sensations. The quieting and calming effect of music can also produce other desired autonomic, immunologic, endocrine, and neuropeptide changes. Thus, the immediate influence of music therapy is on the mind state, which in turn influences the body state, producing a hypometabolic response and a balance of body-mind-spirit.

GENERAL EXPLANATIONS

Bodymind Connections

Our entire body responds to sound, whether we consciously hear the sound or not. Even though we can consciously tune out the sounds of airplane or automobile traffic, our bodies cannot. There are many sounds that in fact assault our body because they are not in harmony with our fundamental vibratory pattern. On the other hand, it is possible that musical vibrations that are in tune with our fundamental vibratory pattern could have a profound healing effect on the entire human body and mind, affecting changes in emotions and in organs, enzymes, hormones, cells, and atoms. Musical vibrations theoretically could help restore regulatory function to a body out of tune (i.e., during times of stress and illness) and help maintain and enhance regulatory function to a body in tune. The therapeutic appeal of music may lie in its vibrational language and ability to help bring the body-mind-spirit in alignment with its own fundamental frequency without having to appeal to the left brain to work.[26]

Imagery, Emotions, and the Senses

Music elicits a variety of different experiences in individuals. During relaxation and music therapy, clients reaching an altered state of consciousness may visualize settings, peaceful scenes, images, or may experience various sensations or moods.[27] Music passages can evoke scenes from fantasy to real life. Melodic patterns can evoke love, joy, and deep peace.

During music therapy and relaxation, individuals can be guided in experiencing *synesthesia*, or a mingling of senses.[28] Musical tones can evoke color and movement, or tastes can evoke shapes. Many children spontaneously "see" sounds and "taste" textures.[29]

Music and color can be expressed in terms of vibrations. When color is translated into music vibrations, the harmonies of color are 40 octaves higher than the ear can hear. A piano spans about 7 octaves. If the piano keyboard could be expanded another 50 octaves higher, then the keys played at these higher octaves would produce color, rather than audible sound.[30]

One musical selection entitled "Spectrum Suite" (see Resources at the end of chapter) is designed to evoke colors. While listening to this selection, clients are guided in focusing on seven main energy centers known to exist in the body. In Eastern culture these centers are called *Chakras*. Each energy level is then associated with a specific musical tone and a specific color. For example, while focusing on the spine (the first energy center), the client is guided to hear and feel the keynote of C resonating in the spinal area and image the vibrations of red bathing this area of the body.[31]

Uses and Outcomes of Music Therapy

Music has been used as a vehicle to foster a variety of desired outcomes. One such outcome is enhanced creativity. Creativity involves the development of new ways of association. It is determined by how one approaches and considers things, rather than by one's education or professional qualifications.[32] Creativity incorporates the unexpected, the unknown, and the peculiar. It can be enhanced by relaxation wherein the busy mind settles into a more quiet and receptive state. Through visualization the mind can envision new ideas and ways of thinking. When appropriate music is played, alpha and theta brainwaves occur, which are known to stimulate creativity.[33]

Music and movement and/or tonal exercises have been used to help clients become aware of their bodies and the energies released in them. Such techniques are used to achieve body-mind balance and to release blocked energies. Therapists have used musical instruments as another form of music therapy, particularly with disabled individuals. Various instruments are played by clients during the therapy to develop the qualities of perseverance, perceptiveness, concentration, and initiative and to promote perceptual-motor coordination and group interaction.[34]

Music has been used as a vehicle to improve learning.

When individuals demonstrate high psychophysiologic stress levels, learning is inhibited or blocked. When music and relaxation are combined, students become relaxed and learn better. Their learning can become more fun, and they are more fully involved in the experience and process.[35] Music has been used also as a catalyst during the process of accelerated learning. Some of the techniques that involve music-learning are Suggestology™, Super Learning™, Optimalearning™, and Accelerated Learning.™[36]

Music is used to correct and reprogram unhealthy unconscious thought patterns. Audiotapes are now available in the marketplace to repattern thought processes. Such tapes are enhanced by music. Their aim is to put the listener in a relaxed and balanced state. During relaxation, the reprogramming message is delivered to the deeper unconscious mind where the new thought pattern will ultimately reside. Such self-help tapes frequently include desired affirmations or suggestions combined with meditative music or white noise.[37]

Music can be used to facilitate reframing of past memories and experiences.[38] In achieving an altered state of consciousness, the unconscious mind can remember complete details of an individual's past experiences that the conscious mind may have forgotten. Past memories and experiences can be remembered and relived. When the conscious mind remembers such experiences, they can then be reframed or reorganized to produce a more healthy and positive experience.[39]

Music has also been combined with subliminal suggestions for self-help or enhanced learning. The subliminal technique delivers verbal messages to the individual at a volume so low or through a change in speed or frequency so fast that the conscious mind cannot perceive it. The conscious mind responds to the music while the unconscious mind absorbs and responds to the verbal suggestion.[40]

Music has been used to evoke imagery for a number of therapeutic ends. It is likely that clients who have difficulty imaging may be helped by the addition of relaxing background music. Appropriately selected music can activate right-hemispheric functioning and release a flow of images.[41]

Cathie E. Guzzetta

Bonny has developed an innovative approach to listening to music combined with the use of imagery called *Guided Imagery and Music* (GIM).[42] GIM is the conscious use of imagery that is evoked by relaxation and music. It is a method of self-exploration, self-understanding, growth, healing, and transformation. In this approach, one listens to classical music in a relaxed state, allowing the imagination to come to conscious awareness and sharing these experiences with a guide. The guide helps integrate the experience into the listener's life.

Bonny and Savary describe their work in their book, *Music and Your Mind*.[43] They have also founded the Institute for Music and Imagery (formerly called the Institute for Consciousness and Music), a nonprofit educational institution dedicated to furthering the use of music and the arts as agents of healing, renewal, and change (see Resources at the end of the chapter). The Institute engages in research and writing to expand human consciousness through music. It provides workshops and training for therapists who are interested in incorporating GIM into their practice.

Music Therapy in Clinical Settings

Music can act as a catalyst to facilitate mental suggestion and enhance a client's own self-healing capacities. Thus, music has the potential to be useful in the treatment of many health problems, such as cardiovascular disease, hypertension, migraine headaches, gastrointestinal ulcers, Raynaud's disease, and cancer. Mind modulation exists in the autonomic, immune, endocrine, and neuropeptide systems. As a result, every tissue, end-organ, and cell is capable of responding to mental healing suggestions.

Several hospitals are using relaxation music to reduce stress and pain in hospitalized patients.[44] Music has been used in birthing, counseling, and massage rooms; during physical therapy; in helping stroke, burn, and cancer victims; with brain damaged and multiply handicapped children; and in psychiatric hospitals, addiction treatment centers, and prisons.

A recent study investigated the effects of music and

relaxation on the psychophysiologic stress levels of patients admitted to the coronary care unit with the presumptive diagnosis of acute myocardial infarction.[45] There were statistically significant reductions in psychophysiologic stress in the music and relaxation group. The experimental group had lower heart rates, blood pressures, psychologic anxiety scores, higher peripheral temperatures, and fewer complications than the control group. Other outcomes related to music therapy can be found in the *Journal of Music Therapy*, which publishes research articles that explore the use of sound and music as they affect physiology, behavior, emotions, learning, and therapeutic outcomes.

Selecting Appropriate Music

Selecting the appropriate music for use in music therapy is an important and challenging task. There is no doubt that musical selections can influence the outcomes of music therapy. No one musical selection or any one type of music works best for all people in all situations. Musical selections that are relaxing and meditative to one client can be disruptive and annoying to another. Moreover, the music that some individuals identify as relaxing to them may, in fact, not be physiologically relaxing at all.[46] In addition, the music preference of the nurse, which changes as he or she matures, can influence the type of music selected.

Most music is not composed for the purposes of relaxation and healing. Thus, it is important to choose the appropriate music for the desired response. Individuals associate relaxing and displeasing events in their lives with certain kinds of music.[47] This conditioned learning response will influence their music preference and perception of whether the music selection is relaxing. Although music experts tend to agree that rock music does not evoke psychophysiologic relaxation (even if the individual thinks it does), many experts also agree that soothing classical, spiritual, or popular music also may not be relaxing for some clients.[48]

Musical selections (i.e., popular, classical, operatic, folk, jazz) should be judged for their soothing and relaxing qualities. A variety of selections should be available when working with clients because it is difficult to predict the client's music preference and the response to the particular selection. When musical selections with words are chosen, the analytic left brain tends to pay attention to the message. Clients may concentrate on the words, their messages, and their meaning, rather than allowing themselves to concentrate and flow with the music.[49] Thus, selections without words are recommended.

New Age Music. Most traditional musical selections are based on tension and release. Such music is designed to create a sense of anticipation followed by a sense of relief. The sense of anticipation is used most in popular and classical music. The tension-release music may be emotionally exciting and helpful in eliciting imagery, but it is not designed to relax most individuals.[50]

A new type of music has evolved for the purpose of "orchestrating human instruments." The goal of this music is to allow the bodymind to choose whatever response mode that it needs to operate at a higher level of efficiency. This new kind of music has been called *nontraditional, meditative,* or *New Age* music. Nontraditional meditative music potentially has a wide appeal because it is designed to transcend personal taste. There is no recognizable melody and no harmonic progressions to which we have been conditioned to respond. Frequently, there is no central rhythm or natural beat. Nontraditional music requires neither intellectual analysis nor emotional involvement. It is a vibrational language that helps the bodymind attune itself with its own pattern or resonance. The music tends to flow endlessly and serves as a vehicle for relaxation, self-absorption, and contemplation.[51] A word of caution is necessary, however. Not all music labeled as "New Age" can be judged as relaxing and meditative. Evaluate New Age musical selections to determine their soothing and meditative qualities.

Hospital Music. Relaxing music selections have been developed by a variety of companies and individuals (see Resources at the end of the chapter). Some have been developed specifically for use in the clinical setting. For example, Halpern has created several nontraditional long-playing music selections that contain up to 8 hours of continuous relaxing music. These tapes are designed for patient use in hospitals during surgery, childbirth, and postoperative recovery.

Helen Bonny, has also developed a set of music tapes called *Music Rx*™ for use in various hospital settings. Music Rx was tested at two hospitals in a study using intensive care and surgical patients. Patients participating in the Music Rx had reduced heart rates, greater relief from pain, and positive psychologic ratings.[52] The Music Rx tapes use classical selections and are designed to reduce stress, provide a pleasant diversion, and quiet mood states. Music Rx is recommended for patients in the critical care units and operating and recovery rooms, as well as other inpatient and outpatient settings.

It has been suggested that, as we learn more about how vibratory frequencies and patterns affect our bodymind, healing compositions will be composed to strengthen our altered vibratory patterns and bring them back to balance.[53]

Individual Preference. Individuals should evaluate their response to various types of music. Many people already intuitively know how they respond. Although different musical selections can produce various effects, the fullest effect occurs when the listener is appropriately prepared to experience the sounds. The therapeutic effect of music is lessened when individuals are angry, distracted, critical, analytic, or resistant. With a relaxed and receptive bodymind, music has the potential to enter the body and play through it, rather than around it. Thus, some form of relaxation exercise is recommended before the music experience.

Depending on the individual's psychophysiology, mind state, and mood, music can produce different feelings at different times. An important rule to follow when listening to music is the *iso-principle.*[54] The iso-principle matches the individual's mood to the appropriate music to obtain the best results from the experience. Music that matches the individual's mood helps achieve an altered state of consciousness because it is as if the mind and feelings are vibrating at a certain frequency and are satisfied when

Evaluating Your Response to Music

1. Set aside 20 minutes of relaxation time.
2. Find a comfortable position.
3. Find a quiet uninterrupted place.
4. Check your pulse rate.
5. Observe your breathing pattern (fast, slow, normal).
6. Assess your muscular tension (pain, muscle tightness, shoulder stiffness, jaw and neck tension). Are you loose, limp, sleepy?
7. Evaluate your mood state (angry, happy, sad).
8. Listen to the music for 20 minutes. Let your body respond to the music as it wishes: loosen muscles, lie down, dance, clap, hum.
9. Following the session, assess your breathing pattern.
10. Assess your muscular tension (more relaxed? more stimulated? tighter? tenser? calmer?).
11. Evaluate your mood state.
12. Record the name of the music selection and your before-and-after responses in a music notebook for use when developing your own therapeutic tapes.
13. On a separate page in your notebook, recall and write down the many ways that music has empowered your life psychologically, physically, and spiritually. Include your most dramatic, intimate, and emotional memories associated with music. You will begin to realize the importance of sound in your life and recognize its healing potential.

the music is in resonance with that frequency. For example, if you are feeling carefree and gay, it is not advisable to play solemn music.

Create your own tapes that match your moods and your musical preference. If your mood is tense or angry, you might start out with a short selection (3 minutes or less) of music that resonates with your mood, and then add selections that increasingly move you to a relaxed state. Before creating your own tape, spend some time experimenting with music.

162

Nursing Diagnoses

Nursing diagnoses compatible with music therapy interventions described in this chapter and that are related to the nine human response patterns of Unitary Person are as follows:

- Exchanging: (Music therapy can be used to enhance coping and recovery with all diagnoses in this category)
- Relating: Social isolation
- Valuing: Spiritual distress
- Choosing: Ineffective individual coping
  Noncompliance
- Moving: Sleep pattern disturbance
- Perceiving: Alterations in self-concept
  Disturbance in body-image
  Disturbance in self-esteem
  Hopelessness
  Powerlessness
- Feeling: Alterations in comfort: pain
  Anxiety
  Fear

When selecting your own nourishing music, you should experience a variety of musical selections. Pay attention and become aware of what is happening to you when listening to specific selections. No one can direct you in what music will work best for you. You must discover that for yourself. It is important to identify your preference, your moods, and your specific psychophysiologic state at the moment.

Try "experimental listening."[55] Listen to various types of music at different times of the day and week. Spend 20 minutes listening to each type of music and then systematically evaluate your response to the selection. The steps below outline the psychophysiologic parameters to assess when evaluating your response to specific types of music. Based on your response, create your own relaxation music tape of 20-30 minutes in length. The more regularly you use the tape, the more effective it will become.

Cathie E. Guzzetta

Experiencing music can be a holistic experience. As more individuals come to realize that music can be a principal source of healing and stress reduction, they will take great care to select their music.

Notes

1. Antoine de Saint Exupery, *The Little Prince* (New York: Harcourt, Brace, & World, Inc., 1971), p. 16.
2. Hans Jenny, *The Structure and Dynamics of Waves and Vibrations* (Basel, Switzerland: Basilius Press, 1967), p. 1ff.
3. Steven Halpern and Louis Savary, *Sound Health: The Music and Sounds that Make Us Whole* (San Francisco: Harper & Row, 1985), p. 33.
4. Cathie E. Guzzetta, "Physiology of the Heart and Circulation," in *Cardiovascular Nursing: Bodymind Tapestry*, ed. Cathie E. Guzzetta and Barbara M. Dossey (St. Louis: C. V. Mosby Co., 1984), pp. 104-153.
5. Ibid., pp. 115-116.
6. Steven Halpern and Louis Savary, *Sound Health*, pp. 33-37.
7. Ibid., p. 37.
8. Ibid., p. 39.
9. Cecilia Schulbert, *The Music Therapy Sourcebook* (New York: Human Sciences Press, 1981), p. 13.
10. Peter Michael Hamel, *Through Music to the Self* (Boulder, CO: Shambhala Press, 1979), p. 166.
11. Helen Bonny and Louis Savary, *Music and Your Mind* (New York: Harper & Row, 1973), p. 15.
12. Peter Michael Hamel, *Through Music to the Self*, p. 174.
13. Helen Bonny and Louis Savary, *Music and Your Mind*, p. 14.
14. R. McClellan, "Music and Altered States of Consciousness," *Dromenon* 2 (Winter 1979): 3-5.
15. Ibid., pp. 3-5.
16. S. Krippner, *The Highest State of Consciousness* (New York: Doubleday & Co., 1972), pp. 1-5.
17. Don G. Campbell, *Introduction to the Musical Brain* (St. Louis: MMB Music, Inc., 1984), pp. 14-65.
18. Ibid., p. 54.
19. Ibid., p. 45.
20. Helen Bonny and Louis Savary, *Music and Your Mind*, p. 90.
21. R. Beebe, "Synesthesia with Music," *Dromenon* 2 (Winter 1979): 7.
22. Don G. Campbell, *Introduction to the Musical Brain*, p. 14.

23. I. Altshuler, "A Psychiatrist's Experience with Music as a Therapeutic Agent," in *Music as Medicine*, ed. D. Schullian and M. Schoen (New York: Henry Schuman, 1948), p. 267.
24. R. McClellan, "Music and Altered States of Consciousness," p. 4.
25. Don Campbell, *Introduction to the Musical Brain*, pp. 20-22.
26. Steven Halpern and Louis Savary, *Sound Health*, pp. 39-43.
27. Helen Bonny and Louis Savary, *Music and Your Mind*, p. 30.
28. Jake Page, "Roses are Red, E-Flat is Too," *Hippocrates*, September-October 1987, pp. 63-66.
29. Jean Houston, *The Possible Human* (Los Angeles: J. P. Tarcher, 1982), pp. 47-48.
30. Steven Halpern and Louis Savary, *Sound Health*, p. 183.
31. Ibid., p. 185.
32. Steven Halpern and Louis Savary, *Sound Health*, p. 115.
33. Don Campbell, *Introduction to the Musical Brain*, pp. 62-63.
34. Cecilia Schulbert, *The Music Therapy Sourcebook*, p. 104.
35. Steven Halpern and Louis Savary, *Sound Health*, p. 116.
36. Ibid., p. 119.
37. Ibid., p. 136.
38. Ibid., p. 129.
39. Helen Bonny and Louis Savary, *Music and Your Mind*, p. 31.
40. Steven Halpern and Louis Savary, *Sound Health*, p. 137.
41. Helen Bonny and Louis Savary, *Music and Your Mind*, pp. 96-97.
42. "Guided Imagery and Music Brochure" (Port Townsend, WA: Institute for Music and Imagery, 1986), p. 1ff.
43. Helen Bonny and Louis Savary, *Music and Your Mind*, pp. 13-41.
44. Steven Halpern and Louis Savary, *Sound Health*, p. 58.
45. Cathie E. Guzzetta, *Effects of Relaxation and Music Therapy on Coronary Care Patients Admitted with Presumptive Acute Myocardial Infarction*, Department of Health and Human Services Division of Nursing Grant NU-00824, August, 1987.
46. Steven Halpern and Louis Savary, *Sound Health*, p. 46.
47. Peter Michael Hamel, *Through Music to the Self*, p. 169.
48. Ibid., p. 169.
49. Steven Halpern and Louis Savary, *Sound Health*, p. 98.
50. Ibid., p. 142.
51. Peter Michael Hamel, *Through Music to the Self*, p. 142.
52. Helen Bonny, "Sound Spaces: Music Rx is Proven in the ICU," *ICM West Newsletter* 2, no. 4, (December 1982): 2.
53. Steven Halpern and Louis Savary, *Sound Health*, p. 104.
54. Helen Bonny and Louis Savary, *Music and Your Mind*, p. 43.
55. Bibi Wein, "Body and Soul Music," *American Health*, April, 1987, pp. 67-74.
56. Steven Halpern and Louis Savary, *Sound Health*, p. 150.

Cathie E. Guzzetta

SUGGESTED READINGS

Clynes, M. *Music, Mind and Brain*, New York: Plenum Press, 1982.
Drury, N. *Music for Inner Space*, San Leandro, CA: Prism Press, 1985.
Johnston, W. *Silent Music.* London: Collins Press, 1974.
Priestley, M. *Music Therapy in Action.* London: Constable, 1975.
Rudhyar, D. *The Magic of Tone and the Art of Music.* Boulder, CO:
Shambhala Press, 1982.

RESOURCES

Relaxation, Imagery, and Music Tapes
Bodymind Systems, 910 Dakota Drive, Temple, TX 76501
Halpern Sounds, 1775 Old County Road, #9, Belmont, CA 94002
Mystical Rose Books and Tapes, P. O. Box 38, Malibu, CA 90265
Narada Distributing, 1804 E. North Ave., Milwaukee, WI 53202
Sound of Light, Box 1244, Boulder, CO 80306
Source Distributing and New Age Co-op, P. O. Box 1207, Carmel
Valley, CA 93924
Sources Cassette, Dept 99, P. O. Box W, Stanford, CA 94305
Inner Guidance System, GWYNEDD, Plaza 2, Suite 301, Spring-
house, PA 19477
Fortuna Records, 11 Kavon Ct., Navato, CA 94947
Aura Communications, P. O. Box 5256, San Diego, CA 92105
Valley of the Sun Publishing, P. O. Box 38, Malibu, CA 90265

10

The Music Therapist:
Creative Arts Therapist and Contemporary Shaman

JOSEPH J. MORENO

In considering the historical development leading to the current applications of music therapy as a professional discipline, it is crucial to remember that music therapy is not a recently developed modality. Rather, music therapy as a profession is only a recent and specialized line of development of the continuing 30 thousand-year-old shamanic traditions of music and healing still being practiced throughout the world. By comparison, music therapy in the United States has had little more than a 30-year history of professional recognition.

Music as therapy, without being described as "music therapy," is currently a flourishing practice in countless tribal and other nontechnological societies in Asia, Africa, Australia, America, Oceania, and Europe. That so much of the music of these cultures is oriented toward healing traditions becomes particularly apparent in the ethno-musicological literature. A survey of world music traditions (May, 1983) covers 19 representative culture areas, with individual chapters written by some of the world's foremost ethnomusicologists. It is remarkable, for example, that the chapters on the musics of Indonesia, the Australian Aboriginals, several subSaharan African cultures, the North American Indian, Alaskan Eskimos, South American Indian music, and aspects of other cultures are overwhelmingly oriented toward the role of music and healing in the shamanic tradition. The chapter by Olsen, "Symbol and Function in South American Indian Music" (1983) is devoted almost entirely to the role of music in shamanic practice. Singing and drumming are discussed in relation to their roles as the principal stimuli utilized to induce states of shamanic ecstasy. Indeed, this chapter is a substantial treatise in itself on music and healing practices in tribal cultures.

In the chapter examining the black music of South Africa, John Blacking (1983) refers to the highly social nature of subSaharan music in general, where individual parts may interlock in rhythmic polyphony (the hocket technique) to create the whole. His description of this kind of performance is an ethnomusicological expression of the concept of rhythmic entrainment that has become the focus of a growing body of music therapy research: "Anyone who has performed in such ensembles will know just how the music generates a change of somatic state when all the players or singers of different parts slot into a common movement."

The "common movement" that Blacking refers to is analogous to the "phase locking" that occurs in rhythmic entrainment, when two or more objects that are pulsing at nearly the same time tend to "lock in" and begin pulsing at the same rate. In this can be seen a common element between the rhythmic connection that can exist between the shaman and patient and between the music therapist and client. In both instances, rhythm can bring the two together on a level that is distinct from verbal communication and that is perhaps even more basic and significant. It seems unlikely that these world traditions of music and healing could have survived for 30 thousand years unless they had been found to be empirically effective (Harner, 1982). This legacy poses a special challenge for the music therapist to interpret its significance for contemporary music therapy theory and practice.

A serious reexamination of these living world traditions of music and healing in shamanic practice can help to: a) enhance our understanding of the relationship of music therapy to other psychotherapeutic modalities, b) clarify the role of music therapy in response to current trends in

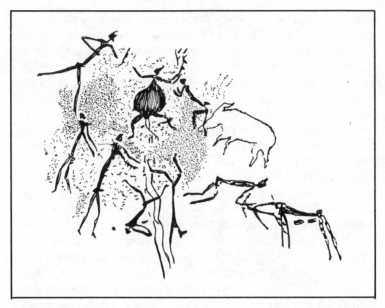

Figure 1. Impression of prehistoric rock art of the Federation of Rhodesia and Myasaland.

holistic healing and the integration of the creative arts therapies, and c) clarify points of understanding about the most basic meaning of music as a therapeutic modality.

An examination of prehistoric documentation can be highly revealing. The illustration in Figure 1 is based on a Bushman rock painting from Zimbabwe in Southern Africa that is estimated to be about 26 thousand years old (Huffman, 1983).

This painting seems to represent some of the earliest visual documentation of music and healing and to illustrate the musical element within a holistic paradigm. Huffman (1983) describes the central figure as a mother goddess surrounded by dancing figures presumed to be in a trance state. The male figure in the upper right is clapping to accompany the dancers and providing the rhythmic musical support that sustains the trance. Lewis-Williams (1981) has drawn on Bushman ethnography to support explanations of Bushman rock art that emphasize trance performance. The Bushman medicine men still enter trance during medicine dances, and these beliefs are shared by Bushman groups throughout Southern Africa. Furthermore, Lewis-Williams' trance metaphor has demonstrated relevance to rock art, compatability with anthropological theory, predictive potential, and simplicity. Other interpretations, in contrast, have little explanatory power because they are merely ad hoc inductions (Huffman, 1983). It has also been demonstrated that prolonged violent rhythmic dancing may cause hyperventilation (Jones, 1954) that also contributes to trance.

This superficially simple 26 thousand-year-old painting can have a stunning impact if one considers its full implications. Within the painting there seems to be a perfectly explicit depiction of the holistic integration of the creative arts therapies in healing (i.e., music, art, dance and drama).

The music is illustrated by the clapping accompaniment, and the dance appears to be clearly depicted. Art is represented by the very creation of the painting, and the implied healing ritual would represent a dramatic experience enacted between the group of participants and the spirit world.

According to Huffman (1983) the symbolic components of the painting, such as the wavy lines, represent bees, which were special power animals to the Bushman, and the special powers attributed to the figure interpreted as a menstruating goddess further suggest the enactment of tribal myths in healing ritual.

Prehistoric paintings such as this one strongly suggest a prehistoric connection between music, art, dance, and drama in the healing process. This integration of the creative arts therapies, this interdisciplinary cooperation, which the respective American organizations for music, art, dance, and drama therapies are just beginning to initiate was probably well established 26 thousand years ago. The painting also suggests that the group therapy process, another relatively new trend in psychotherapy, has always been as integral to tribal healing rituals as it is today.

The holistic integration of music, art, dance, and drama in healing rituals in both historic and contemporary practice in cultures throughout the world provides a strong empirical model from which to formulate an approach to music therapy relevant to the mainstream of Western culture.

The shaman, whether referred to as a "medicine man," "witch doctor," or by any other term, is the prototypical healing figure and music therapist, and has always been a multidisciplinary practitioner—a holistic healer. A shaman never specializes in only music, or art, dance, or drama. Instead, he or she naturally integrates all of these elements into practice. For example, in American Indian culture the Navajo medicine man or woman would never only sing a medicine song to function as a specialized kind of "music medicine man," and then call upon other healers to carry out the ritual dances, do the sand paintings, the dramatization of the tribal myths, the verbal interactions with the patient, and so on.

And yet, as absurd as it might seem, this separation represents precisely the kind of therapeutic compartmentalization and overspecialization that occurs in our own culture. Professional training programs tend to create single focus therapists who lack the necessary breadth of background to holistically draw from sources in the other creative arts. Although there exist a few progressive institutions in which teams of creative arts therapists work together cooperatively, it is certainly the exceptional institution in which all of the creative arts therapies are fully represented in treatment programs. Greater versatility on the part of individual therapists might be a more feasible goal than that of having teams of four creative arts therapists in every institution.

By contrast, the medicine man or woman not only integrates sources from all of the creative arts, he or she never holds a compartmentalized view of a patient. Traditional healers view patients from a broad social perspective,. and never attempt any cure without full consideration of their patients' emotional, spiritual, and physical state. They would never consider the musical part of the treatment as an element separate from the whole—or in any way separated from the total needs of their patients. Their "goals," if they would express themselves in those terms, would not focus on a single aspect of their patients—like some goals characteristic of the behavioral approach to music therapy, that is, "the patient will make more positive statements" or "the patient will spend less time in isolation." Rather, the medicine man or woman looks at the patient as a total human being and thinks in terms of the patient's total life adjustment.

This holistic model certainly has many immediate implications for the education and practice of the music therapist, as well as for all therapists working in the creative arts. In this writer's view, it is unfortunate that music therapists in their professional training in the United States do not receive instruction in art and art therapy, and that dance therapists do not receive instruction in drama and drama therapy, and so on. The model of the traditional healer suggests that the professional training of the music therapist include at least introductory level courses in art, dance, and drama and their therapeutic applications. In this way, music therapists, although still retaining a primary musical identity, could enrich their work by holistically integrating sources from the other creative arts.

In practice many music therapists often do involve their clients in therapy experiences that integrate music with the other arts, such as music and movement or music and art expression. However, they typically lack the training to pursue these directions with any real depth or confidence. These practices seem to reflect their feeling that a one-dimensional music-only approach is too limiting, both for themselves as therapists and for their patients. At the same time, many music therapists who do integrate the other creative arts into their practices may do so with misgiving, as if they have somehow betrayed the purity of their discipline. The shaman's holistic model should dispel all of these doubts.

A further implication from the shamanic model is suggested for the music education of the music therapist. Shamans typically have to deal only with patients from their own culture group. Musical materials, as assimilated through the culture, need only reflect the music of a homogeneous cultural group. However, the music therapist who lives in a multi-cultural society needs to develop some degree of ability in a wide variety of ethnic musical genres in order to enhance the possibilities of establishing musical communication with patients from diverse ethnic backgrounds. The use of these ethnic musical associations might not always be indicated in practice, but the music therapist should certainly have the necessary breadth of musical background to utilize these possibilities when they are called for. This suggests that a holistic music education for the music therapist should include required coursework in world music or ethnomusicology.

The shaman is a specialized figure in tribal cultures. The shaman is more than a medicine man or woman administering herbal medicines and functioning in a medical way. The shaman has more visionary abilities. A shaman is defined by anthropologist Michael Harner (1982) as ". . . a man or woman who enters an altered state of consciousness—at will—to contact and utilize an ordinarily hidden reality in order to acquire knowledge and power and to help other persons."

Central to the shaman's task of entering the state of altered consciousness that is crucial to the healing process is the use of rhythmically hypnotic and repetitive supportive music, most typically in the form of rhythmic drumming. Neher (1962) investigated the role of rhythmic drumming as a physiological stimulus in trance inducement by attempting to replicate the shamanic drumming stimulus in a controlled laboratory experimental situation. In this manner, the experimenter was able to closely monitor subject responses. Neher's research indicated that the experimentally controlled drum beating induced symptoms of trance-like states similar to those observed in shamans in an altered state of consciousness. Unfortunately, it is very difficult to measure the physiological responses of shamans and patients in real healing situations, as the intrusive nature of attempting to introduce monitoring equipment into highly sacred and private ceremonies minimizes these possibilities. Neher's data indicated that:

1. A single beat of an untuned drum contains many frequencies, so that the different overtones are transmitted over different

pathways in the brain. He concluded that the resonant sound of a drum can stimulate larger areas of the brain than a less complex single frequency sound.

2. A drum beat contains many low frequencies, and the frequency receptors for low frequencies are so much stronger than the delicate high frequency receptors that the listener can tolerate low frequency pitches for a longer time before pain is felt. As a result, more energy can be transmitted to the brain with a drum than with a higher frequency stimulus.

3. Electroencephalogram (EEG) measurements of Neher's subjects indicated that the typical tempo of tribal drumming, replicated in the experimental setting, was close to the basic rhythm of alpha wave production (8-13 cycles per second). Additionally, the drumming produced an auditory driving of the alpha waves leading to a trance-like state in the subjects.

Finally, the subjects reported that they had experienced unusual perceptions in the trance-like state similar to those described by traditional healers, indicating an altered state of consciousness. Neher's research seemed to have experimentally provided measurable physiological data that supported what has long been empirically experienced and understood by traditional healers. However, it is possible that Neher's data were critically flawed in that he was unable to control for movement artifact in his EEG measurements (Achterberg, 1985).

Rouget (1985) believes that music should ultimately be seen as more than only a rhythmic stimulus in trance inducement. Rouget suggests that though music is the principal means of manipulating the trance state, it does this by "socializing" it more than by simply triggering it. This process of socialization varies from culture to culture, according to the ideological system within which trance takes place. While Rouget emphatically rejects Neher's conclusions, short of definitive data on this highly complex issue, the relationship between the psychological and physiological role of music in trance inducement remains an open question.

In order for shamans to be effective healers, they need to enter a state of "non-ordinary reality," an altered state of consciousness. This altered state is necessary to free the shamans so that they can "travel" (in shamanic terms) to the spirit world, either in order to remove harmful spirits from the patients or to restore beneficial ones. Shamans are well aware that these spirits do not exist in "ordinary reality," and, in any case, a "spirit" is perhaps no more of an abstraction than such theoretical concepts as "id," "ego," "super-ego," and other analytic constructs (Harner, 1982).

In order to reach the spirit world, shamans must be internally focused and able to fully concentrate on the task at hand. Therefore, the music (drumming, or other rhythmic musical stimuli such as chanting or the playing of rattles, etc.) is often made or supported by an assistant or group of assistants so that the shamans will not have to be distracted by the actual music-making. The music affects the shamans psychologically and physiologically by supporting an alpha state in the manner previously cited (Neher, 1962), and also blocks out any distracting stimuli. For the experienced shaman, the musical stimulus alone can immediately trigger the response whereby he or she enters an altered state of consciousness. This is a response that has been conditioned by association with all previous similar experiences.

The hypnotically repetitive rhythmic music can be seen as a sedation of the left hemisphere of the shaman's brain, the hemisphere that might otherwise be concerned with distractions of "ordinary reality." This sedation then liberates the right hemisphere of the brain to travel to the spirit world, a journey that is integral to the healing process. In more poetic shamanic terms, the drum is seen as the shaman's horse that allows him or her to fly to the sky to encounter the world of the spirits (Eliade, 1974).

The musical stimuli have values for the patient as well. Rhythmic music also allows the *patient* to enter a receptive semi-hypnotic state that reinforces belief in the power of the shaman and of the healing ritual. Shamans may also make use of special medicine songs that symbolize the power of the ritual and further enhance patients' faith in the ability of shamans to heal and in their commitment to their patients in calling upon the sacred songs. As Frank (1974) has stated, "The success of all methods and schools

Joseph J. Moreno

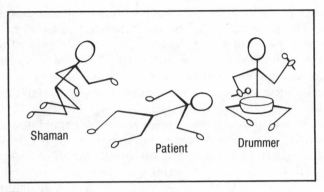

Figure 2.

of psychotherapy depends in the first instance on the patient's conviction that the therapist cares about him and is competent to help him."

Figure 2 illustrates the physical arrangement of the most basic shamanic music and healing situation. In this model, the oldest psychotherapeutic context known to humankind, it can be seen that music is intrinsic to the psychotherapeutic process. Without the musical support, shamans in most cultures would find it difficult to travel to the spirit worlds.

This model also provides a basis for suggesting that music contributes an essential element to therapy that should never have been eliminated from modern Western therapies. For example, in Western-oriented culture, a verbal therapist such as an analyst has many therapeutic goals in common with the shaman. Like the shaman, analysts need to minimize distracting left brain stimuli in order to focus on a right brain intuitive connection with the patient. The analyst also tries to process the patient's experiences by evaluating them in relation to his or her own life experiences and knowledge, just as the shaman "brings into play his or her past experience of affliction and transcendent realization in relation to one who is now suffering" (Halifax, 1979). This process requires a great deal of introspection, concentration, and a high level of sensitivity to the patient's feelings and needs. The shaman seeks to contact the appropriate guardian spirits and connect these to the needs of the patient.

176

Despite their differences in approach, both the shaman and the analyst need to be able to focus entirely on the process of the moment, sensitize themselves to the needs and feelings of their patients, and to remove themselves from their ordinary state of being. However, the shaman takes advantage of the facilitating support system of music, of which the analyst and patient are entirely deprived. The analyst is still able to complete his or her task, but the process is that much more difficult for both therapist and patient.

Music therapists, in common with shamans, take the fullest possible advantage of music in the therapeutic process. In music therapy, the musical element becomes the primary focus. The musical element in music therapy in Western culture takes on an even broader role than the music in traditional healing. Without the universally shared worldview and unquestioning faith in the healing ritual that is such a supportive element in those tribal cultures in which shamanic healing occurs, the music becomes the binding force. The musical experience alone can create a bond between therapist and client, help to summon the client's regenerative forces and a belief in the therapist's healing ability, and ultimately realize a contemporary Western expression of the traditional music and healing rituals.

Finally, the traditional interactive model of shaman, drummer, and patient (see Figure 2) suggests that music therapists should not lack the confidence to fully interact with their patients verbally and to pursue in-depth verbal processing of their patients' experiences and feelings. There should be no separation in theory or practice between the musical and verbal elements in music therapy—neither should be used separately. Called for is a holistic integration.

It is of interest to further examine the shaman's characteristic use of musical assistants. By making frequent use of an assistant to help in the physical act of music making, shamans free themselves to travel without distraction to the spirit world. Music therapists often follow this model intuitively, by utilizing, when possible, a cotherapist to make music so that they can interact more directly with the patients. Also, technology has provided an always available musical assistant through the medium of recorded

Joseph J. Moreno

music, which can meet the music therapists' same needs
of physical and mental liberation. However, sometimes
shamans may create their own musical support, just as
music therapists can also function entirely independently.

Observing music and healing rituals in various world
cultures provides contemporary evidence of the continuity
of these traditions. Balinese culture in Indonesia provides
many interesting examples. Trance is a common form of
ritual practice in Bali and serves many functions. Trance
provides a kind of emotional outlet for people living in a
highly ritualized and predictable culture, often serving as
a kind of exorcistic function, and always in the context of a
musical setting. Associations with the special gamelan
music played during the trance dance is trance-inducing,
just as the drumming becomes trance-inducing for the
shaman. Usually, young girls are chosen to be trance
dancers, called upon, for example, in rituals designed to
ward off epidemics. These prepubescent girls represent a
kind of purity to the Balinese that allows them to be entered
by the gods, as evidenced by their trance-like state. The
dancers, in turn, incite many of the participant observers
to go into trance as well.

The recent use of the Paiste Sound Creation Gongs in
Europe as a specialized instrument and approach in music
therapy is directly derived from Indonesian traditions.
The Sound Creation Gongs are a set of eleven untuned
gongs, designed for work in music therapy. Each gong has
a unique and contrasting timbre. The sound polarities lend
themselves to the expression of emotional polarities (i.e.,
calm vs. anger) and gong sounds have the additional value
of being unconditioned sound stimuli, with the potential
of being able to elicit relatively spontaneous musical
responses not limited by previous musical associations.

In Indonesia, the large gong in the Javanese gamelan
is the most honored and the most sacred instrument. Special
offerings to the gong are made weekly to appease the spirits
that live within and around it (Lindsay, 1979). In general,
Javanese gamelan performers associate performance of the
music with a state of peace and detachment, again reminiscent
of the shamanic alpha state. These connections between

gamelan music, trance, exorcism, the Indonesian and Western uses of the gong, and even in the Western re-creation of gamelan style instruments in the Orff Schulwerk (also broadly utilized in music therapy) are all representative of the continuing links between modern music therapy and traditional music and healing. The Orff xylophones, created for use in music education and therapy, were modeled directly after the Indonesian gamelan instruments. Like the gamelan xylophones, they have the possibilities for providing the immediately gratifying music making that can be so useful in therapy.

In a variety of contemporary African cultures it is still possible to observe healing rituals that in their integration of all the creative arts in the healing process provide a striking parallel to the image previously discussed and portrayed in Figure 1. In Southern Africa, the Shona people of Zimbabwe have healing rituals called bira ceremonies (Berliner, 1981). The rhythmic music played by the mbira is intrinsic to the ceremony.

In Shona religion, a basic tenet is that after people die their spirits continue to affect the lives of the living. The living must try to continue to maintain good relations with the spirits of the departed. If they do not manage these relationships effectively, the Shona consider it inevitable that they will have serious problems of some kind. When the problems cannot be dealt with in any other way, the Shona organize a bira ceremony. The whole family or community gathers to summon the ancestor's spirit for help, and the shaman serves as a spirit medium.

In the context of the highly rhythmic mbira music, which is played all night, along with continual dancing and the drinking of specially prepared ritual beer, the shaman becomes possessed by the spirit, then "becomes" the spirit, and only then can he or she help the patient (Berliner, 1981). As is suggested in Figure 1, the Bushman rock painting, the rhythmic music and dancing support, the spirit-mediums in their trance-like state. In Balinese culture, as previously stated, the music supports the dancers in entering the altered state of consciousness that is intrinsic to the therapeutic process.

Traditional Music and Healing;
Contemporary Music Therapy Techniques

Many interesting parallels can be drawn between the role of music in traditional healing rituals and a contemporary re-expression of some aspects of these practices in music therapy techniques. For example, a technique such as guided imagery and music has a very obvious relationship with shamanic practice (Kovach, 1985).

In guided imagery and music, the patients rather than the therapist (the symbolic shaman) enter an altered state of consciousness. This is acquired through deep relaxation and concentration on the music, which can induce a trance state similar to that which occurs in shamanism. In guided imagery, the patients travel to their own inner world of conflicts and other personal issues rather than to spirit worlds. In both instances an inner vision is essential.

As in shamanism, the darkened room and the music help the patient to focus on unconscious feelings rather than on the superficial realities of ordinary daily life. During the imagery session, patients are in a different reality, focusing on repressed conflicts or other difficult material that in many ways can be more real than their ordinary reality.

The music therapist, like the shaman, is still necessary to help patients verbally process their experiences and gain insight into their feelings. Another interesting parallel is that the changes in mental imagery in response to the varying character of the supportive music in guided imagery are similar to the changing shamanic visions in response to changes in the tempo or timbre of the drumming.

Achterberg (1985) has stressed the continuum between the shaman's use of imagination in healing and the growing use of imagery in general medical practice. Imagery is a pervasive element in shamanic healing that is fully adaptable to the cultural context of modern medicine and to applications of music therapy with a specific medical focus. For example, in the work of Rider (1987), improvised music, rhythmic entrainment and imagery are combined for the purposes of pain management and for measurable disease control. This is exemplified by the case of a diabetic patient who demonstrated a marked decline in blood sugar variation in response to this personalized approach to music and imagery. As Achterberg (1985) has stated, "the finest medicine will be produced by those who take the best from the shaman and the scientist."

Still another parallel can be seen in the integration of art and music in music therapy, that is, the patient freely draws in a self-expressive way in response to selected music stimuli analogous to the use of sand painting and music in the healing rituals in the Navajo culture of the American Indian. Although the approaches are entirely different, there does exist the common element of art and music expression integrated into the healing process.

In the same manner, the integration of music with dance or movement expression in music therapy has a direct relationship to the kind of ritual depicted in the Bushman rock painting in Figure 1. Music and hypnotherapy and music and psychodrama (Moreno, 1980, 1984) are two other integrated approaches with obvious relationships to traditional practices that are becoming more accepted in response to a growing holistic consciousness in the field of music therapy.

Directions for Future Research

Music therapists should become involved in collaborative field research with ethnomusicologists to study music and healing rituals from a multidisciplinary perspective. Ethnomusicologists have studied tribal music and healing ritual (Bahr & Haefer, 1978), but often the focus of the research has been on the musical and ritual elements of the healing, without real attention to either the immediate or long-term effects of the healing upon the patient.

Collaborative research between music therapists and ethnomusicologists could combine serious study of the music and ritual along with the maintenance of data on the patients' responses to treatment. This kind of research would also help to determine the possibilities of adapting some of these traditions of music and healing techniques to the mainstream of Western music therapy. There is a sense of urgency regarding this research because many of these traditional healing practices are rapidly disappearing in response to urbanization and other acculturative influences.

Toward an Independent Theory of Music Therapy

Music therapy as a therapeutic modality has tended to explain itself in terms of the frame of reference of other psychological theories, such as behavioral therapy, psychoanalytic theory, and others. In this manner, the music therapist working in a behavioral context conceptualizes music as a positive reinforcer to realize a contingent goal, or in psychoanalytic terms conceptualizes music as an experience that can be ego supportive and expressive of the libido without superego censure. These explanations of music therapy theory, through the framework of other psychological theories, point to the fact that an independent theory of music therapy that would explain itself largely in its own terms is still lacking. An exhaustive study of the common elements in music and healing rituals throughout the world could provide the data needed to develop this kind of theoretical basis for a more independent theory of music therapy that would express itself primarily from a music frame of reference.

This could represent a major breakthrough in an understanding of the music therapy process. Building the entire theoretical constructs of music therapy on a foundation of controlled research, based only in a Western culture setting, eliminates from consideration all of the continuing world traditions of music and healing, of which music therapy as a profession is only one extension.

The deepest aspects of these rituals cannot be experimentally replicated because they are such an intrinsic part of the various culture systems in which they are practiced. Despite this, they can and should be studied, both in the field and through the extensive anthropological and ethnomusicological literature. Again, despite the vast cultural differences between tribal societies and modern Western cultures, there are many commonalities in the use of music in healing in both settings.

Music therapy related research has amply demonstrated and measured the effects of music on human behavior, both psychologically and physiologically. Music itself has been explained from the point of view of the physics of sound and from artistic, musicological, and ethnomusicological frames of reference. Nevertheless, despite the vastness of all this knowledge, the modern music therapist in practice is not so far removed in many essential ways from the traditional healer. The conceptions and the terminology have changed, but music still serves much the same purpose that it always has. The connections between tribal practices and contemporary music therapy are too strong to be ignored or merely dismissed as an historical legacy. They are vital and living connections that should be strengthened rather than severed.

In considering the historically persistent role of music in healing throughout the world from a Jungian point of view, it would appear that music has a strong archetypal significance to the human species. Shamans have always been intuitively aware of the archetypal power of music in healing, and this is evident in the spiritual and dramatic power of their practice. Music therapists in Western culture may diminish this connection with the archetypal power of their therapeutic medium of music when they fail to maximize the emotional depth of their work. The borderline between recreational music and in-depth music therapy could be partially measured by the extent to which the music therapist creates musical experiences of deep emotional meaning for clients and engages them in serious experiences. The music therapist needs to approach the power of the shaman, who takes the spiritual depth of the work for granted.

Music therapists can learn a great deal from the shamanic model: to grow in imagination, in sensitivity, in awareness of the archetypal power of the musical experience, and in the creative and expressive freedom of their work.

Jung, who had a good musical background, eventually stopped listening to music. He felt irritated "because music is dealing with such deep archetypal material and those who play don't realize this" (Tilly, 1956/1977, p. 274). The

Joseph J. Moreno

shaman, by contrast, has always been close to the archetypal significance of music, and this sensitivity can be incorporated into the work of the contemporary music therapist. Deeply impressed by a music therapy demonstration, Jung went on to say, "I feel that from now on music should be an essential part of every analysis. This reaches the deep archetypal material that we can only sometimes reach in our analytical work" (p. 275). The archetypal work of the traditional healer can provide an exciting and liberating model that can open new possibilities for a renewed dynamic and spiritual emphasis in music therapy.

References

Achterberg, J. (1985). *Imagery in healing: Shamanism and modern medicine*. Boston: Shambhala Publications.
Bahr, D., & Haefer, R. (1978, Jan.). Songs in Piman Curing. *Ethnomusicology, XXII.*
Berliner, F. (1981). *The soul of mbira*. Berkeley: University of California Press.
Blacking, J. (1983). Trends in the black music of South Africa. In E. May (Ed.), *Musics of many cultures: An introduction*. Berkeley, CA: University of California Press.
Eliade, M. (1974). *Shamanism: Archaic techniques of ecstasy*. Bollingen Series 76. Princeton, NJ: Princeton University Press.
Frank, J. D. (1974). *Persuasion and healing* (rev. ed. p. 165). Baltimore: Johns Hopkins University Press.
Halifax, J. (1979). *Shamanic voices* (p. 317). New York: Dutton.
Harner, M. (1982). *The way of the shaman* (p. 25). New York: Bantam Books.
Huffman, T. N. (1983, June). The trance hypothesis and the rock art of Zimbabwe. In J. D. Lewis-Williams (Ed.), *New approaches in Southern African rock art*. The South African Archaeological Society. Goodwin Series, *IV.*
Jones, A. M. (1954). African rhythm. *Africa 24,* 26-47. *Studies in African music* (2 Vols.). London: Oxford University Press.
Kenny, C. (1982). *The mythic artery*. Atascadero: Ridgeview Publishing.
Kovach, A. M., Stein- (1985). Shamanism and guided imagery and music: A comparison. *Journal of Music Therapy, XXII* (3).
Lewis-Williams, J. D. (1981 a). *Believing and seeing: Symbolic meanings in southern San rock paintings*. London: Academic Press.

Lindsay, J. (1979). *Javanese gamelan*. London: Oxford University Press.

May, E. (Ed.), (1983). *Musics of many cultures: An introduction*. Berkeley, CA: University of California Press.

Moreno, J. (1980). Musical psychodrama: A new direction in music therapy. *Journal of Music Therapy, 17* (1).

Moreno, J. (1984). Musical psychodrama in Paris. *Music Therapy Perspectives, I,* (IV).

Neher, A. (1962). A physiological explanation of unusual behavior in ceremonies involving drums. *Human Biology 34* (2).

Olsen, D. (1983). Symbol and function in South American Indian music. In E. May (Ed.), *Musics of many cultures: An introduction*. Berkeley, CA: University of California Press.

Rider, M. S. (1987). Treating chronic disease and pain with music-mediated imagery. *The Arts in Psychotherapy, 14* (2). 113-120.

Rouget, E. (1985). *Music and trance: A theory of the relations between music and possession*. Chicago: University of Chicago Press.

Tilly, M. (1956, 1977). The therapy of music. In W. McGuire & R. F. C. Hull (Eds.), *C. G. Jung speaking* (pp. 274, 275). Princeton, NJ: Princeton University Press. (Original 1956, *In Memoriam, Carl Gustav Jung*. Privately issued by The Analytical Psychology Club of San Francisco, 1961).

11

Music in Attitudinal Medicine

ARTHUR W. HARVEY

Does music have a role to play in medicine today? I recently visited an elderly patient in the hospital who was nervously awaiting a C.A.T. scan. I placed headphones on her and began to play a tape of baroque music. Within just a few minutes, her respiration slowed, color returned to her face and her *attitude* was transformed from one of panic and fear to one of peace. Music is currently being used in many areas of medicine, including labor and delivery, neonatal care, ICU, CCU, pediatric cardiac catheterization, pre- and post-operative care, coma units, surgery, dentistry, neurology, psychiatry, gerontology, rehabilitation, oncology, pain and stress management, as well as many others.

As in the days of ancient Greece, music as a healing art today is gaining credibility in its partnership with medicine. In the mid-fifteenth century, after the development of printing, physicians learned that Pythagoras had healed the sick by charms, incantations, or music. Plato taught that music alters the soul and the soul in turn alters the body, and Galen used listening to music to provide health-giving activity. For the next several centuries, music was an integral part of medical theory and practice.

Francis Bacon, in an address to King James I, described such an alliance between music and medicine.

This variable composition of man's body hath made it as an instrument easy to distemper; and therefore the Poets did well to conjoin Music and Medicine in Apollo, because the Office of Medicine is but to tune this curious Harp of man's body and to reduce it to Harmony.[1]

Several recent developments in the concept of medicine have facilitated a new attitude towards the roles that music can play in medicine today, as well as "for times to come." Such an attitude is evident at the University of Louisville School of Medicine in the developing Program for the Arts in Medicine, in the Division of Behavioral and Attitudinal Medicine, with which I am associated.

Since the mid-nineteenth century, medical training and practice has focused predominantly on dealing with physical components and the illnesses and diseases that need to be treated for recovery and rehabilitation. While that is still the major component of standard medical practice as it exists today, during the past few decades (coincidentally with the development of the creative arts therapies movement), an awareness of the interconnectedness of mind and body, as well as growing interest in concepts of wellness and preventive medicine, have resulted in new paradigms for the role of music in medicine.

Early in this century, awareness of the connection between mind and illness led to the development of the field of psychosomatic medicine. Evidence that negative thoughts and feelings can contribute to bodily illnesses eventually led to interest in the possibility of positive thoughts and emotive states promoting health. Evolving from awareness of and acceptance of the reality of an interconnectedness of mind and body, behavioral medicine was established, along with psychobiology and most recently psychoneuro-immunology. Each of these current emphases in medical practice places importance on attitudes. Since attitudes are both cognitive and affective functions of the brain/mind which affect the body, and since music has such a powerful effect upon both thinking/feeling and physiological processes, music can have an important role to play in attitudinal medicine.

In a recent article in *The Journal of the American Medical Association*, Norman Cousins wrote that it is necessary in medicine today "to create a balanced perspective, one that recognizes that *attitudes* such as a strong will to live, high purpose, a capacity for festivity"[2] are important in enhancing the environment of treatment. Ellen Langer, in *Psychology Today* stated that "a wide body of recent research has been devoted to investigating the influence of *attitudes* on the immune system, which is thought to be the intermediary between psychological states and physical illness."[3] In *Who Gets Sick: Thinking and Health,* Blair Justice wrote, "What goes on in our heads, then, has far-reaching influence on not only our nervous system but also the immune system, the hormone system and our health."[4] Hinkle and Wolfe at New York Hospital-Cornell Medical Center were among the first researchers to identify what distinguishes those who stay well from those who get sick. After twenty years of studies on several populations, they concluded that "a good *attitude* and ability to get along with other people"[5] characterizes those with a low frequency of illness. Immunologists have theorized for years that stress hormones affect an individual's immunity. Robert Good of Memorial Sloan-Kettering Cancer Hospital was one of the first authorities to recognize that "a positive *attitude*, and a constructive frame of mind can alter our ability to resist infections, allergies, autoimmunities or even cancer."[6] The discovery that our *attitudes*, beliefs and moods influence the chemical messengers that carry on communication among the cells of the nervous, endocrine and immune systems has given us better understanding of both how we get sick and how we get well and maintain good health.

That music is a major contributor to our attitudes today is without question. The awareness of and application of music as a specific intervention in health care for the purpose of facilitating both psychological and physiological health is an idea whose time has come. Charles Darwin, looking back on his seventieth year, said:

If I had my life to live over, I would make it a rule to read some poetry and listen to some music at least once a week, for perhaps the parts of my brain now atrophied would thus have been kept alive through use. The loss of these tastes is a loss of happiness.

Thomas Jefferson wrote, "Music furnishes a delightful recreation for the hours of respite from the cares of the day, and lasts us through life."

Attitudes are changing. Psychiatrist Carl Hammerschlag, as many others, offers a variety of techniques to change the attitudes of patients, including suggesting "that they hike up a mountain . . . ponder the flight of a young eagle . . . sing them a song. . . ."[7] Raymond Bahr, Director of Coronary Care at St. Agnes Hospital, Baltimore, Maryland, asserted that, "Without a doubt, Music Therapy ranks high on the list of modern day management of critical care patients. . . . Its relaxing properties enable patients to get well faster by allowing them to accept their condition and treatment without excessive anxiety." Anaesthesiologist Ralph Spintge, one of the organizers and currently executive secretary of the International Society for Music in Medicine, has been instrumental in documenting the importance of music in medical treatment and thus in providing momentum for the change in attitude concerning its significance. In a recent article he wrote:

Physiological parameters like heart rate, arterial blood pressure, salivation, skin humidity, blood levels of stress hormones like adrenocorticotrophic hormone ACTH, prolactin, human growth hormone HGH, cortisol, beta-endorphine, show a significant decrease under anxiolytic music compared with usual pharmacological premedication. EEG studies demonstrated sleep induction through music in the preoperative phase. The subjective responses of the patients are most positive in about 97% (of 59,000). These patients state that music is a real help to them to relax in the perioperative situation and during surgery in regional anaesthesia.[8]

Although there are many individual and organizational uses of music in medicine today, as well as a growing body of literature supporting the important functions that music can play in health care, a brief examination of several recent publications dealing with mind/body healing either totally omitted references to music or included minimal material dealing with the importance of music in mind/body healing (i.e. *The Healing Brain; Minding the Body, Mending the Mind; The Psychobiology of Mind-Body Healing; Super-immunity;* and *Your Emotions & Your Health: New Dimensions in Mind Body Healing).*[9] Several recent publications by physicians (*Music in Medicine; Rehabilitation, Music and Human Well-Being; The Life Energy in Music; Music and the Brain; Music Therapy in Child Psychosis;* and *Tone Deaf & All Thumbs* as well as an earlier work, *Music & Your Emotions*[10]) give encouragement to the possibilities of music becoming an accepted component of medical practice in Western culture, as it has been in other cultures of the world for centuries.

In a recent publication, Miao Hongshi, M.D., reports on music electrotherapy in China today, as well as music electroacupuncture and music electroacupuncture anesthesia. Doctors in several hundreds of hospitals in China have been studying the uses of music in both functional diseases and the treatment of organic diseases, with very positive results.[11] Research in music applied directly to the body as a vehicle for healing has been studied extensively in Norway, Finland, Germany, England, Denmark and most recently in the United States. Initial development of VibroAcoustic Therapy has indicated its application in a great variety of patient conditions, including: Rett syndrome, autism, spastic conditions, abdominal/colic pains, digestive problems, lumbago, stress-induced depression, muscle cramps, insomnia, circulatory deficiency, as well as other physiological illnesses.[12]

With increasing awareness of cymatics and the principle of entrainment (covered in other sections of this book) providing impetus for the utilization of music as a positive vibrational source in medical application, there is growing interest in many centers around the United States in developing technologies such as Betar, The Genesis System, Somatron, Trilax and Multivib, and using them as one component of medical treatment. Current and future work in bio-vibrational-electromagnetic energy resulting from musical stimuli, or producing musical sound patterns, is certainly a realistic possibility in the near future. Because music as vibrational patterns affect and respond to cellular and sub-cellular vibrations, prescriptive sound patterns may become a part of traditional medical practice in the future, as they have been in Native American, African, Tibetan and other cultures through specific healing chants, songs and tones. A recent publicity release from International Management Group stated, "The Science of Sound can detect life-threatening illnesses two years before conventional medical tests, so proves American Scientist, Dr. Valerie V. Hunt."

In a publication, *The Healing Within: Medicine, Health and Wholeness,* Robin Price elaborates upon the implications of a radionic principle:

The body is a series of harmonies in which dis-harmony is related to dis-ease has led to the possibility that the wrong harmony may be displaced by the harmony appropriate to the affected organ. A practitioner in this advanced field has pointed out that the human body is analogous to a symphony; though every cell is essentially the same, each has its particular function and operates within its own organic system at an optimum harmonic rate. A machine now exists which is said to implant into the misdirected structure the corrected harmonic frequency. By correcting the signal and feeding it back into the affected organ, the machine, it is claimed, can stabilise cases and even reverse them. Cases involving un-alleviated pain, patients wearing pacemakers, and psychopathic cases are not appropriate for this treatment; however, arthritis, stress and tension are said to answer well; also cases of drug addiction, since the drug in question may be safely emulated by frequency and so gradually diminished. It is obvious that if this system is viable, the exchange of one frequency for another may have profound implications for the treatment of certain cancers; this assumption remains to be tested.[13]

That music produces both physiological and psychological changes in individuals is assumed. Mirandola wrote, "Music produces like effects on the mind as good medicine on the body."[14] A classic study was made in 1948 by Alexander Capurso to determine a categorization for moods evoked by music. From a selection of 105 musical compositions most frequently performed, 6 categories of mood effects were determined:

A. Happy, Gay, Joyous, Stimulating, Triumphant
B. Agitated, Restless, Irritating

C. Nostalgic, Sentimental, Soothing, Meditative, Relaxing
D. Prayerful, Reverent
E. Sad, Melancholy, Grieving, Depressing, Lonely
F. Eerie, Weird, Grotesque.

In 1937 Kate Hevner developed a mood wheel, an arrangement of 66 adjectives in 8 related groups, for classifying emotional expressions of musical selections.[15] Most recently the work of Dr. Manfred Clynes in the development of sentic theory has utilized computer science to show 8 essentic forms of emotions, (love, hate, grief, joy, no emotion, reverence, anger and sex) and has developed an explanation of why music evokes emotional states.[16] (See chapters by Clynes in this book.)

Why and how music produces changes in attitudes is discussed in a variety of disciplines as diverse as philosophy, psychology, psychoacoustics, neurology, music therapy and music education. Awareness that music produces attitudinal changes is important. The complexity of the mind/brain/body response to music is illustrated in this description by Aldous Huxley:

Pongioli's blowing, and the scraping of the anonymous fiddlers had shaken the air in the great hall. This moved the air in Lord Edward's membrana tympani; the interlocked malleus, incus, and stirrup bones were set in motion so as to agitate the membrana of the oval window and raise an infinitesimal storm in the fluid of the labyrinth. The hairy endings of the auditory nerve shuddered like weeds in a rough sea; a vast number of obscure miracles were performed in the brain, and Lord Edward ecstatically whispered "Bach!"[17]

Music has the capability of energizing or ennervating, exciting or calming, distracting or focusing, pleasing or irritating, uplifting or degrading, as well as healing or harming. With our current understanding that our psychological state has a direct effect upon our physiological state, and awareness that music affects our psychological state, a strong justification for the need for music to serve many roles in the developing field of attitudinal medicine is evolving.

With the concept of health care moving today toward a more holistic model, and the recognition that wellness is a product of healthy body/mind/spirit interactions, and that medical treatment is effective only when the whole person is treated, music may be an important asset in creating the appropriate environment for healing. Many hospitals have music therapists on staff. Hospitals throughout the world are beginning to provide listening equipment in connection with surgical procedures, offering patients a choice of tapes. Programs such as "Music in Residence" at the Washoe Medical Center in Reno, Nevada, where musicians Susan Mazer and Dallas Smith spend full days in specific units of the hospital presenting live performances, provide a powerful therapeutic tool that affects health care providers and patients, as well as visitors.

Programs where music is an acknowledged contributor in furthering the realization of healing health care consistently report a reduction in the need for pain medication, a reduction in expressed level of frustration of both staff and patients, and an increase in positive attitudes towards involvement in recovery. I initiated an effort to assist attitudinally with the medical staff at the University of Louisville School of Medicine by offering of a lunch-time musical respite at our Genesis Center that I called *Eine Kleine Lunchmusik*. Carlyle wrote:

Give us, O give us the man who sings at his work! Be his occupation what it may, he is equal to any of those who follow the same pursuit in silent sullenness. He will do more in the same time . . . he will do it better . . . he will persevere longer. One is scarcely sensible to fatigue while he marches to music. The very stars are said to make harmony as they revolve in their spheres.

Throughout history there have been accounts of music serving as a vehicle for healing. For music to become an established component of Western health care in the years ahead, widespread application of the following is needed:

1. Medical school education needs to include music as an important component of its program. I created and taught a course on music and medicine for medical students and created a medical school chorus and instrumental ensemble

at the School of Medicine where I taught. In addition I
was invited to speak to medical students on music and
medicine at other medical schools in the United States
as well as in Germany and Australia. Attitudes toward
medical practice begin during medical school.

2. Hospitals need to schedule regular in-service training
sessions for staff dealing with uses of music in health care.
For over fifteen years I have been presenting seminars for
health professionals, including "Music in Health Care,"
"Music and Health," "Therapeutic Uses of Music," and
other related topics, through the College of Allied Health
and Nursing at Eastern Kentucky University, where I have
been professor of music. In addition I helped found Music
for Health Services Foundation, which has sponsored three
national conferences on music and health, where health
professionals and musicians shared creative uses of music
in health care practice. These conferences have resulted
in invitations by hospitals to provide staff training in the
uses of music in their facilities. As attitudes change, practices
change.

3. Musicians need to be as skilled in the science of their
art as they are the art of their science. Understanding
neurophysiological processes, clinical procedures, and
technological possibilities, along with musical competence
and aesthetic sensitivities, is necessary to establish communication credibility with a profession that is as interested
in knowing the *why* as in knowing the *what* and *how* of
music as a vehicle for healing. The Program for the Arts
in Medicine of the Division of Behavioral and Attitudinal
Medicine was established within a school of medicine
under the leadership and inspiration of Joel Elkes, M.D.
This is the only such program I am aware of. It provides
a model for research and validation of musical interventions
in all phases of health care.

4. We need to create and recreate musical works that
take into consideration known effects from timbral, rhythmic,
melodic, harmonic, tonal/modal, and formal elements
of music and their interrelationships. Matching musical
style to perceptual response style may be essential for
healing. Knowledge of vibrational relationships between

frequencies and organic functioning, such as several New Age composers have theorized, may be important to explore. Stylistic effects upon neurological functioning, as postulated by Alfred Tomatis, M.D., with classical music and Georgi Lozanov, M.D., with baroque music, needs to be examined and applied in health care.

Although I have focused on the healing roles of music in medicine, specifically attitudinal medicine, I am aware of and constantly experience music itself functioning as the physician, as it facilitates well-being, both preventive and rehabilitative. Music can be a prescription for stress reduction, sleep, digestion, pain reduction, neurological functioning, muscle stimulation, perceptual clarification, increased energy, affective control and mood regulation.

On a broader scale, music may be a source of healing for interpersonal and intercultural dis-ease by providing a communicative bridge between individuals and cultures. As John Erskine wrote, "Music is the only language in which you cannot say a mean or sarcastic thing." Perhaps the Doobie Brothers understood the message of this book when they sang "Music is the Doctor of My Soul."

Notes

1. Rosalie Rebollo Pratt. "A Brief History of Music and Medicine." in *Rehabilitation, Music and Human Well-Being.* Edited by Mathew H. M. Lee M.D. Saint Louis, Miss.: MMB Music Inc. 1989. p. 1.
2. Norman Cousins. "Intangibles in Medicine: An Attempt at a Balancing Perspective." *The Journal of the American Medical Association.* Vol. 260, No. 11, Sept. 16, 1988. p. 1610.
3. Ellen J. Langer. "The Mindset of Health." *Psychology Today.* April 1989, p. 49.
4. Blair Justice. *Who Gets Sick: Thinking and Health.* Houston: Peak Press. 1987. p. 13.
5. L. E. Hinkle & H. G. Wolff. "Health and the Social Environment: Experimental Investigations." In A. H. Leighton, J. A. Clausen, & R. N. Wilson (Eds.). *Explorations in Social Psychiatry.* New York: Basic Books. 1957. p. 105.
6. R. A. Good. "Forward: Interactions of the body's major networks." In R. Ader (Ed.), *Psychoneuroimmunology.* New York: Academic Press. 1981. p. xvi.

7. Carl A. Hammerschlag. *The Dancing Healers: A Doctor's Journey of Healing with Native Americans.* New York: Harper & Row. 1988. Cited in *Your Personal Best* Vol. 1, No. 6. October 1989. p. 14.

8. Ralph Spintge. "Music as a Physiotherapeutic and Emotional Means in Medicine." *Musik, Tanz Und Kunst Therapie.* 2/3 1988. p. 79.

9. Robert Ornstein and David Sobel. *The Healing Brain.* New York: Simon and Schuster, 1987, Joan Borysenko. *Minding the Body, Mending the Mind.* Reading, Mass.: Addison-Wesley Publishing Co., 1987; Ernest Lawrence Rossi. *The Psychobiology of Mind-Body Healing.* New York: W. W. Norton & Co., 1986; Paul Pearsall. *Superimmunity.* New York: McGraw-Hill Book Co., 1987; Emrika Padus. *The Complete Guide to Your Emotions & Your Health: New Dimensions in Mind/Body Healing.* Emmaus, Pa.: Rodale Press, 1986. (This publication did include a significant number of references to music.)

10. Ralph Spintge MD, Roland Droh MD. *Music in Medicine.* New York: Springer-Verlag. 1986; Mathew H. M. Lee. *Rehabilitation, Music and Human Well-Being.* Saint Louis, Miss.: MMB Inc. 1989; John Diamond, MD. *The Life Energy in Music.* Vol. I, II, III. Valley Cottage, NY: Archaeus Press. 1981; MacDonald Critchley, MD and R. A. Henson, MD. *Music and the Brain.* Springfield, Ill.: Charles C. Thomas, Publisher. 1977; Rolando O. Benenzon, MD. *Music Therapy in Child Psychosis.* Springfield, Ill.: Charles C. Thomas Publisher, 1982; Frank R. Wilson, MD. *Tone Deaf & All Thumbs.* New York: Vintage Books, 1986; Emil A. Gutheil MD, *Music & Your Emotions.* New York: W. W. Norton, 1952.

11. Miao Hongshi M.D. "Music Therapy in China." In Rosalie Rebollo Pratt and Barbara Hesser (Eds.) *Music Therapy and Music in Special Education: The International State of the Art.* Isme Edition Number Three. Saint Louis, Miss.: MMB Inc. 1989.

12. Olav Skille. "VibroAcoustic Therapy." *Music Therapy.* Vol. 8, No. 1. pp. 61-77.

13. Robin Price. *The Healing Within: Medicine, Health and Wholeness.* Monograph Series No. 23. Kent, England: Institute for Cultural Research. 1986. p. 12.

14. Emil A. Gutheil, M.D. *Music & Your Emotions.* p. 56.

15. Kate Hevner. "An Experimental Study of the Affective Value of Sounds and Poetry." *American Journal of Psychology.* Vol. 49. 1937. pp. 419-434.

16. Manfred Clynes, D.Sc. *Sentics: The Touch of Emotions.* New York: Anchor Press/Doubleday. 1978.

17. Dennis C. Monk. "The Mind's Ear." *Designs for Arts in Education.* July/August 1989. p. 17.

III
Potpourri of Music's Potential

There's music in the sighing of the reed;
There's music in the gushing of the rill;
There's music in all things if men had ears.
    Lord Byron, Don Juan

Vibration, pulse, rhythm, tone, color, intensity—these define music and its power in performance. But new fields of study and ways of observing the effect and affect of music and sound are emerging. The "music of the spheres" can now refer to anything from the measurement of individual brain waves to the vibrational wave of the earth rotating around the sun.

This section presents new thoughts, systems and perspectives that use music and sound as healing tools. The viewpoints are varied and individual.

Philosopher Herbert Whone introduces us to music "energy" as creation, word and spirit. Harvey Walter, M.D., explores music's healing powers as shown in the anthroposophical writings of Rudolph Steiner. Jonathan Goldman, director of the Sound Healer's Association, networks us into the great variety of methods being explored in sonic entrainment. Then in my article I summarize some of the work with imagery, music and physiological structure. Jill Purce and Sister Miriam Therese Winter give us personal insight into sound and their lives.

12
Music—The Way Out of the Maze

HERBERT WHONE

In a world of multiplicity "energy," in every sense of the term, has been scattered and peripheralized. It is because of this that human beings, fascinated by peripheral things, have lost touch with their fundamental being. By way of analogy with music, a human being is like a harmonic of a fundamental tone; the harmonic may be far removed from the fundamental tone, but it is part of that tone and would not exist without it. So identified are we with our partial existence ("partial" is another name for a harmonic) that we take the mystery of our life for granted: the countless intelligences operating in the physical body, the mystery of sight and of hearing, are little in our consciousness. And, to bring us to the subject under discussion, the fact that we are capable of uttering sounds, perhaps the greatest mystery of all, likewise does not warrant a moment's thought.

It is strange to contemplate that the creatures of the world might, after all, have remained mute. But this was not in accordance with the Creator's design. Rudimentary sounds peculiar to each creature emerged during the evolutionary process, and these ultimately gave way and were transcended by the complex, all-embracing language(s) used by humans. "In the beginning was the Word," says St. John; now, at a special point, after aeons of preparation there came into existence beings capable of making their own words, their *own* order through sound. What then is the connection between the Word and the word? Both are terms made by humans, but let us try to see the significance of the fact that the same term is used for the Divine and the human levels. To do this we will first consider generally the power that sound has in human life.

We can see that from the beginning the fall or involution undergone by humans as spirit beings is a form of spell-binding; the fascination of the music of the world has lulled them to sleep. Humanity has been enchanted— sung to sleep. In the depths of that condition, we are given the capacity to make our own sound, which is in effect a means of escape, a means of breaking the spell. To disenchant ourselves, or to di-spel the spell, we can do one of two things. In either case, we have to make a sound back into the very material world which has ensnared us. The first thing we can do is to spell out letters, that is, make the sounds of the letters which constitute the name of a given entity, and on the principle of resonance gain power over it. We can see this indicated in the Rumplestiltskin fairy story. This is a complex process, as spoken sounds are impure through the presence of a multitude of clashing harmonics in the resonating chamber, the mouth. The second thing we can do, on a less complex level, is to resonate a given physical object by knowing its precise vibrational frequency. This is most clearly illustrated by taking a relatively uncomplex substance with a pure sound, like a wine glass, and causing it to sing out by forcefully voicing its natural pitch, its own sound. The power over it is made even more remarkable if we increase the vibrational input and over-resonate it so that the glass actually breaks into pieces. In this way, pure music (as indicated in the story of Orpheus and his lyre) has power in the material world. Such vibrational techniques, on the principle of resonance, are now used in a more refined way for treating specific localized illnesses. As we may imagine, such power is dangerous, for an inaccurate frequency input may inadvertently affect areas other than the ones being treated, for all sound has power and resonates something somewhere. For this reason, human beings are not prematurely given secrets they might abuse for egotistic purposes.

What has to be understood, however, is that the very

Sound that is the ground of creation is also capable of destruction, of breaking up physical bondage. Such a concept of *Sound* is limitless in its implications, and has to be seen more as an activity of Mind, in fact as the Word of God, an ordering power which goes down through the planes, ending up in and as physical substance. At this point, as has been pointed out, a remarkable thing occurs: the created life forms, vibrating internally at their own particular frequencies, begin the movement to break out of that encapsulated state, to free themselves from it, to make their own small sound. This is the magic key we have to bear in mind in our reflection upon the sound which ultimately came to be spoken, sung and played by humanity. It is a key of true magic.

If we reflect for a moment we can see that the effect of any sound upon us is truly remarkable. Once I observed a herd of reluctant pigs being goaded into a waiting van; the noise was almost unbearable, except to those working with it and immured to it. Shortly after that, at a certain abbey early on a spring morning every bird in the vicinity seemed to have congregated for a glorious song of joy. One might almost describe what I heard as sonic embodiments of the difference between hell and heaven. Certainly one would not lull a child to sleep by the former, or rouse an army to battle through the latter. There is an appropriate sound, it seems, to all feelings, joys, fears, hates, in fact to the whole gamut of inner life. What I am affirming is simply that music has power, that sound has the power to affect us all at different levels of our being. The question is, what constitutes that power?

At this point we can look at the power inherent in the spoken word, in the vowels or consonants normally used, not forgetting the connection between the Word and the small word. Let us look at some of the sounds employed. For example, the sound of the letter *R* is not soothing; we could disturb calm or focused attention by making at close range a continuous *R* sound rolled with the tongue. No other sound is more likely to fragment psychologically or physically; an analogy in life is the pneumatic drill breaking up concrete. On the other hand, were we to be in a lethargic or stupefied condition, an input of *RRRR*s might be quite useful to break through our inertia—more efficacious perhaps than medicine. At the other extreme, in the sound of the letter *M* we have essentially an inner hum, a vibratory energy circling within the substance and finding release only through the nose. Clearly we cannot make much impact on the outer world by the repetition of this sound. *M*, in fact, affirms the vibrating life of substance. It is a female letter, as in *ma, matter, matrix, mum, "keep mum,"* and so on. We cannot stimulate activity by a letter *M*; an orator with an orbit of *M* sounds would have no spell. But we may, on the other hand, counter overstimulation or mental excitement and soothe disturbed emotions by a gentle *hmmmmmm* sound. Similarly the sound of *H* is utterly different from the sound of *G. G* is a sound that makes an almost total block of power at the throat level. It denotes the fixity of earth, the hard unyielding compaction of matter which is the spirit's tomb. H is a sound unqualified by hardness, not different from the breath that is the life force which keeps in us the connection with the outer cosmos and the inner self. All consonants may be looked at in a similar way.

With the vowels or basic sonants, we need to start from an open *A* sound, as in *arm*. From this unmodified sound, one of two things may happen. Either the sound may be constricted by the tongue into the top of the head (as *i* in hit, or *e* in feet) which has in it an element of pain, or it may be pushed out from the abdomen, the very antithesis of the head sound. The tight *i* is, as creation itself, a constricting factor on energy, and the *u* is the energy pushed out of that constriction. Taking *A* as the central sound of the heart, we may see here the connection with the threefold being of humans, head, heart and will or thinking, feeling and doing. We are suggesting that the sounds people make are not arbitrary but a natural expression of their feelings about their condition on earth, and also that these sounds are tied up with universal principles of which humanity is a reflection and an embodiment. We are suggesting, moreover, that at root level, the meaning of these sounds are and have been at one time, common to all people. This is why words of power in different religions have common elements: they derive from the common sounds and wisdom of antiquity. Existentially, of course, we find confusing differences between languages due to many factors; essentials have been watered down and error has occurred in every language. Consequently, now we have to aim at finding roots in order to understand the meaning of the words we use. We are in the midst of a confusion of tongues, of religious beliefs, and of personal differences of many kinds. All levels exist simultaneously; the more peripheral something is, the more misleading. In all things it is necessary to find roots.

We have said that the ability to make sound is, in a sense, a way of return. Our relationship with the world is inevitably a dual one; while expressing joy at the creation of which we are a part, we experience at the same time a profound sense of loss. In a deep sense, creation is a restraint upon freedom. In music we express the dance of life, but also the yearning to recover what has been lost. We may pray silently from the heart, but we express the prayer through our ability to produce sound via our voice or an external instrument, which is merely an extension of the human instrument. The minor third of folk music testifies to this common yearning or act of prayer. Of course, any music gives voice to *all* the conflicts inherent in human life, at best offering a sense of their resolution. Small humanity pitted against the majesty of the universe occasionally bridges the gap, and art has fulfilled its function. Resolution is indispensible to human well-being. Composers may have extended music's frontiers beyond the harmonic system, but the harmonic system is indigenous to and reflective of cosmic order: it is based on mathematics and ratio, and above all on resolution from discord, as in the moving of notes back to a tonic center or the returning of foreign keys back to the home one. The principles inherent in one stretched string cannot be effaced from our consciousness, which holds within it nature's principles of structure, which for us is beauty.

For those who are non-musicians, it may be well to say that simple intervals, such as the octave, fifth, and fourth, are nothing more than simple frequency ratios: 1/2, 2/3, and 3/4 respectively. They are pleasing to the ear because of this proportion. It is only when frequency ratios are inexact giving complex ratios such as 223/239.8 that they become non-beautiful, which is why a slightly out of tune violin drives us to distraction: if played in tune, it is at least tolerable, even if unmusical. The power of sound has certainly been abused for upon such principles tortures have been perpetrated. Again, however, in the question of intervals, we are faced with universals. On this objective level, for instance, the nature of and the power in the perfect fifth affects us in the same way; though subjectively, due to imposed tradition or personal experience, the sound of the fifth makes us laugh, cry, or become paralyzed by fear. Behind all differences are roots; behind the particulars are universals.

We have said that the ability to make sound is our greatest gift, that our small sound is a way of return to the all-comprehensive Sound, which is the Spoken Word, the Word of God. What we see is our imperfect understanding: it is the creative artist in us that struggles from the human condition to make that rare breakthrough to the suprahuman wordless level. Such breakthroughs, catching the eternal level, redeem the whole of human existence: it is why performers have a special role in life, and why the aim of all artists in whatever sphere is to refine and refine again their work. Of course there are as many signatures as there are people; the sound *is* the person. One may have imagination but lack clarity, or have impetuous drive but lack sensitivity. The permutations are limitless. Acquiring a technique in the world of music is a much misunderstood term. If there is a technique at all, it is the drawing out and integrating of all parts of the person.

For the musician, however, the most potent way out of the locked situation is in making music that gives the illusion that there never was a lock in the first place. The key that does the unlocking is in the word "play." Clearly, with regard to our existence, rigid acceptance of the inertia of the physical world is death to the spirit: it is necessary to see that the physical is itself an illusion, that all is encapsulated spirit. That gives us room to move, to play; we are not taken in, and we have a light relationship with our own substance, which enables us to escape the trap. In like manner players of music transcend limits layed down and do not conform to fixed formulae but make their way out through unpredictable factors such as portamento, vibrato, the holding of points of tension, the suspense inherent in breathing, and in a sense of flow which is the true meaning of rhythm. Their sense of play has nothing to do with precise order or with unformulated power, but belongs to feeling or sensitivity. These levels of order and power are necessary, but it is feeling that relates the poles and effects a reconciliation between them.

In music, therefore, we live among and are moved by two worlds, one of mathematics and immutable universals, and the other of the expression of the human condition, in which we effect a release through a play which is possible only through the integration of the parts of our being. Here too, in the latter, we are dealing with factors that are common to all people: there may be personal differences, but artists, willy-nilly, are the vehicle of laws much higher than themselves. They cannot avoid, of course, revealing personal differences. The player of a violin is particularly vulnerable in this sense, as that instrument is the most sensitive register of all the player is as a human being.

It is not generally understood how much the bowed instrument, in its perfected seventeenth-century form, is a symbol of fundamental principles, especially that of the Father-Mother aspect of the Creator. The bow is obviously the masculine initiating force, and the violin essentially the feminine receiving agent, merely an enclosed volume of air awaiting stimulus from the bow. Once contact is made, creation ensues, the fingers differentiating the sound as the Son differentiates the universe. The question is, what sort of sound is made as a result of the connection between the two? What is the nature of their relationship?

To produce a beautiful sound violinists must draw upon, and out of themselves, two different things: initiative transmitted via the bow, and sensitivity in the response to that initiative via the instrument. These are two aspects of the player's being, and in the balance between power, which is not crudely aggressive, and receptive substance, which is not inert but alive and responsive, each player is seeking to unite his or her own masculine and feminine sides. In the finest players the bow and instrument appear to be working as a unit. Always sound players make externalizes the degree to which they have related these poles in themselves; it is a polarity deriving from the Father-Mother, Spirit-Matter aspects of the Godhead, and there can be no greater mystery than that relationship.

It is obvious from this that our sensitivity to our own substance is an important issue, especially in the field of playing a stringed instrument. Without this sensitivity how can the clarity of thought (technique), the feeling life, and the energy operate. The fact that the parts of the violin are named anthropomorphically—belly, back, ribs, neck, waist—is an indication of a mystery which is not normally thought important enough for inclusion in textbooks. Its implications, however, are limitless.

More directly of course, all men and women make their own unique sound via their voices. The threefold structure—heart, head, will—must reveal itself in all its subtleties. Such sounds are being emitted and received by human beings every moment of the waking day. We are surrounded and permeated by sound; in fact, on the level we have discussed, we *are* sound. The question of what we allow to be transmitted from ourselves to others, and what we allow to enter our own systems is everyone's privilege to decide. I suggest—to sum up a subject that needs an extended symphony rather than a brief sketch—that the purer the quality of the music played and the more consciously used are our words, the more we may relate to the Spoken Word and the nearer we may draw to the fundamental Tone (t-one) to which all belong and all will return.

13

Music as a Means of Healing:
Rudolph Steiner's Curative Education

H. WALTER, M.D.

A doctor who tries to penetrate into the nature of the arts from the standpoint of Spiritual Science will find music and its significance in healing a source of great inspiration.

He will be filled with a sense of reverence for music when he learns from Spiritual Science that the origin and well-spring of the sounds is the spiritual world—the true home of man as a being of soul and spirit; and when he realizes that man—the microcosm formed and created from out of the cosmos—is, in body, soul and spirit, himself music.*

That music occupies a special place among the arts is still realized today. There are very few who are wholly devoid of any feeling for music. Subconsciously we realize its heavenly origin and that its forces have an uplifting, freeing and healing influence upon the soul. Indeed forces that are akin to the soul and spirit of man work more directly in music than in the other arts.

The influences of music were experienced much more concretely in the epoch which lasted until the Middle Ages, when the seven Liberal Arts were cultivated, when Grammatica, Rhetorica, Dialectica, Arithmetica, Geometria, Astronomia and Musica were recognized as *Beings* who could lead the seeking soul of man to the Goddess Natura whom they served.

---

*This article was written before the use of inclusive language began. "Man" refers to men and women, all humankind, and "he" and "him" to anyone.

For the man of those times, an understanding of music was a stage upon the path of knowledge which he strove to reach and where the relationships between Nature, Universe and Man were revealed to him. So too, music was something that the doctor of those days could apply in his work of healing, either out of inner knowledge which he himself possessed or out of tradition.

When we go back into still more ancient times, we find that in the Mysteries, music was also used as a help in the healing art.

The Mysteries indeed were centres for the cultivation of music, as we realize when we think of Bardism. Bardism was closely connected with the Druidic Sun-Mysteries and the last echoes of Bardic art lasted on into the Middle Ages, albeit then in a decadent form. The Bards were poets, minstrels, teachers and healers—men who had actual experience of the divine-spiritual world through the art of music, and so were able to be channels for the power and wisdom of the Gods to flow into mankind. Again we are reminded of David, who as an initiate of the Mysteries was such a master of the art of music that he was able to soothe and quell the rage of King Saul.

In the Greek Mysteries, where Apollo, the father of Aesculapius, was honoured both as the Sun-God, the God of healing and music, the element of music was a means of education and was widely applied in the art of healing. Men still felt the presence of the healing and all-purifying Sun-forces in the music of that age.

The lyre—called the 'attribute' of Apollo— was regarded as a kind of symbol of the human body, upon which the Sun-Spirit played heavenly melodies in order that man's soul and body might be formed in beauty and that the unfolding of his forces of soul and spirit might be strengthened.

It was everywhere realized in those times that the Apollonian art—which included singing and the playing stringed instruments—had a most beneficial effect upon the soul and body of man and harmonized his inner being.

The phrygian legend of Marsyas tells us that Silenus—who carried off the flute discarded by Pallas Athene and challenged Apollo to a contest in which he (Silenus) was vanquished—was doomed to suffer bodily torments. This legend portrays a transition from an earlier to a later evolutionary stage of humanity with its different methods of musical culture.

It indicates, as well, the contrast between wind and stringed instruments, and how by their very nature they correspond to a different interpenetration of the physical, bodily elements by the soul and spirit. Only when there is inner balance and harmony between the bodily nature and the soul and spirit can man be healthy in the true sense of the word.

Now these Apollonian Mysteries of which Greek Mythology contains the echoes, lead us back to still more ancient times, when the evolution of man was impelled and guided by lofty Spiritual Beings. For in the age of Greek culture it was no longer possible, as it was in times of hoary antiquity, for man to rise directly to the spiritual worlds where the speech of the Gods, the Divine Creators, resounded in the Music of the Spheres; the Gods had themselves to come down to the Earth and guide the evolution of man onwards to the future.

Rudolf Steiner once spoke in a lecture of how, in pre-Grecian times, one of these Beings influenced Europe, inaugurating a wonderful culture of music, which was a mighty impulse in the further development of the human race. This Being was the real founder of Bardism. Rudolf Steiner told us further that all traditions which, later on, the Greeks associated with the God Apollo, point back to him. What he was able to impart to civilization through the cultivation of music, was to be the germ for the future development of man's faculty of *logical thought*.

This happened in the age we call the Third Post-Atlantean epoch, when the *Sentient Soul* in man unfolded, and consequently when he was particularly sensitive to all that could still be communicated to him through music, from the spiritual world.

The *Intellectual Soul* did not begin to unfold in man until the following epoch—that of Greek culture. And we can see clear evidences of how, side by side with the wonderful musical culture associated with the names of Homer,

Orpheus and Apollo, the musical element in itself began to be an object of study to the rationalizing, reasoning mind of man. We have an example of this in Pythagoras who taught the laws of music in his school but always, of course, from the point of view that as cosmic laws they are at the basis of all creation, of Man as well as of Nature.

This was a decisive moment in human history, for it denoted a transition from such remnants of ancient clairvoyant faculties as were still possessed by man, to the on-coming period of the development of the *Consciousness Soul* in which we are still living today.

In the course of this epoch man was to learn to know himself as a self-conscious, independent individual in the world and consequently to create music out of his own inner experiences, out of his individual soul and spirit. And today we stand at a point in the development of consciousness where from the inner realization of his own inner freedom, man must enter into a new understanding of and relation to music.

Anthroposophy has indicated the way to this. In certain lectures on music, Rudolf Steiner gave the fundamental principles which showed how music can be used in medicine and in education, and the following paragraphs are intended briefly to explain how we have begun to apply these principles in our methods of Curative Education.

Wonderfully illuminating was the picture given by Dr. Steiner in these lectures on music when he spoke of the heaven of fixed stars and the Zodiac as being the heavenly 'instrument' upon which cosmic melodies are played by the Planetary Gods as they move in their orbits.

Again he gave a picture, showing how our faculty of speech—which is to be regarded as a later development of a primeval, wholly *musical* mode of expression—arose when the soul of man (of which the vowel sounds are the expression) began to form the consonant sounds out of the forces of the body which was itself created by the Zodiacal forces.

And so as man learnt to sing and then to speak in the course of the ages, his soul and his Ego revealed themselves more and more through his physical body. The physical body of man is the most perfect musical instrument. Its range of possibilities is infinite. As an individual Ego man must learn gradually to master and use this body as his instrument and servant.

The process whereby, in the course of evolution, the soul and self of man take possession of his bodily nature is also reflected in music, which through the ages has developed into the forms we know today. Rudolf Steiner has said that it was only towards the end of the Graeco-Latin epoch of civilization that man began to experience the interval of the *third* as well as that of the *fifth.*

The reason for this is that by that time the soul was able to descend more deeply into the body, consequently man was then beginning to distinguish himself as an *individual* being of soul and spirit from the universe around, and to experience himself as an entity within the limits of his skin. This gave rise to his experience of the interval of the third in music.

From now onwards, man was conscious of the source of musical creative power *within* his soul, and music became an expression of his own sentient life. Major and minor became the modes of expression in music for joy and sorrow, for the inner expansion of the soul (major) and a submergence of the soul in the physical body—a process connected with pain (minor). Experience of the interval of the *seventh* leads back to old Atlantean times, whereas man of the present age is only just beginning really to have some experience of the *octave.*

It is easy to perceive from these indications how music can be adapted and used for healing and educational purposes, if, that is to say, we have true insight into the stages of the child's development and the various tendencies to illness in the growing human being.

Through the different periods of life the child has to recapitulate briefly what the whole race has had to develop in the long course of the different epochs of civilization. Diseases are disturbances in this evolutionary process— caused either because the being of soul and spirit descends too deeply into the bodily nature or else because the soul and spirit can only unite inadequately or imperfectly with the body.

H. Walter, M.D.

Against such tendencies to illness, especially in the age of childhood when the processes of development are still in full flow, we have a significant healing agent in music.

Think, first of all, of the child up to the seventh year of life. Through birth he has received his physical body which on the one side has been built up according to cosmic law during embryonic life, but in which, on the other side, the forces of heredity are interwoven.

The physical body serves the child as a kind of model which—up to the time of the change of teeth—has to be transformed by the forces of soul and spirit into as suitable an instrument as possible for the individuality. The individuality—the soul and spirit—must master the forces of heredity.

This first life-period represents, in a certain sense, a repetition of that stage of evolution when, with the help of Divine Powers, human souls began to adapt themselves to and enter into possession of the bodies that had been created for them, while they lived, for the most part, in spiritual worlds.

At this age (up to the seventh year) the child is, in his whole being a sense-organ, because the 'sentient body' is still hovering around the organism; through his senses the child is still closely interwoven with all that is happening in the environment. Every impression—and through the impressions forces from beyond the earth—all press inwards and become involved in the process of bodily transformation.

Hence at this age the child is highly sensitive to music. Music that is suited to his age comes, as it were, to meet and mingle with his soul, and, as a result, his forces of soul and spirit are awakened and supported in such a way that through the senses, i.e., from the head, they can work down into the bodily organization and give rise to healthy, formative impulses. At this age of life, therefore, we have a most valuable agent in music when we find evidences of disturbances in the processes of development and growth, difficulties in walking or speaking, indeed even when actual malformations have existed from birth.

Music can be used in the education of such children to support and strengthen the processes of healing. Melodies composed on the old pentatonic scale will be particularly suitable for purposes of Curative Education because the child, with its dreamy existence, is as it were borne along by the surrounding world, and since its organism is not fully prepared, cannot really experience the interval of the third. If we sing rhyming songs composed on the pentatonic scale and accompanied by the lyre to a child whose soul longs to persist in a dreamlike existence remote from the Earth, we shall be able to stimulate him to take delight in the world around.

We speak to the soul of such a child by this music and the soul begins to glow at the prospect of the earthly life it is facing. The life-forces begin to stir in the limbs and we can strengthen this process still further by playing music with strong rhythm and beat to the child, or letting him make the movements of Eurhythmy with his arms and hands to the accompaniment of the music. This promotes the life-forces in the limbs and metabolic system and lays a healthy foundation for the later development of the *will*— which as we know is intimately connected with the metabolic processes.

Not until the ninth year of life is it normal for a child to be mature enough really to experience the interval of the third as it exists in our modern scale. At the age of nine, the soul has descended more deeply into the body and the child begins to be aware of himself as an individual being within his organism.

If we let a child of this age listen to the harmonies of major and minor chords, we shall be able to bring inner balance into the soul's relationship to the body on the one side and to the outer world on the other. The harmonies will work through the senses and influence the development of the faculty of speech.

Gradually, for instance, we shall begin to pass over from major to *minor* keys in the case of a child who cannot bring himself sufficiently into connection with his body. On the other hand we shall work more with *major* keys in the case of a child who has, as it were, sunk too deeply into his bodily nature and hence takes little interest in the outer world. This interest in the outer world should normally awaken between the ninth and tenth years and go on developing until the age of puberty.

Even in disturbances which express themselves in irregularities in breathing and in blood circulation we shall be able to use music as a healing agent, during the years when, as we know, the child's rhythmic system is unfolding and developing.

If we then add the experience of the *octave* in education and for purposes of healing, the child's development is still further promoted. For as Rudolf Steiner has said, the experience of the octave—which is the repetition of the tonic at a higher level—will help the child on the one side to strengthen his inner being as a citizen of the Earth, and so on the other side to rise above the lower elements in his being, to free his higher Self and thus master and control the still unpurified desires and passions arising in his inner life. In this sense, full and complete experience of the octave in music is a thing of the future.

Thus all the elements of music can be used to assist the development of the child between the ages of seven and fourteen, when together with the inner unfolding of the soul, the first germs of the faculties of thinking, feeling and willing are beginning to quicken.

We can use the whole scale, with the different intervals and keys; we can use melody to which, above all, the child's nervous system will respond; we can use rhythm which stimulates the inner forces of will in the very limbs themselves; and we can also use major and minor chords to guide the feeling into the right channels and bring harmonizing influences to bear upon the soul and thence upon the breathing and circulation of the blood.

Even a healthy child of this age needs music to assist the development of his powers of soul, and as for a sick child, the more varied the possibilities for experiencing music, the better, whether it be by listening, by learning himself to sing or play such instrumental music as is suited to the needs of the individual soul.

We shall bear in mind, above all in the care and education of ailing children, that the different musical instruments, like the different parts of the physical body, will help the soul to express different moods, also that the various *kinds* of instrumental music appeal to the soul in different ways.

So, for instance, all percussion instruments—used in an orchestra for the emphasizing of rhythm and beat—stimulate the will-activity in the limb movements, together with the delicate metabolic processes that are involved.

Music played on the lyre or kindred instruments will tend rather in the direction of strengthening the forces in the inner being which press on to become tone and word and are related, chiefly, to the *head*-system.

Wind instruments as the bearers of the melody proper and stringed instruments (violins, etc.) as the expression of the harmonic elements, have a particular connection with the ebbing and flowing life of *feeling*, hence with the upward and downward flowing breath and stream of blood with their foci in the middle, rhythmic system of the human being.

Further possibilities of music as applied in Curative Education have been revealed in the indications given by Rudolf Steiner for certain exercises in Speech and Tone Eurhythmy—the new Art of Movement inaugurated by him. Again, for the treatment of sick children, we give special exercises in *Curative Eurhythmy*. It would lead too far afield in this article to enter more deeply into a description of these exercises or to speak in greater detail of their effect upon the formative, rhythmic and harmonizing processes in the being of man. An introductory chapter on the subject will be found in *Fundamentals of Therapy*, by Rudolf Steiner and Dr. Ita Wegman.

From what has been said in this brief survey, however, it will be clear what far-reaching possibilities are contained in music for Therapy and Curative Education, if we are able to unfold a delicate insight into what is lacking in a child who is ailing in body and soul.

What has been said here, by way of example, is merely intended to indicate principles which have already proved their worth to teachers and educationists. Starting from these principles, all manner of ways open out before doctors and those engaged in the work of Curative Education, enabling them to promote health in the whole being of children whose development of body and soul would otherwise be arrested or stunted.

This work has many joys in store, for again and again we find such children blossoming forth in their whole being when their souls are warmed, strengthened and developed by music. Music is indeed a 'food of heaven' for the soul of man.

We have tried and are trying in our work of Curative Education to apply all the indications given by Rudolf Steiner in lectures and personal conversations on the subject of music as a healing agent. Treatment of this kind needs infinite patience because in most cases results must necessarily be slow in coming, but although as yet we are still at the initial stages, the experience already behind us is a most wonderful encouragement to continue our work in the light of these teachings.

14
Sonic Entrainment*

JONATHAN S. GOLDMAN

All life consists of rhythmic processes. From the simple pulsations of a single-cell organism to the rising and falling of our breath, life is filled with rhythm. This rhythm is also called "periodicity," meaning that the activity of something falls in cycles.

Much of life is directed by the external rhythms of nature. For example, the earth spins on its axis and rotates around the sun, and around our moon orbits the earth. We attune ourselves to the cycles of the sun and the moon, following the different rhythms they create. With day and night, different behavior is created; we usually get up with daylight and go to sleep at night. When our light-dark cycle is disturbed, as when we take a long jet flight, our ability to function in the new environment is affected for a day or two. We call this "jet lag." Different behavior due to rhythm also occurs for the different seasons of the year and the response of nature to this. Not only our sleep patterns, but our eating patterns, digestive patterns, even our harvesting and mating patterns are affected by the rhythms of these cycles.

Sound and Frequency

Sound can be understood as being rhythmic. Sound takes

*Rearranged and edited from a presentation at IV International MusicMedicine Symposium, 1989, at Rancho Mirage, California.

the form of waves, which are measured in cycles per second (hertz or hz). This periodicity is rhythmic in nature. Each cycle of a wave may be recognized as a pulse of sound. Each individual frequency that we measure may be understood as being rhythmic, for the number of cycles per second that make up that frequency creates a rhythm. Low notes pulse much slower than high notes. The lowest note on a piano produces a frequency that vibrates at 27.5 hz; the highest note on a piano vibrates at 4,186 hz.

The range of hearing for the human ear varies immensely. The upper range for "normal" hearing is between 16,000 and 20,000 hz. The bottom limit of what we can hear is around 16 hz. We cannot actually hear very slow pulsed notes, below the threshold of hearing, as single tones, but we can perceive them as being rhythmical in nature. These extremely low frequencies (called ELFs) sometimes can even be counted. In particular, sounds pulsed in the range of 0.1 hz to 8 hz are perceived as being rhythmic in nature. Events slower than this are not perceived as part of an ongoing rhythm, while faster events are heard as a single tone.

Entrainment and Resonance

Entrainment is an aspect of sound that is closely related to rhythms and the way these rhythms affect us. It is a phenomenon of sound in which the powerful rhythmic vibrations of one object will cause the less powerful vibrations of another object to lock in step and oscillate at the first object's rate. This phenomenon of nature has to do with the conservation of energy. It seems that nature finds it more economical in terms of energy to have periodic events that are close enough in frequency to occur in phase or in step with each other.

An excellent example of entrainment is illustrated by Itzhak Bentov in his book *Stalking the Wild Pendulum.* If you have a room full of pendulum-type grandfather clocks and start the pendulums in motion at different times, they will all swing differently. However, if you walk out of this room and come back the next day, you will find that all the pendulums are swinging together at the same rate. This locking in step of rhythms is entrainment. It was discovered by the Dutch scientist Christian Huygens in 1665.

Entrainment is actually an aspect of resonance. Resonance may be defined as the frequency at which an object most naturally wants to vibrate. One object may set another object into motion if it shares the same resonant frequency. If, for example, you strike a tuning fork of 100 cycles per second and bring it near another tuning fork of that same frequency, the second tuning fork will be set in motion. Even though it has not been struck, the second fork will begin to vibrate and sound merely by being in the same field as the vibrating tuning fork.

We have all seen a singer break a glass with his or her voice. This is another example of resonance. This also occurs between two guitar strings, one struck and one unstruck. Resonance is a cooperative phenomenon between two objects that share the same frequency. With resonance you are meeting the natural vibrations of an object with its own vibrations, thereby setting it into motion. Thus resonance may be conceived of as being passive in nature.

Entrainment, on the other hand, seems to be active. With entrainment you are changing the natural oscillatory patterns of one object and replacing them with the different oscillatory patterns of another object. You are actively changing the vibrations (the frequency or rhythm) of one object to another rate.

The oscillators of television sets, radio receivers and other similar equipment lock on to each other and entrain. With television sets, when you turn the knobs you are adjusting the frequency of your set's oscillators to match the frequency of the station's oscillators. When the frequencies come close to one another, they suddenly lock, as if they "want" to pulse together. Usually, the fastest oscillator will force the slower ones to operate at its pace. Living things are like television sets in that they also oscillate; they pulse, they vibrate, they have rhythm. These rhythms of life allow for entrainment.

Entrainment is found throughout nature. Fireflies blinking on and off entrain with each other. Female college roommates often have menstrual cycles that synchronize together.

Muscle cells from the heart, when they move closer together, suddenly shift in their rhythm and start pulsing together, perfectly synchronized.

This entrainment also takes place when two people have a good conversation. Their brain waves oscillate synchronously. Such entrainment is seen in the relationship between students and their professors. Psychotherapists and clients entrain with each other, as do preachers and their congregation.

Within our own bodies, we are constantly locking in our own rhythms. Our heart rate, respiration and brain waves all entrain to each other. Slow down your breath, for example, and you slow down your heart beat and your brain waves. Conversely, if you are able to slow down your brain waves, you can affect your heart rate and respiration. This is one of the principles of biofeedback.

It has been found that the frequencies of pulse, breathing and blood circulation, as well as their combined activities, all function harmonically. That is, their rhythms are strictly coordinated in whole number ratios—two to one, three to two.

Brain Waves

Our brain waves pulsate and oscillate at particular frequencies that can be measured, just like sound waves, in cycles per second. There are four basic delineations of different brain wave states, based upon the cycles per second of the brain. They are:

Beta waves—from 14 to 20 hz. They are found in our normal waking state of consciousness. Beta waves are present when our focus of attention is on activities of the external world.

Alpha waves—from 8 to 13 hz. They occur when we daydream and are often associated with a state of meditation. Alpha waves become stronger and more regular when our eyes are closed.

Theta waves—from 4 to 7 hz. They are found in states of high creativity and have been equated to states of consciousness found in much shamanic work. Theta waves also occur in state of deep meditation and sleep.

Delta waves—from .5 to 3 hz. They occur in states of deep sleep or unconsciousness. Some of the newer brain wave work indicates that a state of deep meditation produces Delta waves.

Two other delineations of brain-wave activity have been noted by some researches:

High Beta—from 23 to 33 hz. They are associated with hyperactivity and some types of anxiety.

K Complex—over 33 hz. They usually occur in short bursts and are often associated with the "aha" moments, when there is a sudden integration of ideas or experiences.

External Rhythms and Internal Processes

As the functions of the human body can entrain to each other, it is possible to use external rhythms to affect the internal mechanism of heart rate, respiration and brain wave activity. This ability to affect internal rhythms by external means seems fairly logical and matter of fact. Yet research into this area did not make its way into scientific journals until the 1970s, when studies began to report that resonance and entrainment of bodily processes can occur in response to external sound and musical rhythms. In his paper "On the Effects of Lullabies" Johannes Kneutgen reported on the soothing effects of lullabies played for infants and noted that breathing rhythms became synchronized with the rhythm of the music. A paper by Janet and Hobart Landreth called "Effects of Music on Physiological Response" reported that heart rate changes were directly related to changes in tempo.

One series of extensive studies by Harrer and Harrer called "Music, Emotion and Autonomic Function" explored some of the effects that emotional musical experiences have on the autonomic nervous system, including blood pressures, pulse rate, respiration, galvanic skin response and muscle tension. The authors found that heart rate was sensitive to both music volume and rhythm. They also found that some subjects tended to synchronize either their heart beat or their respiratory rhythm to the music.

In 1980, Sheila Ostrander and Lynn Schroeder's book *Superlearning* brought to the public some awareness of the potential abilities of music to entrain. They examined the Lozanov Method of education, that originated in Bulgaria. In part of the program music is used to help induce states of consciousness effective in heightening the learning process. Music pulsed at about 60 beats per minute was found to be helpful in inducing an alpha state.

Lozanov utilized baroque music in his work. Almost immediately after the book appeared, sales of baroque music climbed dramatically, due to its use in various learning acceleration programs. However, close examination of the Lozanov Method revealed that only the adagio sections of certain baroque pieces were effective. In Bulgaria Lozanov had limited access to music. It has since been found that much "New Age" music is pulsed at this 60 beats per minute and is as effective as baroque music in entraining brain waves in listeners.

These cited studies of the 1970s, as well as information in *Superlearning*, did not seem to contain conclusive data about the ability of external rhythms to entrain internal rhythms. An external rhythm of 60 beats per minute should reduce the heart rate and a much faster rhythm should raise it, but the change was not always directly proportional; 60 musical beats per minute would not always produce 60 heart beats per minute. For example, some heart beats might go down from 72 to 64 beats per minute, and others might reduce to 68. This differentiation makes data for certain research studies inconclusive, though it does not rule out the ability of external rhythms to entrain internal rhythms.

It is also important to understand that different individuals being tested had the ability consciously to fight against external rhythms and not be affected by entrainment to them. An additional factor is that the strength of response to the entraining rhythm may vary from person to person.

Monroe's Entrainment of Brain Waves

During the time much of this research on the various effects of external rhythms and heart beat was being conducted in universities and medical centers, a great deal of private research was being conducted on using, not specific rhythms to entrain heart beat, but specific frequencies to entrain the brain. This work was pioneered by Robert Monroe of the Monroe Institute.

Robert Monroe was a business executive with a background in broadcasting. He was director of the Mutual Broadcasting System and owner of a group of radio stations and cable television corporations in the southeast. When Monroe began having spontaneous out-of-body experiences in the 60s, he started private research into the effects of different frequencies on various states of consciousness. Part of Monroe's experience with out-of-body travels involved hearing different frequencies which he felt triggered the experiences. He felt that sound somehow could play a role in helping others achieve similar states of consciousness, and with the help of a research team, he set out to discover if he could control or drive the brain with sound waves.

Through trial and error and probably a lot of intuition, Monroe discovered that specific frequencies could produce entrainment of brain waves. He found that, much like a glass resonated by a pure tone, the brain resonated when bombarded with pulsing sound waves. Monroe called this a *frequency following response*, or FFR, and patented this effect in 1975.

The frequencies Monroe used to entrain the brain were in the same spectrum as the brain waves themselves—from .5 hz to about 20 hz. These are frequencies that the human ear is incapable of hearing. However, working with a psycho-acoustic phenomenon called beat frequencies, Monroe found that it was possible to create very low frequencies from much higher sound.

At the same time that Monroe was doing this work, Dr. Gerald Oster, a biophysicist at the Mt. Sinai School of Medicine in New York, was independently investigating the effects of this beat phenomenon. The phenomenon is this: If you use two independent sound sources, for example a tuning fork of 100 cycles per second and another of 108 cycles per second, they produce a tone that waxes and wanes in a pulsing wah-wah-wah sound or beat. The rapidity of the beat equals the difference between the two frequencies. In the above illustration, between the two tuning forks of 100 and 108, you would create an 8 cycle per second beat frequency. If the sound comes from an external source, such as a loudspeaker, the beats can be heard with both ears or with only one ear, which is called a "monaural" beat frequency. The phenomenon of beat frequencies is described in many psycho-acoustic journals.

If the frequencies of the two sound sources are applied separately, one to each ear, a "binaural" beat frequency is created. This beat frequency is not an actual sound, but only a frequency difference between the two actual sounds. This sound is "heard" within the brain itself; the binaural beat frequency is created by both brain hemispheres working simultaneously. Thus, in his attempt to discover a technique to entrain the brain, Monroe found a way to sonically synchronize the left and right hemispheres. In thousands of experiments using an EEG to monitor the brain waves of people hearing a different signal in each ear, he verified that binaural beats could indeed entrain or drive brain waves. The entrainment or frequency following response did not take place only in the area of the brain responsible for hearing, or only in the left and right hemispheres; the entire brain resonated, the waveforms of both hemispheres becoming identical in frequency, amplitude, phase and coherence.

This paper is not on the potential uses of brain synchronization, which may have remarkable implications for education, but rather on the ability of external sound stimuli to affect the internal rhythms of the brain. This most interesting side effect—the ability to synchronize the hemispheres of the brain—is mentioned for those interested in further study.

In order for this patented process (which Monroe called "Hemi-sync") to work, it appeared that headphones were necessary. Later work with the FFR, however, indicated that entrainment of the brain still occurred with external sound sources, such as stereo speakers, if they were given enough separation in the room. While the effects were not quite as rapid or as powerful as with headphones, sonic entrainment still took place.

Other Work on Brain Entrainment

Monroe is the creator of this technology. However, he is not the only person who is utilizing sonic phenomenon to entrain the brain. A number of other private institutions utilize similar processes. One person, a non-sectarian monk named Brother Charles, is head of M.S.H. Associates, which specializes in using sound to enhance and accelerate consciousness. Brother Charles was a disciple of the Eastern spiritual leaders Swami Paramahansa Muktananda. He found that through the new sonic entrainment technology it was possible almost instantly to induce states of deep meditation, normally not available to people without years of meditational practice. Brother Charles uses a process called "phasing," which employs a mechanism very similar to Monroe's to create altered states of consciousness. Indeed, it is the innate ability of the brain to detect waveform phase difference which gives rise to binaural beats.

An additional aspect of this sonic entrainment technology, brought to my attention by Sherry Edwards, a researcher at Ohio University, is that if the carrier waves creating the beat frequencies are harmonically related to the beat frequencies, a more powerful sonic entrainment occurs. According to Edwards, the most powerful form of entrainment to induce 7 hz., for example, involves using two differentiated signals that are harmonic multiples of frequencies of 7—say 49 hz and 56 hz. For entrainment of 6 cycles, you would work with a multiple of 6—perhaps 60 and 66. Thus far there has not been much available research regarding this. It does make sense, however, and I mention it for those interested in working with this technology. Ronald deStrulle, director of Holistic Programs, Inc., of New York, utilizes a process which seems to be in agreement with Edwards' thoughts on entrainment.

One of the most popular entrainment frequencies being utilized these days is that of 7.8 cycles per second. Both Ronald deStrulle and scientist Robert Tollaksen have created different tapes utilizing this frequency. DeStrulle's is called "Geo-Magnetic Field Entrainment," while Tollaksen's is simply called "Earth Hertz." It is of interest to note that the earth's ionosphere, the electromagnetic field around the earth, has been measured. This is called the Shumann Effect, and it appears that the frequency of the earth is somewhere around 7.83 cycles per second, which is identical to the alpha wave rhythm of the human brain. Itzhak Bentov, author of *Stalking the Wild Pendulum*, theorized that persons vibrating at these frequencies during meditation would entrain with the geomagnetic energies of the earth and lock in resonance with it. There are also some researchers who, like Bentov, believe that this 7.8 hz frequency is the resonant frequency of the human body.

It has been suggested by Dr. Robert Beck that perhaps this frequency is a "cosmic carrier of information" and could be the "drummer" to which psychics, healers, dowsers, etc. are entrained. By listening to tapes of the 7.8 hz it may be possible that listeners are able to resonate with the frequency of the earth's aura. Both deStrulle and Tollaksen have reported rather remarkable therapeutic experiences from those who have utilized these frequencies.

The original innovator and creator of this entrainment process, Robert Monroe, does not utilize beat frequencies of 7.8 hz or those in the alpha frequency spectrum. Most of the beat frequencies in his tapes, such as "Way of Hemi Sync," focus more on delta and theta waves mixed with beta frequencies. Additionally, unlike many of the other recordings to be discussed, Monroe does not deal with one specific frequency but with many.

Tom Kenyon, head of Acoustic Brain Research in North Carolina, produces various sonic entrainment cassettes called "WaveForms." Along with "Differential Signaling," Tom's term for the Hemi-Synch process, he also utilizes the pulsing of low tones at specific rhythmic patterns to entrain the brain into the desired state. He claims that an advantage of this form of entrainment is that a person with ear deafness can still get the entrainment, whereas in differential signaling, there would be no entrainment since one of the signals is not being received. Tom has worked with researchers using a 24 channel Neuromap EEG recording of subjects after they listened to his WaveForm tape. This research showed a shift of dominant alpha brain activity and a powerful increase in theta (4-8 hz).

Dr. Jeffrey Thompson, a chiropractor working with sound at Sound Sphere Productions has produced the "Isle of Skye," which incorporates music as well as the sonic entrainment technology. This tape, according to Dr. Thompson, "contains specific frequency modulation designed to induce the production of Alpha and Theta waves in the human cerebral cortex. . . . I use multiple variations of Alpha and Theta wave frequencies, phasing the wave forms through the 3.5 to 13 hz. range." Jeffrey uses a number of other sonic therapies besides these tapes, and his work merits further investigation.

The use of music to accompany these sonic entrainment frequencies is becoming more and more common. Many of Monroe's tapes utilize music as well as the Hemi-Sync frequencies, with most of the Hemi-Sync frequencies at a subliminal listening level. These subliminal frequencies have been found to be as effective as the audible ones.

It is important to understand that with these extremely low frequencies any music which may accompany the sounds must be pulsed slowly. As discussed before, music pulsed at about 60 beats per minute is ideal for helping to induce alpha states. If music pulsed a good deal faster were used, the entrainment of the heart to faster rhythms would clash with the slow brain waves pulses created by the beat frequency process. The effect would be minimal, if it existed at all. Therefore, slow music must be utilized.

"Dolphin Dreams"

The relationship between rhythms and brain wave frequencies is utilized and applied in the Spirit Music recording of "Dolphin Dreams." This is a sonic environment created as a tool for meditation and birth. It features the sounds of the ocean, human heart beat, dolphin sounds and choral voices. The choral voices utilize a wordless melody containing the "Ur" song, a descending melodic minor tune that is found in lullabies throughout the world. Along with these sounds, there is a choir chanting the Sanskrit mantra "Om." This sound was detuned in each channel to be slightly out of phase in order to create the "Schumann" resonance of 7.83 hz.

Some of the dolphin frequencies heard on this recording also resonated in this 7.83 hz range, with the dolphins utilizing a vibrato effect in order to create this frequency. Scientists at the Aspen Research Center have found that not only do dolphins create this frequency, but they have also been attracted to 7.83 hz when it was sent out via sonic instrumentation during underwater research.

In choosing the correct heart beat for "Dolphin Dreams," researchers experimented with a number of different pulsed heart beats. At first the heart beat of an infant in utero was tried, but the heart beat of the infant's mother was found to be equally if not more effective for calming. A heart beat of 60 beats per minute was also tried, since it is so favored by the Lozanov Method, but a heart beat of 48 to 50 beats per minute was finally found to be most effective for working harmoniously and harmonically with the other soothing sounds on the recording.

Tibetan Bells, Peruvian Whistles

"Sonic entrainment" as used in this paper is a relatively new term. Yet, sonic entrainment as a phenomenon has been used by medicine men and women and shamans from different cultures since prehistoric days. The ability to create altered states of consciousness through drumming, chanting and music is probably as old as music itself. Jeanne Achterberg in her book *Imagery in Healing* notes, for example, that analysis of shamanic drumming encompasses a frequency range of from .8 to 5.0 cycles per second, which she refers to as "theta driving capacity."

Tibetan bells, or Ting-Sha's, have been utilized in Buddhist meditation practice for many centuries. An examination reveals that the two bells, which are rung together, are slightly out of tune with each other. Depending upon the bells, the difference tones between them create ELFs somewhere between 4 and 8 cycles per second. This falls exactly within the range of the brain waves created during meditation and helps shift the brain to these frequencies. It is little wonder that Tibetan bells are experiencing a world-wide increase in popularity as tools for increased relaxation and reduction of stress.

Peruvian whistling vessels are ancient pipe-like instruments, originally found buried with mummies in Peru. For quite a while it was thought that they were just water jars. Then, some people began to experiment with them, blowing on them as whistles. The psychoacoustic effects of actually blowing these vessels are quite amazing and powerful.

Recently, replicas of these whistling vessels have been made available for experimentation and research. The entire cranium of the person blowing them seems to act as a resonating chamber—an effect that cannot be reproduced on a record. These vessels are usually blown in sets of seven and they create tremendous beat frequencies.

The March 29th, 1988, science section of the *New York Times* was devoted to these vessels. The headline read "Complex Whistles Found to Play Key Roles in Inca and Maya Life"; the subtitle read "Much more than toys, the whistles were genuine musical instruments." Stephen Garret and Daniel Statnekov tested the tonal ranges of these vessels using spectrum analysers and frequency meters. They suggested that, rather than being primarily utilitarian liquid containers as anthropologists regarded them, the bottles were specifically produced as whistles. Dr. Garret found that curious sounds were produced when two or three bottles of the same culture were blown simultaneously. Their higher notes would interact to produce deep lower notes that could not be tape-recorded but heard only in the ear, where the effect is generated. He said, "The idea is that these low frequency sounds were important religious rituals for changing states of consciousness." Such vessels were undoubtedly sacred tools, used under the guidance of a shaman or priest and utilized only at specific times and for specific purposes. Listening to these whistling vessels makes one truly appreciate the possibility of profound knowledge of sound among ancient cultures.

The Peruvian whistling vessels and the Tibetan bells are two examples of shamanic tools that employed the concept

Jonathan S. Goldman

of sonic entrainment for the brain. Numerous other ancient cultures knew of these principles for using ELFs to alter consciousness and applied them in their instruments, drumming and chanting.

Today, healers and therapists working with sound and music have the potential of following in the paths of the ancient shamanic traditions, combining magic and mysticism with modern science and technology. These healers and therapists are responsible for being aware of new discoveries of the use of sound and music in this manner.

Hemi-Sync and Other Uses of ELF

The technology of creating sonic entrainment may turn out to be a most important aspect of the therapeutic use of sound and music. Private research from various people working with this technology has indicated very promising results. However, the available literature is at this time mostly anecdotal, and experiental data is limited.

As creator of this technology, Robert Monroe and the Monroe Institute have done the most research for the longest period of time with their Hemi-Sync, particularly in the area of using sound to enhance education. A number of subjective studies have shown that groups of students in various age groups using tapes with Hemi-Sync had higher test scores and grades than control groups not using the technology. Hemi-Sync has also proved to be of help in the areas of learning disabilities, cerebral palsy, mental retardation, autism, uncontrolled seizure disorder, emotional disturbance, and Down's syndrome. Sonic entrainment is also being utilized for pain control, stress reduction and relaxation.

Ronald deStrulle, cited earlier, utilizes an entrainment frequency of about 1.45 hz, which he calls a "Tri-Thalamic Entrainment Format." It is designed to create entrainment between the hypothalamus, pituitary and pineal centers of the brain. Brother Charles is experimenting with this frequency in a select group of test subjects, and he also believes it stimulates the pituitary gland.

While there is little research to indicate the effects of

230

utilizing frequencies such as 1.45 hz, it is certainly an area of research that may prove enlightening. In a letter, deStrulle wrote that several doctors and audiologists from the New England Dyslectic Center Group have been obtaining excellent results with dyslexia by using Tri-Thalamic Format and that a study was presently being conducted which indicated profound improvement with Alzheimer's patients. We have been unable to confirm these reports, but they indicate the possibility of great inroads in this area.

It seems likely that in the area of neurological illnesses and brain injuries, sound, and in particular sonic entrainment, may prove to be the most effective, especially when this technology is combined with other sonic technologies such as those developed by Dr. Alfred Tomatis. Hemi-Sync has been utilized with stroke and aphasia patients with seemingly considerable success. If, as has been indicated, it may be possible to resonate specific portions of the brain using particular frequencies, it may therefore be possible to treat all manner of physical and emotional ailments using sound in this manner. Hopefully, we are just at the very beginning of some very powerful therapies which will utilize this technology.

Cautions

At the same time, it seems that caution is needed. If such frequencies stimulate the pituitary, for example, what effects would occur from long-term exposure to them? It has been suggested that these frequencies could be dangerous as well as healing, perhaps bringing on premature strokes and other imbalances in the brain. We do not know.

Sonic entrainment is by no means the cure-all or the answer to all the potential uses of healing with sound, but it certainly is an important development with astounding possibilities. As with all new discoveries, there is equal concern about misuse. With technology as simple as this, it is becoming increasingly easy for anyone with a bit of recording equipment to produce tapes that create sonic entrainment. The ease with which such tapes may also be obtained and used without discretion is of equal concern.

Jonathan S. Goldman

Without proper research and study, we may be unleashing a Pandora's box to an unsuspecting public. It is important that the long-term effects of some of these frequencies being utilized should be studied, and that we determine whether they are beneficial or dangerous.

We are currently at the forefront of using sound to affect the body, mind and spirit. These are exciting times with many new discoveries and developments. The potential areas of use may be limited only by our imagination.

Bibliography

Achterberg, Jean, *Imagery in Healing*. Boston: Shambhala, 1985.

Allesch, Christian G., "A Study of the Influence of Music on Pulse and Respiration Frequency." *Zeitschrift fur experimentelle und angewandte Psychologies*, 1981, Vol. 29.

Atwater, F. Holmes, "The Monroe Institute's Hemi-Sync Process," Unpublished research, Monroe Institute, 1987.

Beck, Bob, "ELF Waves and EEG Entrainment," from *Kiplinger Magazine*, Jan./Feb. 1988.

Bentov, Itzhak, *Stalking the Wild Pendulum*. Rochester, VT: Inner Traditions, 1988.

Berendt, Joachbim-Ernst, *Nada Brahma: The World is Sound*. Rochester, VT: Inner Traditions, 1987.

Broad, William, "Complex Whistles Found to Play Key Role in Inca and Maya Life," *New York Times*, Tuesday, March 29, 1988.

Burns, Linda, "Conversation with Linda Burns."

Clynes, Manfred, and Janice Walker, "Neurobiologic Functions of Rhythm, Time and Pulse in Music," *Music, Mind and Brain*, edited by Manfred Clynes, New York: Plenum Press, 1982.

DeStruelle, Ronald, "Letters to Jonathan Goldman," October 10, 1989, November 12, 1989.

Fonatana, Alberto E. & Loschi, Julia A., "Combined Use of Music with Sound of Heart Beats and Respiration Rhythms in Psychotherapy," Acta Psiquiatrica y Psicologic de America Latina, March, 1979.

Goldman, Jonathan, *Awakening the Lost Chord*, Spirit Music, 1984.

Harrer and Harrer, "Music, Emotion and Autonomic Function" in M. Critchley and R. Henson (Eds), *Music and the Brain*, London: Wm. Heinemann, 1977.

Hutchinson, Michael, *MegaBrain*, New York: Ballantine Books, 1987.

Kenyon, Tom, "Acoustic Brain Research," Acoustic Brain Research, Inc., 1989.

Krier, Beth Ann, "Meditation on Tape: Enlightenment Made Easy," *Los Angeles Times*, January 30, 1987.

Landreth, Janet E. & F. Hobart, "Effects of Music on Physiological Response," *Journal of Research in Music Education*, Vol. 22, 1974.

Leonard, George, "The Silent Pulse," New York: E. P. Dutton, 1978.

Morris, Suzanne Evans, "The Structure of Metamusic," *Breakthrough*. Faber, VA: Monroe Institute of Applied Sciences, 1987.

Morris, Suzanne Evans, "The Effects of Music and Hemi-Sync on a Child with a Seizure Disorder," *Breakthrough*, 1983.

Myers, John, "Human Rhythms and the Psychobiology of Entrainment," Unpublished, Bell Communication Research, 1988.

Ostrander, Sheila & Lynn Schroeder, *Superlearning*, New York: Putnam, 1982.

Varney, Karen, "Metamusic with Hemi-Sync as an Adjunct to Intervention with Developmentally Delayed Young Children." Virginia Commonwealth University, 1988.

15
Sound in Mind and Body

JILL PURCE

To watch the effect of sound on matter is to witness life itself coming into being. Hans Jenny, a Swiss engineer and doctor, influenced by the work of Rudolph Steiner, made it his life work to demonstrate this. He vibrated all kinds of materials with sounds in a variety of ways. He used liquids and pastes and fine powders and subjected them to different kinds of sounds. As I watched, I saw heaps of matter which had no form take on the precise and exquisite patterns that I had seen in nature. The longer the sound was maintained the more differentiated these patterns became. If the materials or the sound changed, so did the patterns.

This is extremely significant. If sound can introduce form and pattern into matter, then it is essential to understand the nature of sound.

The inspiration of Dr. Jenny's work started me in my research. I looked into all the traditional literature on the creative power of sound. I realized that this theme is common to many traditions that consider sound a great force in the universe.

Creation Through Sound

When I began looking into these traditions I found that even quite widely distant peoples had the idea that the world itself came into being and continued to come into being through sound, that the coming into being is a sonorous event. This is found in the East and West. We can understand it as a metaphorical description of a vibratory universe, which means that human beings have always known that everything in the world has its identity because of the periodicity and regularity of its movement, and that this is what makes one thing separate from another and gives it form.

St. John's Gospel says, "In the beginning was the Word, and the Word was with God, and the Word was God." Almost identical words can be found in the Hindu tradition. So the beginning is sound, and also language. Furthermore, in these traditions the beginning comes about not only through sound and the word but through the allocation of names—as in the Bible, when Adam names everything. When you give a name to a thing it has a separate identity because it has one name, not another name, which means that it is something "recognizable." In this way you have the beginning of language and thought. So you have creation through vibration and you have creation through language.

To technologize the world you need language and differentiation, but to be in the present, to experience "treeness" for example, you need to be able to suspend naming and language. Normally when you look at a tree, you say "tree" to yourself. Immediately after saying the word your mind starts on its trajectory of inner chatter, of tree associations related to the past and future. Objects thus named conjure up things undone yesterday and regretfully still to be done tomorrow. The moment you name something you are thrust into time—naming actually creates a past and a future. If you want not to be in time, but want to remain in perceptual contact with treeness, then you cannot name it as "tree," for that separates it from you as an object. People have devised different ways of tricking the mind so that they can be in a state of perceiving treeness or can be "tree-ing."

You have to undo the skill of naming which we have been taught since birth and for which we get good examination marks. You have to be able to use it when it's appropriate and not use it when it isn't. Sonorous yogas are devised for just this purpose. They either splinter the attention, giving it so much to do that you forget to think, or create a closed circuit of attention. Using your voice and listening to the sound you are making at the same time enables you to go beyond the dualism of language and separation from the world. When you see that something is different from yourself and also that everything is different from everything else, language arises. The separation of me and not me is the separation all traditions try to overcome so that we can be in a state of unity. Sound is one of the most effective ways of going beyond separation.

Finding a Living Tradition

The magical and healing qualities of sound were taken for granted by most peoples of antiquity, and particularly by the Egyptians, Greeks, and East Indians. In searching for places where knowledge of this had survived, I found myself studying within various traditions. A precise understanding of the use of sound and voice has survived in the Tibetan tradition. This is because of the peculiar situation in Tibet where a medieval spiritual culture was preserved. In medieval Europe we had certain similarities in our own spiritual tradition. We also had cave-dwelling hermits who performed extraordinary miracles. These abilities have been almost entirely lost through the age of so-called enlightenment. But this tradition survived in Tibet, perhaps because of its geography or the rare atmosphere of the high Himalayas. For generations and generations Tibetans have studied the mind and developed a highly sophisticated science of mind. There are vast numbers of words in the Tibetan language which are in some way qualifications of mind.

The Tibetans talk about three aspects of the human being: body, voice and mind. The location for "body" is in the head, "voice" is in the throat and "mind" is in the heart. For Tibetans there is no identity between mind and brain, as in the West. The voice acts as an intermediary between the subtle realm of mind and the more physical realm of body. It is seen as a bridge between the material and the nonmaterial. Speech, voice, sound, and subtle breath or *prana* are all connected.

It is not only Tibetans who consider sound as a bridge—the idea is very widespread. Sound is often considered as an intermediary for the translation of spirit into matter and of matter into spirit through the agency of human beings. If spirit can become matter through sound, then matter can become spirit, again through sound. Sound has been used in almost all places and times as the means for travelling the path of transcendence—for transforming matter back into spirit. You can see this almost literally in that you can use the sound of an object to break it apart. For example, if you listen to the sound of a wine glass and sing that note back at the glass, you can smash it with your voice. So you can decompose form with sound physically, and you can transform it with sound spiritually.

Within the Tibetan tradition of Dzogchen the aim is to relax into a state of contemplation and to live your life with integrity, so that the implications of your actions are apparent in the clarity of every moment, so that you live like fish in water—as if riding the waves of the Tao you leave no traces and lead an impeccable existence causing no disturbances. If you cannot do this, then you would try to understand the reason. You might have a blockage or an energy disturbance which prevents it. In this case there are many kinds of practices which would help. Sound is often used to bring about a state of clarity and contemplation.

Mantra

In India, too, the voice is important for transformation. Perhaps the most common form of such practice in India—and also in Tibet—is the use in mantra. Mantras are sacred sounds preserved in the ancient languages, even in languages which are no longer understood. Certain sounds are used for specific illnesses or problems caused by particular beings, and there are mantras to bring you into a state of clarity or emptiness. Other mantras tune you into the lineage of teachers in which you are participating. Working with the particular sounds that have been used by masters of the lineage allows you to tune into and share in their attainment. You are tuning into all those who have ever used the mantra.

Mantra is used throughout the world. For example, among the Sufis, the mystics of Islam, forms of mantric chanting are combined with rhythmic movements of the body and rhythmic breathing to bring one into a state of transcendental ecstacy or spiritual bliss. Most liturgies are chanted or sung, including the Christian liturgy. The Sunday services of matins, communion and evensong when people chant psalms, sing hymns, and intone prayers together, are a form of spiritual entrainment. Everyone is tuning together. When you change from speaking to singing, something very interesting happens. Singing unites people, and that is why all countries have a national anthem.

Shamanic Ground

The great world religions have superimposed themselves over the indigenous shamanic traditions which had existed for hundreds of thousands of years. Many of the sonic yogas of Tibet and India are very ancient and existed long before Buddhism. Exercises of chanting, rhythmical bodily movement and rhythmical breathing were incorporated into the great religions. There are many such practices, like the whirling of the dervishes. They spiral and rotate while breathing and praying, along with the voice of the flute, which is very similar to the human voice. Sufis say that the body of the dervish is like the body of the flute through whom God is blowing.

Teaching Sound

I have found certain similarities in the principles behind the ways sound has been used for spiritual purposes. These are useful for people who feel alienated from their own spiritual traditions and can benefit from the understanding of those who used their voices for spiritual purposes in the past. We are rediscovering the voice, this magnificent tool which we carry around with us all the time. Ordinarily we use our voices unconsciously, but we can begin to use them in a way that ancient traditions have understood—for our own transformation.

Liberating the voice means liberating a human being. It is our means of expression. It is the way in which our breath is made conscious, and our breath is our way of exchanging ourselves with the world. We breathe the world in and we breathe ourselves out into the world; it is a constant relationship which goes on mostly unconsciously. The use of the voice is one way in which this becomes conscious. If you know what you are doing you can change this relationship completely.

Breathing in itself is an art of great precision. You can choose different kinds of breathing, depending on the kind of state you want to enter or the experience you want to have or the part of yourself you want to contact. First you must learn ways to breathe. In addition you try to change the breath for chanting, and at the same time you chant in order to change the breath. You do both in order to change the nature of your being so that you can go beyond the chattering mind and be in the nature of the mind itself.

Usually breathing is fast and high and tends to emphasize the inbreath. A fast, high concentrated inbreath is fine for rebirthing or work with hyperventilation or if you want to uncover emotional material. To go beyond emotional material, beyond the activity of the thinking mind, you lower the breath and work with the outbreath. There are many ways to lengthen the breath and change your whole pattern of breathing.

It is not just making sound that is important. Being able to listen to it is essential if you are trying to go beyond thought. When you listen you are completing a circuit of attention, and it is this circuit of attention which enables you to go beyond the thinking mind. It is important to listen and to make sound at the same time.

In addition, sound can be used to liberate you from the pattern of anxieties, which is stimulated and nourished by every perceptual experience. Each perception initiates naming (language and thought) and therefore comparison in time with past and future. We are immediately excluded from the present by our regrets and fears. The persistence of these negative thought patterns starts by affecting our emotions and energy, and then brings about physical changes at the body's weak points, which can ultimately result in pathology.

Through using sound to work on the morphogenetic field of a person, in other words the resonant potentiality of his or her own healthy state, that person can be maintained in health. In English to be healthy is to be sound; we talk about being sound in body and mind, to be of sound mind. To be in tune like this is to maintain a state of health. Each person has a sound quite distinct from that of another person, and you can learn to bring your whole being into resonance with it. In doing this your voice should get lower, fully resonant and much richer, so your whole being is resonating when you use your voice.

Furthermore, you can learn to go within your own sound to discover and reveal the inside of the sound through harmonic or overtone chanting. This way of working with sound is of ancient shamanic origin. It brings out the internal core of the sound, which can be heard as separate notes over and above the note you are singing. This is a magical thing to do either alone or with a group. You have a sense that you are evoking angelic beings—which of course in antiquity and even medieval times were thought to be sonorous. At the same time you use the tongue to differentiate and make audible parts of your own voice which were undifferentiated and unconscious. And because tongue movements are linked directly to thinking, you are also stimulating little used neural pathways.

An Experiment with Children

Recently, at a summer school I gave for school teachers of the arts, I discussed with the teachers how the period of assembly in schools has become a problem for them. The law in England enforces Christian prayers during school assemblies; the law in the United States forbids them. In both cases teachers do not know what to do with this period but are not permitted to abolish it. The real aim of an assembly is to tune the pupils and teachers into something higher than themselves so that the activities of the school can be harmonious, so that the development of the children can carry on smoothly. Therefore it is a very important period, but its importance has been forgotten and the original intention lost.

In the next workshop I gave, in London, surprisingly there were five school teachers, including the supervisor of music teaching in London, a teacher of mentally handicapped children and a teacher of Montessori. A week later I was invited to teach in a primary school. I had the chance to use an assembly as a period for tuning together, using sound in a way that it has always been used, yet in a way which was non-denominational. In addition, I taught ten-year-olds in the morning and seven-year-olds in the afternoon. The supervisor of music teaching and various other interested people sat in on the experiment.

I asked the children to describe their experiences on listening to certain kinds of sounds, harmonic chanting and so on. The children were immediately transfixed. They asked the most precise and brilliant questions. They got right to the central point immediately. They knew exactly what was going on. They were completely spontaneous. I expected them to imitate each other, but each one was quite different, yet rooted in a common source of experience. The children were relating truly cosmic visions. They themselves were thrilled.

Later we had a period in which children painted what they had experienced. The teachers who came were amazed by what happened. They said that they had never seen the children so spontaneous. Children who rarely spoke told us about their experience. The paintings of these children were extraordinary and very moving. Out of the darkness sprang brilliant rainbow colors, luminous waves and beams, with balls of light floating in space. The children were so excited they started to write poetry too. One poem made me cry. Parents reported that the children came home ebullient, bursting with what had happened to them.

Transformation of Humanity

If you can bring this out in children from an early age

then it really might be possible to transform society. And nothing short of the transformation of humanity is needed at this point in time. Transformation means living our lives in ways which are harmonious with our environment and with other people, facilitating the illumination of others and the illumination of life on earth.

Since the voice is an instrument of transformation that we carry about with us all the time, it is one of the most powerful and also most readily available means for this end. If we open our ears so that we can hear our own voices, our voices can become a means of transformation for ourselves and others.

16

Imagery and the Physiology of Music

DON G. CAMPBELL

Imagination is not the talent of some men, it is the health of every man.

Ralph Waldo Emerson

[Deeply listening to music] opens up new avenues of research I'd never even dreamed of. Because of what you've shown me this afternoon—not just what you've said, but what I have actually felt and experienced— I feel from now on music should be an essential part of every analysis. This reaches the deep archetypal material that we can only sometimes reach in our analytical work with patients. This is most remarkable.

Carl Jung

Music is the archetypal ordering of sound. It patterns and reinforces the powers of listening, attention, and memory for people of every culture. Music is not only art and a refined form of beauty's expression, but it is also the subtle and dynamic power that unifies breath, rhythm, and tone of the human body. Every thought, feeling, and movement has its own musical qualities. Music and physical bodies share similar organizational patterns of system and structure. Our pulse and heartbeat have a rhythm and tempo; breath has pattern and flow in our bodies. Just as the interrelatedness of the systems in the body, such as respiration, heartbeat, brain wave patterns, and the nervous system, create a connected whole being, the components of melody, harmony, rhythm and tonal color create a counterpoint of systems that make music a living body of sound.

The rhythm of music has significant, measurable effects on the heartbeat and the breath, causing alterations in these two basic elements of life. Fast music with a constant, driving pulse can accelerate our heartbeat and modify muscle tension and skin temperature, while slow music will subdue these same physical responses. Mellow music with no consistent rhythmic pattern may promote a sense of physical release in us; if we are under high stress it may also impart the feeling of safety. Fast music that is non-melodic, with an irregular rhythmic pattern, and loud sounds can easily bring discomfort to our bodies and minds. When imagery or suggestion is blended with any mode of music, physical responses are enhanced.

Every style of music creates a unique, non-verbal language that may modify how we control our conscious mind. For example, certain types of music prolong our feelings of a safe, inner space in therapy; others keep the body in rhythmic physical patterns compatible with aerobic exercise. In addition, music has the remarkable ability to alter our perception of time, so that thought processes and physical processes seem elongated. Curation and healing are easier to effect under these circumstances.

Health professionals have made widespread use of imagery during the last decade for ameliorating many physical, mental, and emotional disorders. Complex use of myth, story telling, and guided meditation has created remarkable inroads in psychotherapy for greater understanding and control of mind-body systems. The innovative research of Anees Sheikh, Jean Houston, Jeanne Achterberg, Helen Bonny, Carl Simonton, and Akhter Ahsen has generated a large body of data on the effects of thought and imagery on the physical body. Many researchers are even beginning to focus on how mind-body interactions can have profound effects on our immune systems. Yet, we are still neophytes in the art of framing the "whole" picture of the mind-body relationship.

Imagery and Healing

Until the seventeenth century in Western culture, a healthy mind-body relationship was seen as essential to overall health. Descartes' proposal that the mind and body are separate, independently functioning systems changed the entire course of Western medicine, logic, and civilization. Eastern and shamanistic cultures never made the split between body and mind, and holism has never been alien to their concept of physical or mental health. The re-integration of mind and body is now on the forefront of health care, as are Eastern modes of healing.

A simple example illustrates how the images surrounding chosen words can influence the outcome of health care. A small child with a bleeding cut on the arm is brought to the school nurse. "That cut looks deep," states the nurse crisply. "I will put something on it. It will hurt and sting only for a few minutes." The child cries and looks tense, distressed, and fearful. By changing the image through different words and inflection, a different healing environment can be created. Softly, the nurse says, "Oh, my, I know that cut was a surprise. I will put something on it. This will feel warm and wet, so that you'll feel better very soon." The child relaxes and talks about the accident and is curious about the nurse's treatment. Imagine how the use of music in situations like this could further enhance the healing environment.

The following six elements, all essential for the successful process of integration of music, imagery, and healing, actually flow together to form a circle, each building upon the other and contributing to form.

1. *Music modifies environment.* Music shapes and colors the surrounding atmosphere. Sound gives added dimension to the emotional ambiance of a given space. Music in an environment is like wallpaper—it can make a space or situation feel lighter, more spacious, safer, enhance its beauty, or it can make it seem more dense, cluttered, tense, or boring. For example, slower baroque music played in an emergency room may create a less frantic pulse for the nurses and doctors at work. (Although this may be helpful

for controling an excess of emotional tension in this environment, it could be decidedly hazardous when adrenaline is needed by the staff in a crisis.) In the emergency waiting room, baroque music, the piano music of George Winston, or light popular music could reduce the stress of this situation far more than a "Miami Vice" television program. A dentist could alter the environment for patients by playing light classics to assist relaxation; active music could be used to invigorate hospital or elderly patients who have not been able to exercise regularly. However, music for setting a mood or giving more space and comfort to a physical setting is not curation or therapy; it is simply a way of providing individual ease and comfort in a stressful environment.

Familiar music will create an environment that feels safe. This is especially true for children. Some new age music without strong melodies or rhythms is effective in creating safety. Slow pieces from the baroque and classic periods or new recordings like "Relax With the Classics" (selected by Charles Schmid of the Lind Institute in San Francisco) are also excellent choices for lessening the sense of vulnerability in an environment.

On the other hand, unfamiliar, strange, or music foreign to one's culture may generate an uneasy feeling. This effect has been used in curious and amusing ways. For instance, in British Columbia a fast-serve market piped the music of Montovani and Strauss waltzes into its parking lot so that the loitering teenagers would not hang out there. They immediately left and did not come back. In Edmonton, Canada, businesses played Mozart and Bach into a city park to drive away drug dealers and their clients, and it worked. Dr. Maria Simonson of John Hopkins University found that rock music causes people to eat faster and to eat more, while slow string music such as Montovani makes them eat more slowly. We are only beginning to discover the many uses of music.

2. *Music modifies our relationship to time and space.* Music can slow down or speed up our sense of time. Surprisingly, our mind's ability to perceive time is modified by whether our ears are in a horizontal or vertical position, and to

what degree. The vestibular system of the ear (a series of canals filled with fluid in the inner ear that tell the brain whether we are lying down, sitting, standing, or on our heads) sends different messages to the brain's internal clock, depending upon body position. Blood flow to the vestibular system is affected by position, which in turn affects vestibular function. Additionally, when we are lying down the vestibular system is not constantly working to determine the exact position of our bodies, and this slowdown also affects our internal clock and our "sense" of time. Consider how slowly time seems to pass when you are lying in bed on a sleepless night, but how quickly it passes when you are up and in the midst of an engaging project.

Music and language seem to create more images and associations when we are lying down than when the ear is in other positions. The effects of image on the body in this position seem more direct than while we are sitting or standing. Listening to a live concert in a vertical position stimulates quite a different response in us neurologically and physiologically than it does when we listen to the same music at the same volume while lying on a couch.

The term "new age music" has come to encompass many styles: the synthesized sounds of Vangelis and Kitaro that create vast colors and space within music, sounds not available with traditional instruments; Tibetan, Gregorian, and Shamanic chanting; jazz; Native American, Japanese, Indian and other flute music; angelic vocal music; and even some white-sugared sounds. The sense of time expansion and reduction is one of the major components that has been observed with "new age" or ambient styles of music. This genre has contributed markedly to our awareness that sound changes the space-time relationship. This awareness process, if used thoughtfully, is one of music's magical keys that can be harnessed for our own transformation and for the benefit of others.

Music creates a time-ordered reality. Its structure can give organization and meaning to the world around us. Classical, baroque, or romantic styles enhance our sense of time-reality and logic, help order our thoughts and images, and facilitate learning. Release from the urgent sense of time pressure in overstructured situations can occur with the flowing, ambient style found in new age music. Experimentation with styles of music and listening postures can yield other helpful results.

3. *Effective visualization incorporates both the concrete and the metaphorical.* It is important for our emotional and spiritual growth and development not to get stuck in either the concrete or the metaphorical. For people who tend to be overly associative, concentrating on "getting concrete" through the technique of visualization is important. The development of the critical thinking process becomes essential to growth.* For people who think too concretely and find it difficult to form creative associations during visualization, then encouraging more free association becomes paramount. A balance between these two approaches is required for effective curation.

Many people believe that they are unable to image because they do not "see" visual pictures, even though their thoughts may be very intense during the process. On the other hand, those with the ability of eidetic imagery have extraordinarily accurate and vivid recall of almost photographic visual images. Again, the two polarities of visual ability are evident. Balance of the inner visual mode can be enhanced through the use of music along with visualization. Music can bring the quality of association to eidetic images. "See yourself resting in a comfortable reclining chair outside on a warm spring day." The careful choice of music with this image could either induce intense association or strengthen the visual picture.

4. *Imagery incorporates the emotional along with the visual.* Jeanne Achterberg clearly defines imagery as that which "provides communication between perception, emotion and physiological change." It is important to realize that image is not just an inner visualization of a picture or form but encompasses much more. Sensory qualities must be included for a thought to be a true image. One, a few, or all of the senses may be involved. Music with image has

---

*See the work of Jean Piaget for more thinking along these lines. Also see *Rhythms of Learning*, D. Campbell, Zephyr Press, 1991.

profound effects upon the emotional and spiritual levels of self-awareness.

Imagery often occurs spontaneously. Dreams, daydreams, visions, and memories all connect us to imagery, especially when stimulated by related sensory input. Hearing a song that was played at our high school prom may recall a potent image; the smell of chocolate chip cookies freshly baked another. Imagery can be induced through reading, listening to music, story-telling, prayer, or active, creative daydreaming. Image-making (imagination) may be creative or factual; it may be as simple as a passing thought or feeling, or as vastly complex as a dream. The words "imagine yourself on the seashore" may evoke a long story in our minds or just bring on drowsiness.

Long guided imagery sessions can be used to stimulate profound healing of the psyche, and may result in healing on the physical level, too. In this type of session, information from the subconscious may become readily available to a therapist for clinical analysis. Imagery can become our major connection between the inner and outer worlds, between the subconscious and the conscious.

5. *Music can effect physical and mental curation, which is known as physioaudiation.* This domain is rapidly gaining prominence as a useful method to repattern the mind and body and effect curation for a wide variety of disorders. Trained therapists are able to lead imagery sessions with very exacting purposes for enhancing well-being in clients. Or an individual can learn to create scenarios for the use of imagery in reducing stress, increasing concentration and facilitating learning, or for inspiration, motivation, and activation.

Increasing self-expression and the development of self-esteem and self-control can be effectively mediated through imagery and music. This will often provide a starting place for other profound therapeutic benefits—emotional, physical, mental, and spiritual. Various methods in current practice are being developed to effect these types of changes.

The most articulate and widely known method of incorporating imagery and music for curation has been developed by music therapist Helen Bonny. Through experience as a research fellow and therapist at the Maryland

Don G. Campbell

Psychiatric Research Center in the 1970s, where she analyzed the effects of LSD, Bonny developed a process known as Guided Imagery and Music (GIM). Remarkable results have been obtained with this technique, combining relaxation with imagery and music. GIM has evolved over the past two decades into one of the safest and deepest methods of psychotherapy.

The Bonny method is a one-to-one process, incorporating a "guide" or facilitator. Rather than the "guide" simply leading the imagery with specific thoughts, stories, or myths, classical music is used to allow the client to journey into a deep state of relaxation. Clients are encouraged to verbalize the impressions that form in their minds as the music unfolds. The music is consciously selected to pace the client through different states of emotional awareness and remembrance to reach a peak experience; then the client is gradually returned to a safe, quiet and relaxed state. The "guide" then assists the client to integrate the experience. At this point the drawing of mandalas or story telling may be used to enhance the therapy. The goal of the Bonny method is to allow the "dynamic unfoldment of inner experiences in service of physical, psychological and spiritual wholeness."

Other professionals in this field use guided imagery techniques that incorporate a variety of styles of music. For example, ambient, new age music may be used in creating a safe environment to allow for long periods of relaxation. Self-induced guided imagery is now being taught by nurses and doctors to patients for relaxation and development of a sense of well-being. Effects of these guided imagery techniques are demonstrated in brain-wave patterns; alpha and theta waves become more predominant. Even more complex techniques are being developed to guide a patient through a series of sensory associations designed to alter states of consciousness significantly and to have marked effects on the physical body. Progressive and highly trained leaders in guided imagery techniques include Jean Houston of the Foundation for Mind Research in New York; Jeanne Achterberg of the Institute for Transpersonal Psychology; and Anees A. Sheikh of the American

250

Imagery Institute at Marquette University in Milwaukee, Wisconsin.

Current use and research of music for curation include the following:

- Reduction of anxiety.
- Relaxation and lessening of pain following surgery.
- Self-induction of altered states for pain management.
- Lessening or eliminating nausea and vomiting in cancer patients.
- Increasing the capacity for movement in moribund patients following surgery or a prolonged illness or for the elderly.
- Increasing general well-being and mental health.

Caution must be used when using any therapeutic mode for healing. For example, illnesses can be made worse by symptom removal; if you take away the pain that indicates serious illness, you take away the motivation to seek a cure for the underlying disease. Also, some patients with chronic pain find that inducing a relaxed state actually increases their pain. A relaxed state may also cause symptoms of serious withdrawal in clinically depressed patients. Music and imagery may bring on a state of panic in some patients, with release of their superego control. If there are significant psychiatric difficulties contributing to any illness, these *must* be treated in addition to using any music therapy techniques to ameliorate symptoms. Anyone who uses music for healing, either for their own benefit or for others, should be aware that unsuspected effects can occur. One needs to have training to deal with these.

6. *For effective healing, integration and grounding must occur.* Integration and grounding are essential if the use of music in any therapeutic situation is to be both effective and safe. Perhaps the best way to begin learning physioaudiation therapy is to master at least fifty techniques for grounding before starting any imagery techniques. For grounding, select music that is solid, that has a beat. Music for integration needs to impart the feeling of safety—of connectedness to self and to the environment. When using music for

251

meditation, select two types: one to start the meditation process, and one to ground it. As in visualization, any therapeutic use of music requires stimulation of both the associative and concrete modes—the associative to allow for the transformative experience to occur, and the concrete to "bring you back" and to integrate the experience into your daily reality.

Choosing Music for Use in Imagery and Healing

The following music has been selected after experimentation at the Institute for Music, Health, and Education. It is important to remember, when choosing music to create a specific environment, that habituation can occur. For example, two minutes of listening to music to activate may be enough to trigger activation—fifteen minutes may negate the effects. Twenty to thirty minutes of listening to baroque music to enhance concentration is effective— listening longer has less value.

Music Selections that help activate:
- J. S. Bach, *The Well Tempered Klavier*
- Cambridge Buskers, *Not Live from New York*
- Don Campbell, *Dances for a SleepWalker*
- Scott Joplin, soundtrack from *The Sting*
- Eugene Ormandy, *Fireworks*
- Sousa marches
- Mannheim Steamroller, *Saving the Wildlife*
- Tomita, *Snowflakes are Dancing, Cosmos*
- Paul Winter, *Earthbeat*

Music Selections that help concentration:
- Don Campbell, *Angels* (side 2), *Cosmic Classics, Crystal Meditations*
- Eugene Friesen, *New Friends*
- Gregorian Chants
- Mozart, *C Major Piano Concerto* (Elvira Madigan)
- Ranier, *Songs of the Indian Flute*
- *Relax with the Classics, Andante* (Lind Institute)
- Paul Winter, *Sunsinger*

Music Selections that help to relax:
- Don Campbell, *Angels* (side 1), *Birthing, Crystal Rainbows, Runes* (deep relaxation)
- Eno, *Music for Airports, The Pearl*
- Kay Gardner, *The Rainbow Path*
- Jonathan Goldman, *Dolphin Dreams*
- *Relax with the Classics, Adagio and Largo*

Music Selections in concert with Active Imagery
- Beethoven, *Piano Concerto 5 in E Flat Major*
- Brahms, *Violin Concerto in D Major*
- Handel, *Royal Fireworks Suite*
- Haydn, *Symphony 94 in G Major*
- Mozart, *Symphonies in C Major, G Minor; Violin Concerto 5 in A Major*
- Relax with the Classics, Allegro
- Tchaikovsky, *Piano Concerto 1 in B Minor*

Music Selections in concert with Passive Imagery:
- Don Campbell, *Dances for a Sleepwalker, Lightning on the Moon*
- Corelli, *Concerto Grossi 4, 10, 11, 12*
- David Hykes, *The Harmonic Choir*
- Handel, *Water Music Suite*
- Kitaro, *Silk Road*
- Mascagni, *Intermezzo from Cavalleria Rusticana*
- Satie, *Gymnopedies*
- Vivaldi, *Flute concertos*

(For information on where to get any of these tapes that are hard to find, write Institute for Music, Health and Education, P. O. Box 1244, Boulder, CO 80306.)

Since each individual has personal preferences for style and type of music, there is no one best style of music combined with imagery for curation. We can never predict that "*this* will have *that* exact effect" in physioaudiation. It is important to experiment, figure out what works best not what an "expert" says is the proper music for a specific result. Yet absolute care must be taken at all times to keep a client safe. We are apt to become stuck when it seems absolutely necessary to create a system, a pattern, a specific method to heal with sound. No one can ever be *the* expert in the field of physioaudiation. Fostering codependency is ultimately not helpful. Instead, the key is to learn to "re-cognize" one's innate healing ability and to assist others in discovering their own innate healing ability.

The best stance with regard to physioaudiation (and life, too) is mesoteric—not esoteric, not exoteric. One should be both grounded in the esoteric nature of music and in the Absolute, the fundamental, the real. The Tarot card "Temperance" is an excellent example of this philosophy— one foot is firmly on the ground and one in the numinous water.

Listening is essential to being a "sound" healer. "Entrainment," too, is essential; this technique allows the therapist to walk in the same place, the same energy, the same vibration as the client. It imparts the feeling of safety to the one being healed, which is necessary for effective and safe healing. It also gives clients the power of being the healer; this occurs when they know that they are truly being heard.

Healing is a perpetual process, a balanced state of mind, body, and spirit. This work with music and imagery is to pattern one's body to heal and to apply one's innate wisdom for healing. Our bodies know how to heal themselves, and the images and sounds lead into curation.

Integrated with treatment, music as medicine is a rapidly emerging field. We now have the unique opportunity through the utilization of imagery and music to shape a new paradigm—a totally natural and personal method for healing ourselves and others.

17

*Music, The Way Home**

MIRIAM THERESE WINTER

High up in the foothills of the Mountains of the Moon, in the Kabale region of western Uganda, I sat one star-studded evening transfixed by the sound of the wind in the pines. The haunting harmonic took me back in time to the summer when I was seven and sat similarly mes-merized on a stone fence in the Catskills in New York. The Uganda pines stood inside the monastic enclosure of a community of contemplative nuns, and when the night was in the midst of its course, I heard a chanting so pure, so ethereal, it pierced me to the heart. It was a sound I too had once attempted when the chant was my own prayer of praise. I felt an overwhelming ache. I was homesick for the past. Homesick for the candor of childhood. Homesick for that ritual innocence when just to do the deed was sacred, before a shift in theological understanding caused me to reshape my religious response. I was homesick for a long-lost Garden of Eden. There was no way on earth, or so it seemed, of ever returning home.

Home. A wholesome word. A healing word. A necessary word. It has been said that all real sickness is homesickness. We have all felt homesick at one time or another. To be homesick is to be heartsick for the hearth of human warmth and affection. Or soulsick for the felt presence of an abiding Deity. Or sick in spirit because, try as we might to convince

---

*Copyright, Medical Mission Sisters, 1990.

ourselves otherwise, we know we are less than whole. Who among us fully inhabits the house of his or her particularity? It may be said that a part of every one of us is permanently away from home. That alienation wounds us deeply. We are homesick for wholeness, for at-homeness-with our-selves, God, the human family, and all of creation on and beyond what we call planet Earth. We are in need of healing, and healing means coming home.

"The longest way round is the shortest way home," according to an ancient proverb. That bit of common wisdom describes the circuitous journey called life, and in life the key to homecoming is knowing precisely where home is. "Home is where one starts from," says T. S. Eliot.[1] Robert Frost says that "home is the place where, when you have to go there, they have to take you in."[2] Musical theory confirms that home is where one begins one's journey and the locus to which one longs to return. Every key has a note called home. Through all the variations and im-provisations, a dominant urge pulls the composer/performer to return again to home base, which is quite appropriately called a "tonic." To come home is to experience completion, at least momentarily. Music imitates life. One is always in search of one's roots. One is always journeying home.

But again, precisely where is home and what does it mean to "come home"? Contemporary feminist Nelle Morton wrote that the journey itself is home.[3] Home is where the heart is, say the poets and the bards. Where God is, say the saints and the mystics. Where music takes us, say those who know far more than they can tell. Music is "a door opener to the person hidden within a silent barrier of hope-lessness."[4] Indeed home is far more than a place, a route, an odyssey, a reality outside of ourselves. Home is some-where within us, in that place where the truth of ourselves, God, and all of creation unobtrusively dwells. Home in this sense is a metaphor, and when used metaphorically,

1. "East Coker" (1940).
2. "The Death of the Hired Man" (1914).
3. In her autobiographical work, *The Journey Is Home* (Boston: Beacon Press, 1985).
4. Connecticut musician Don McKeever.

the experience of home is existentially female.

Females live life from the inside out and welcome the outside in. The miracle of bringing to birth is something that happens inside of us. Intuition is a wisdom dwelling inside of us. Tears, fears, feelings reveal the inner story. The core of our creativity, of all our nurturing activity, of our homemaking propensity, is nestled deep inside. Every person has an innate capacity to proceed from the inside out, for a part of every person is female. When one is free to live according to this principle, one learns to be at home.

Music comes from the inside out. Through composer, performer, audience, a unique mode of communication wells up from the womb of human ingenuity and spills over into the universe of silences and sounds. Music is external revelation of inward reality. The music of the seas, of storms, and all of creation carries cosmic secrets to the threshold of human consciousness, proclaiming the inner truth of all that lives and moves and has planetary or terrestial being, to whoever has ears to hear. All music, from the simplest tribal beat to the most complex harmonic statement, reflects an integration of inner and outer space. As we become more aware of this integral union of who and how we are in the world, we become more at home with ourselves and others and one with the world and with God. Music can unite us with one another, and in that process of at-one-ment, we are comforted and healed.

Polarizing forces at work in the world have contributed to a divided reality that fragments us inside and out. We seem to thrive on opposition, creating contexts and even contests that set us over against someone or something we must conquer in order to control. A hierarchic, competitive mode permeates society and religion. This fundamental dualism is divisive and destructive to body, mind, and psyche, and we cannot simply will it away. We need to take conscious steps toward unity in every sphere of our lived reality, make efforts at integration through all of our disintegrated lives. To be one with the One Who created us and one with the Creator's creation means striving to integrate our inner and outer truths so that we might be one with ourselves. Such an integration is profoundly healing, and music is a means whereby we might bring this healing integration about.

"Mother and God, to You we sing: / wide is Your womb, warm is Your wing. / In You we live, move, and are fed, / sweet, flowing milk, life-giving bread."[5] When will this kind of song arise within our institutionalized religious rites? To proclaim the maternal aspect of what has been for far too long an exclusively patriarchal Deity is to give credence to the biblical claim that we are in God and that God's own Spirit dwells in each of us. Time and again our thrust toward integration is severed at the roots. If we cannot explore who God is for us or how God is within us, how will we know when we find God? And how can God be at home in us? How will the wounds of such soul-splitting segregation ever begin to be healed? When confronted by systematic insensitivity, the soul's song sustains us and brings us home to God. "Mother and God, to You we bring / all broken hearts, all broken wings."[6]

"Mother earth, sister sea, giving birth, energy, / reaching out, touching me lovingly."[7] God is my Mother. Earth is my mother. I am sibling to all that inhabits the universe with me. What a strange, exhilarating discovery. "Formed from earth's own flesh and bone, / one with silt and sand and stone."[8] It is a blessing, therefore, and not a curse to return to the earth from which we have come. The ancient Lenten admonition must be heard holisticly. "Remember that you are dust and to dust you shall return." The appropriate response is, alleluia, and not, woe is me. The Bible tells us that in the beginning God created the heavens and the earth and then drew humanity forth from the earth. If so, then surely we ought to sing: "From the primal womb we are / called to kinship with the stars."[9] Surely we ought to cherish the earth, our sister, our mother, our kin, cherish all her creatures as if her children were our own.

---

5. "Mother and God" from the author's album, *WomanSong*.
6. Ibid.
7. "Mother Earth" from the album, *WomanSong*.
8. Ibid.
9. Ibid.

We must ask forgiveness for the many wounds we have inflicted so viciously upon her, and vow never to harm her again. To achieve this means entering into a new and cosmic relationship with our environment, for the world around us mirrors the myriad ways we might come home to ourselves and be healed. Our music can raise our awareness to this by expressing that intuitive wisdom that surpasses understanding, the wisdom we share with all of creation, for our music is the music of the cosmos, revealing us to ourselves, healing us within ourselves. "It's the song of the universe, as the aeons fall away. / It's the song that the stars sing and all the planets play. / It's a song to the Power neither you nor I can see. / It's a song to the One Who is Mystery."[10]

When we are one with the divine Presence and one with all of creation, we are predisposed to open ourselves up to be one with one another, extending our bonds of kinship beyond the borders of our here and now. Our circle of love is too often circumscribed by the limits of our experience. If we live parochially, we will love parsimoniously, trapped within the suffocating stance of insularity. The poet Edwin Markham wrote: "He drew a circle that shut me out— / heretic, rebel, a thing to flout. / But Love and I had the wit to win: / we drew a circle that took him in."[11] The more we open out to let others in, the more we are whole and healed. Blessed are those who can truly sing, "The life we live extends through a widening circle of friends, / 'til all are caught and held in a circle of love."[12]

Wholeness, healing, integration: that is what the inner journey is about, and it happens when our inner and outer selves, when the world within us and the world around us, when the Creator, creation, and our own creativity merge and emerge as one. We experience this fleetingly through music. I feel it deeply, often through song. It is the closest I have ever come to wholeness, and I suspect to holiness as well. It is where I turn in search of healing, not to be

---

10. "Mystery" from the album, *WomanSong*.
11. "Outwitted," d. 1940.
12. "Circle of Love" from the album, *WomanSong*.

alone in my isolation but in order to center myself within the Center of all my longing, within that Presence, that Power, where all that lives resides. Through music all life can be present to us, and in some sense, present within us. "You spoke a word and stirred a silent spring. / You touched my heart and I began to sing, / to free the music deep in everything. / Now all the earth with its innate melody has meaning for me forever. / You are the song and You are the singing. / All through the longing, You come bringing music."[13] For some, music accompanies their inner journey into wholeness and healing; for others it is the journey itself, the journey into ultimate meaning. When we embrace music as a healing presence, we are already home.

---

13. "You Are the Song" from the album, *WomanSong*.

IV
The Eternal Future
of Sound

Do you know that our soul is composed of harmony?
 Leonardo da Vinci, Notebooks

We know that all living systems are either changing and evolving or static and dying. The rhythms, pulses, tones and energies of sound can efficiently bring changes to living systems. Music can move energy, focus attention and harmonize the mind, emotions, spirit and body.

In this closing section music is acknowledged as a bridge between the spiritual and physical aspects of being. Music thus becomes the art, the sound, the metaphor, the healer, the esoteric symbol, the essence of perception.

As physicians, therapists and musicians begin to consider some of the mystical symbology of music, it may become easier to find language for this powerful world of sound.

This last section focuses on spiritual philosophies. Swami Chetanananda gives us the perspective of a contemporary Hindu, Zen Master Seung Sahn as a Korean Buddhist and Pir Hazrat Inayat Khan as a modern Sufi. Gordon Limbrick and Dane Rudhyar integrate many systems to give insight about holistic views of music and its symbology.

No book can convey the power of sound or the beauty of music. Without the utterance of sound itself, we can only speculate. Thus, it is appropriate in this section to present ideas from a composer, conductor and spiritual philosopher, Kenneth G. Mills, who is devoted to an absolute spiritual attention to Oneness through tone and sound.

18

Dissonant Harmony, Pleromas of Sound, and the Principle of Holistic Resonance

DANE RUDHYAR

Any society or work of art (a musical composition, a painting, a building, a poem, and so on) is a complex whole composed of many parts or units. Whether these units are human beings, musical notes, colored areas, or words does not essentially matter. What matters is the type of organization that makes the units a whole. Two basic types of organization exist. In social organization I have called them the tribal order and the companionate order. In music they are analogous to what I have called the consonant order and the dissonant order.

The tribal order is founded on biological relationship, descent from a community of common ancestors, and a similarity of environment, culture, religion, and way of life. It is the most natural and most easily defined type of relationship. The source from which the tribal community derives its sense of unity—a compulsive, quasi-instinctual feeling-realization—is understood to be in the past, and all members of the tribe are psychically dependent upon an ancestral land. They project their unquestioned feeling of unity upon a tribal god to whom they give personal attributes and with whom they are certain they can communicate, mainly through shamans, prophets, oracles, and eventually an institutionalized priesthood.

In music the harmonic series of fundamental and overtones represents the same kind of order. Each octave of the series symbolizes one generation of the people. The

Dane Rudhyar

One multiplied in tone is like Abraham's seed, whose multiplication in an immense progeny is assured by the tribal god. Octaves of overtones become the basis for the many modes of a consonant and natural music, founded upon the processes of life. Modes manifest in sacromagical tones a kind of consciousness deeply and compulsively rooted in biological activity.

The companionate order begins with a multiplicity of differentiated individuals and has unity as its goal. This goal is difficult to achieve, and it refers to a future condition—a condition in the making. The achievement of this condition of unity (really multiunity) requires the development of a strictly human faculty—understanding—that emerges out of processes of the mind. Thus, while the companionate order is founded upon the will to unity—unity as a goal to be consciously achieved in understanding—it necessitates the activity of the mind.

Mind, however, operates at different ways at different levels of existence. At the biological level, mind is the servant of life. It is the instinctual mind, the function of which is to discover optimum conditions for the preservation and expansion of a biological species. Feelings, emotions, and moods are overtones (as it were) of biology; though eventually these become differentiated and personalized, they can be traced back to their biological roots, even if they should not be entirely reduced to them. These "overtones" operate at the level of the biopsychic mind, which differentiates the personalities of tribesmen from one another but remains the servant of life. It is polarized by the compulsive, repetitive conservation of functional activities intent on perpetuating an original impulse-to-be and on keeping unaltered a prototype, an original form.

The mind operating at the tribal level of organization is therefore oriented to the past. As mind becomes predominantly concerned with solving the problems of transforming and improving the conditions affecting a particular person who feels separate from the community because "special" and having his or her own interests and needs, the mind individualizes. It forgets or loses

264

interest in the collective past of the tribe because it concentrates on solving problems of the personal present. These problems—how to save oneself, for example, or how to profit from a particular situation—are technical problems, that is, they require the individual invention and application of new techniques. Though the mind thus individualizes further, the satisfaction of biological needs and emotional desires for power and comfort makes living in society essential; but the mind in such a state is primarily, and often exclusively, concerned with self-interest and techniques to satisfy it.

Eventually a new kind of mind begins to operate, the "mind of wholeness." Separative self-centeredness and the social and intellectual techniques used to attain power over external things and people and to obtain physical or emotional comfort turn destructive. The principles that form the basis of the companionate order begin to polarize the consciousness of individuals who, though weary of crises and tragedies, nevertheless cling to self-interest and the drive for personal and social power.

These principles had been stated, perhaps many times, by illumined personages and enshrined as ideals to worship— but not to live by. A time comes when their acceptance as a basis for individual and group activity is a matter of actual survival. The mind, transfigured by a new will to unity—unity to be won over the centrifugal passions and self-interests of a multiplicity of competitive egos—becomes the "mind of wholeness." This mind is illumined by the spiritual realization that the whole is not only greater than the sum of its parts but prior to the individual units it contains. Individuals then realize that rather than being primary entities which life's exigencies have gathered into a social whole they are differentiated aspects of a spiritually pre-existent whole. The whole—the society— focuses itself upon the individual in answer to a particular need and for a particular purpose. Thus the companionate order operates wherever a group of individuals, whose minds and psyches have been transformed by such a truly holistic realization, deliberately and irrevocably act, feel, commune, and think as transindividual beings, allowing humanity—or at least their community—to find in them focalizing agents for the release of its power and purpose.

So defined, the companionate principle of organization may seem too ideal and utopian to have any relevance to the vast majority of human beings. Nevertheless, this principle operates in some situations today. To illustrate the difference between the tribal and companionate orders, consider two contemporary gatherings: a family gathering around a Christmas tree and a meeting of delegates to the United Nations. The family gathering is what remains of the tribal order in Western society. The human beings moved by the traditional spirit of Christmas speak the same language, share the same racial, cultural, national, and social background and are probably of the same religion. Personal differences, at least for the time, are forgotten in the celebration of an ancient event which once more vitalizes the great myth of the culture that has formed the collective worldview of the family group.

At the United Nations, however, there are individuals of different races, cultures, nationalities, and religions, who have reached individual status by different paths, and who probably have nothing in common except their common humanity and the will to survive under the critical international situations that have made it imperative for them to meet, discuss, and try to agree. They may dream of a unified mankind, for they know what separateness can lead to, but the actualization of the dream demands constant effort, unceasing vigilance, and faith in a future of which they may be only the architects, not the actual builders. Unity here is in the future. It has to be made before it can be enjoyed. If achieved it has to be "unity in diversity," multi-unity. It can only be achieved through the *harmonization* of differences—which does not mean the reduction of differences to a unity.

Harmony is misunderstood if it is given the same meaning as unity. Its Greek root (harmos) refers to the process of joining together objects previously having a separate existence. Joining boards of wood which had been cut from the same tree so that the patterns made by the grain of the wood match might be called a harmonizing process, but if so it refers to a consonant type of harmony. The process tries to reconstitute a primordial, biological unity. On the other hand, fashioning a crown for the consecration of a king by integrating gold, silver, and precious stones according to an image of symbolic splendor is to produce a dissonant harmony of materials selected for the power, beauty, and sacred significance of their combination.

To produce a consonant harmony one has to retrace the nature of the materials being used to their common source. In music, the perfect chord of the C-major tonality, C, E, G, is a consonant harmony, because the compound notes are harmonics of a lower fundamental C. If this fundamental C has a frequency of 100, the three notes of the perfect chord will have frequencies of 400, 500 and 600. A dissonant harmony is very different. What integrates its components is the realization by a human consciousness faced with it that it is a whole having been endowed with a unifying meaning and purpose.

A tree is of course, a complex whole, but it is a whole issued from a single seed—an original unity. Every part of the tree can be traced back to this physical seed. There is no physical seed to which the materials of a sacred crown can be traced. The crown emerged from a human mind that imagined its form and constituents as *significant symbols* for a particular situation of special importance. A tree operates according to the processes of nature. The creative artist, who gives concrete substance to what he or she imagined, operates according to the needs of the culture or the desires of his or her individual personality.

In somewhat oversimplified terms, then, there is a music of life and a music of the symbol-creating mind. This mind is not the discursive, argumentative, and analytical mind—the intellect—but the mind of wholeness. It is no longer the servant of life processes, which in human beings are psychic as well as biological, but the agent of the will to wholeness. This will is the manifestation of spirit as the principle of unity in operation. Matter, on the other hand, operates according to the principle of multiplicity (and divisibility). In its most basic sense, mind is the harmonizer of spirit and matter; but as a power of harmonization it ultimately serves the purpose of unity, even though it expresses this purpose in the multiple terms of matter.

At a particular stage of human evolution, mind nevertheless becomes fascinated with investigating the quasi-infinite possibilities of formulating what the senses perceive. It tends to become lost in the labyrinths of the divisibility of the materials it investigates. The more names the mind finds to pin down and classify the mirages of a desert world filled with quintillions of grains of sand it calls atoms, the more lost it becomes. Eventually, a bounteous rain transforms this desert into a field of growing lives, and the mind begins to see the world as a "uni-verse," a one-ward reality, wholeness in the making. What it sees is the mind of wholeness. It forever harmonizes dissonances into the immense chord of a space at long last experienced as a plenum of vibratory energy. Space, in its most abstract and most essential reality, is vibrancy. It is SOUND.

When the mind becomes lost in multiplicity, however, it clings to the remembrance of the original feeling of unity. Every universe, every organized system of life, begins in a unitary release of energy. The psychic space of a newborn child vibrates in a simple, pure tone, the AUM tone of its being, still undifferentiated from the mother tone out of which, yet within which, it was born. As a collective psychic entity, every culture—indeed humanity as a planetary organism—has its own AUM tone; and early in the development of a culture-whole this single, pure tone is subconsciously felt or "heard." It is the mother tone that vibrates through the culture's psychomental space, and the members of the culture resonate to it at whatever level they function.

Distraught minds seek rest by trying to reattune themselves to this tone; but even though the tone may be reexperienced in its singleness and vibrancy, the experience means a return to the womb—to a limited, defined space from which emergence once was necessary. Can a weary sunset-consciousness return to the buoyancy of the dawn that was and thereby hope to begin a new day? So to believe is the great illusion of tired minds afraid of letting go of the feeling of being "I." The only way to a new dawn is to accept the mysterious darkness of consciousness mystics call the night of the soul. Only this acceptance can bring to the mind the great dream of the night or perhaps the subliminal experience of space as a sky illumined by countless stars—countless yet all moving as a majestic whole. Out of such experiences a new dawn may come, vibrant with a new creative tone, the AUM of a new day.

Two Concepts of Musical Space

There are two fundamental ways of thinking of space: as an empty container in which a near infinity of entities whirl, moved by a variety of conflicting forces—and space as fullness, a pleroma of being. This fullness of spaces focuses the near infinity of its aspects through a myriad of entities, each of which reveals one of these aspects. I, an individualized person, am one of these aspects of the universal whole, so are you, and so is every other being. In every unit, the whole becomes differently conscious of itself. The consciousness of the whole should not be considered the sum of the consciousness of the myriad beings that are merely its parts, because essentially no entities can be separate as parts. All these entities are the whole itself, defining in a multiplicity of ways the whole's non-dimensional and non-numeratable wholeness of being.

Until very recently Western civilization has been committed to the belief that space is an empty container within which a near infinite number of atoms and larger units move and relate to one another under the pressure of forces of attraction and repulsion. This view pictures each atom as a relatively solid billiard ball, hitting or missing, drawn to or repelled by blindly operating electromagnetic and gravitational forces. Some philosophers believed that these atoms, and their spiritual counterparts called monads, exist forever: that they are the givens of existence. Other philosophers felt that they originated in an immense explosion—which astronomers now call the Big Bang—scattering a metacosmic One into a myriad of particles which after a long process might be drawn back into oneness. Yet what these astronomers, totally committed to the concept

Dane Rudhyar

of an exclusively physical universe, formulate as an explosive beginning, the vitalistically oriented mind sees as an organic process of birth out of a seed.

The concept of space as fullness or plenitude of being can be characterized by the qualificative *holistic*; but this now fashionable term is often used imprecisely, merely as the opposite of analytical or atomistic. The holistic mind is said to deal with any situation as a whole; holistic medicine, for example, is medicine for the whole human being, not only for the person's physical body. The holistic physician not only attempts to cure specific symptoms or injuries but seeks to revitalize the entire organism. An organism is a field of functional activity—a life field. It is an area of space actually reaching beyond the physical skin. The aura (or auric field) of a human being is a space filled with vibratory energies, with sound as well as color, even if average human beings today do not perceive it.

If one speaks of a life field, one can also think of a sound field. The sound field for present-day mankind is our musical space. For practical musical purposes it is represented by the seven octaves of the piano keyboard, a span which is also a series of twelve fifths. Musical space can also be thought of either as an empty container of single, essentially separate musical notes, or as a fullness of tone, a pleroma of sounds. The concept prevalent in Western culture is the first alternative. I am attempting to give a concrete formulation to the latter.

For a human ear, sounds are only potential in the musical space covered by a piano; they have to be actualized by striking keys that set in vibration separate strings producing sounds to which the composer gives the meaning of musical notes, each having its own pitch. But the piano is not only constituted by a ladder of notes; what we hear is the *resonance* of the one sounding board. The whole sounding board vibrates. Sounds are produced by the strings; Tone is released by the sounding board acting as an *agent* for the concretization of the whole musical space defined by the piano structure and its limitations.

Tone (capitalized) indicates or symbolizes the holistic resonance of the entire sounding board when a multiplicity of sounds are generated by the pianist's hands performing swift runs or striking chords. The pianist, however, selects certain notes from among all the possible notes the piano can produce. This selection obeys rigid cultural patterns if the pianist is performing a traditionally tonal kind of music. The selection is primarily conditioned, and to a large extent predetermined, by a collective tradition, secondarily by a particular school of music having its own technique of composition. But the selection can be strictly individual if the composer-pianist believes that all the sounds and all the combinations of sounds the piano can produce are to be used freely by the unconditioned will or emotional impulse seeking to communicate through the hands a state of consciousness (or by the ego to satisfy its desire for what is euphemistically called self-expression).

Consider a sculptor about to work on a block of marble. Let us say that the hands of the sculptor are allowed gradually to release from the chunk of matter a form which the sculptor comes to realize has been held in latency by the stone—a form needing to be actualized concretely because it potentially fills a human need, even if the need is only for beauty. The sculptor fashions a significant artistic object out of the material fullness of space. There are, however, sculptors who impose a predetermined form on the material fullness of space or, especially today, who fasten together assorted pieces of material to make objects according to intellectual esthetic concepts.

I have spoken of the truly creative artist as one who performs "the sacred operation by means of which the fullness of Space-substance would be differentiated into forms."* When I spoke of such artists as "tillers of Space . . . fecundating Space-substance toward the bringing forth of *esthetic* forms," I should have said of *sacromagical* forms, for later I spoke of the creative artist as "the magician evoking form-organisms out of Space, conjuring forth the progeny of Space—realizing the interdependence of all that lives in and still more *from* Space, the great Matrix of

---

*Rudhyar, *Art as Release of Power* (Carmel: Hamsa Publications, 1930).

all forms." From such a point of view the relationship between the constituting parts of an organic form has to be interpreted as the "interpenetration and not the mere juxtaposition" of these parts within a whole.

All these statements can be applied to musical space. When music is an assemblage of notes written down as a musical score, the music extends as an organized collection of notes—the musical atoms of classical physics—in the emptiness of a musical space represented by the sheets of paper of the score. This is the atomistic approach to music. Its horizontal and vertical series of notes—melodies and chords—can be analyzed and divided into their components. These components may be short, repetitive sequences of notes, musical themes, and leitmotifs. Moreover, because the human mind finds itself lost amidst assemblages of seemingly unrelated units, if it cannot discover order relating these units it devises patterns of interconnections and what it calls laws of nature. In Western music the result of this devisal is the tonality system.

The human mind is so conditioned by its need for order and for a system of laws and regulations that it asserts it has discovered them in nature and the physical universe. It is reluctant to admit that its discoveries may well be a projection of its own characteristic structure, thus of its limitations or the limitations of the sense data it is asked by the whole human organism to interpret. Because this human organism operates not only at the biological level but also at the level of collective psychism and personal emotions, the interpretation the mind is asked to formulate should provide sustainment, enjoyment, and expansion for the life functions and for the entire person.

The Western world thinks of the order of nature and the cosmos in scientific terms that belong to the atomistic approach to reality—as *extension* in three-dimensional space, and more recently in four-dimensional space-time. A truly holistic approach would instead establish the required sense of order on the concept of *intention*. Years ago I tried to trigger the realization of a spiritual kind of space in which where God intends to be, there He is.* This space

*"The Search for Ultimates," *Seed for Greater Living* (July 19, 1955).

is nondimensional; it has no measurable distances. It is not the kind of space in which a body has to be physically transported from one place to another in a way our senses or our machines can perceive, analyze, and define. It is not the kind of space in which two objects cannot occupy the same place at the same time (the principle of exclusion on which Western science is based). It is the space of undivided wholeness—pleroma Space.

Having to interpret such a Space, the mind is still obliged to think of different centers or areas of activity and consciousness. They interpenetrate in the true philosophical fourth "dimension" which in reality is not a dimension because it is nonmeasurable. Every center within that Space can be anywhere *if it intends to be there.** In such a Space there is no real distance to be traveled. What is required in order to be anywhere is a determined shift of intention—also of attention. The mind is being refocused from one locality-conditioned state of consciousness to another, every locality (in the physical sense of the term) being a concretized projection of a particular state of consciousness, a projection which fulfills a basic meaning and purpose.

Musical space can be considered from such a holistic point of view, and ultimately experienced. This holistic musical space has one fundamental quality, which I characterize by the capitalized word "Tone." *Tone is the quality inherent in the musical space which the human ear perceives as sound and to which the human mind, developed according to a particular culture, can respond as music.* Tone is brought to a focus by a process of musical organization

---

*The American writer Paul Brunton stayed at the ashram of Sri Ramana Maharshi in India and reported that one day, feeling anxious for his family in New York from which he had had no news, his guru asked him why he seemed so depressed. Told of Brunton's concern, Sri Ramana closed his eyes and after a few moments said, "I have been in New York. What do you want to know that is happening there?"

The modern student of esoteric doctrines may speak of "astral travel," but this is still thinking in terms of dimensional space. To say that the Hindu holy man traveled in a body through an astral realm reveals the modern mind's inability to operate as the mind of wholeness.

Dane Rudhyar

giving rise to sequences or simultaneities of sounds, each
of which has tone (that is, communicable musical meaning)
because it is a focalized aspect of the Tone of the whole.
(Similarly the wholeness of cosmic Space has one fundamental quality, consciousness. Consciousness focuses
itself at various levels through minds, some possessing a
strictly collective character; others, at a particular level
of human evolution and under specific culture-determined
conditions, taking a myriad of individualized forms, each
of which feels itself and claims to be "I, myself.")

The crucial issue is whether the groupings of sounds
organized by cultures into music are interpreted as focalized
objectivations of a particular aspect of musical space for a
particular purpose or as composite sonic entities having
a separate physical identity as themes or leitmotifs susceptible
of being developed, expanded, and transposed in a formal,
culturally conditioned manner. Just as a particular society
(and mankind as a whole) is prior to any person whose
basic patterns of living, feeling, and thinking are formed
and basically controlled by the wholeness (the collective
psychism) of the sociocultural whole, so any particular
piece of music is a product of a particular culture and of
the system of organization dominating the culture. This
system has a particular character and is inspired by a
particular quality of collective living, feeling, and thinking.
This quality is the specific Tone of the culture-whole. But
a culture-whole is only one of the many, relatively fleeting
phases in the evolution of humanity. Its tone is but one
aspect of the all-encompassing Tone of the musical space
which human beings can experience and to which they
may respond creatively in terms of their individual temperament and destiny (*dharma*).

Composers whose sense of music has been trained
according to the rigid traditions of the European culture
find it very difficult, if not impossible, to experience the
wholeness of musical space available to the human consciousness and therefore to experience the quality inherent
in the wholeness of that space, Tone. They experience
Tone only within the limitations imposed by Western

culture. Similarly, most individual persons can only experience Consciousness—the quality of the wholeness of cosmic Space—within the limitations imposed by, first, their culture and, second, the ego that defines their individual character and responses to their physical and social environment.

The most creative and future-oriented musicians of the twentieth century—which does not mean the most famous and most often performed!—have been attempting to expand their musical feelings and their approach to composing or performing music. The more or less conscious and consistent urge to dis-Europeanize and even deculturalize music has driven them to repudiate the organizational rules and patterns of their Western tradition (the European tonality system) and to try to free their musical consciousness from the exclusive use of traditional instruments that produce only particular qualities of sounds. They have done the latter by introducing many types of non-harmonic sounds and noises. These traditionally non-musical sounds exist within the musical space experienceable by human beings. In principle they can be given a musical meaning, but this gift of meaning can be made neither by the intellectual mind, eager for novelty and fame-producing personal "originality," nor by an emotional revulsion against sounds or sound-combinations that have become banal through too much repetition, even though such a revulsion has become fashionable. In order to create a new sense of reality, the gift of meaning must proceed from a consciousness of the whole. It should develop out of the experience of the wholeness of musical space and the innermost realization of Tone as its essential quality.

Holistic Resonance

Tone, the fullness of vibratory Space, the pleroma of all experienceable sounds, can also be called *holistic resonance*, a term which may have a more easily understood, practical significance. The word *resonance* conveys the feeling of an interpenetration of sound vibrations. But I am using the word in a different sense from the one made famous by

Dane Rudhyar

Helmholtz. His experiments with resonators have led musicians along the path of analytical (also materialistic) scientific investigation, and this in turn has led them to misunderstand and exaggerate the importance of harmonics and overtones.

We have already discussed the resonance of natural (the human body, its vocal organs and resonant cavities) and man-made instruments (for instance, a piano or violin). Here the resonance of "musical space" refers to the total resonance of our world of physical matter to the impact of creative power (released by divine or human will or emotions) within the range of vibrations the human ears can hear. This physical world of human experience is not unlike an immense sounding board; and the sounding board of a piano is the best illustration or symbol afforded by Western music, because the seven octaves of the piano symbolize the normal extension of our practically usable musical space.

Should all the piano keys be struck at once, setting in vibration the nearly two-hundred strings, the sounding board would resonate to the full of its capacity for resonance —thus pushing to its limit the tone clusters devised by Henry Cowell (and to a lesser extent before him by Leo Ornstein and Charles Ives). But such a sound would be a symbol of cosmic chaos rather than order. The concept of cosmos implies ordered differentiation, relatedness, and harmonization through interaction and interpenetration. If no atom were related to any other atom, the sum of these unrelated atoms would indeed be a chaos, for a whole is not a sum of unrelated units.

Thus a pleroma of sound is not the sum, within a limited musical field (the range of a particular instrument or of an entire orchestra), of all possible sounds unrelated to one another. A pleroma of sound is an all-encompassing organization of sounds produced by the interaction and interpenetration of a multiplicity of *relationships*, each ensouled by its own tone, all these tones actualizing diverse aspects of the Tone of the whole pleroma.*

---

*Similarly a nation is not actually an aggregation of unrelated individuals, but instead an organization of social classes and groups. Considered as voters the individuals are abstract units susceptible

276

In European music from 1600 to 1800 tonality fulfilled (to some extent) the function of a pleroma of sounds: all the notes interrelated by a rigid tonal structure were considered parts of a musical whole, each note or chord contributing to the integrated tone, or resonance, of the piece. But because this tonality resonance of the whole was related in a quasi-paternalistic way to an originating source, the tonic (the father or tribal great ancestor), the Tone of the musical piece resulted from the fact that all the component sounds belonged to the paternalistic field—the musical space—defined by the tonality system and issued from the tonic note, the original seed.

The pleroma concept basically differs from the tonality concept in the same way that dissonant harmony differs from consonant harmony. Tonality is based (psychologically and philosophically) on the urge to refer the multiplicity of sound-relationships (intervals) to a primordial One—the tonic, or in terms of the harmonic series, the fundamental tone. A pleroma of sounds refers to the process of harmonization through which differentiated vibratory entities are made to interact and interpenetrate in order to release a particular aspect of the resonance inherent in the whole of the musical space, its holistic resonance, its Tone.

In the beginning is the One, the tonic. In the conclusion there is the Whole, the pleroma whose soul quality is Tone. The tonic (or the fundamental of the harmonic series) represents the alpha of musical evolution; the pleroma of sounds, the omega. The sacromagical consciousness of early human beings stressed primordial unity, the monotone endlessly repeated to make sure that the differentiated many would never forget the interrelatedness which they could experience and conceive only in terms of their common descent from the One—biologically the common ancestor and psychically the tribal god. Multi-unity is the end of a cycle of culture, the omega condition of music in and

---

of being added, thus producing a sum. But the success of national polls reveals that the beliefs and reactions of these theoretical individuals mainly depend on the class or group to which they belong. Each class or group represents one particular aspect of the national whole.

through which the wholeness of the whole can be "heard" as Tone.

Concentration on the One leads to a devotional attitude and, in music, to the harmonic series as a principle of differentiation of the one fundamental into the many harmonics believed to be issued from this one root tone. On the other hand, concentration upon the wholeness of any whole leads to the realization of Space as fullness of being. Here "being" refers to being-in-relation, for (from this point of view) Space is the total relatedness of every area of Space to every other area. I say "area" rather than "point" because Space is not to be seen as the sum of all individual points (and even less of abstract points) but as a complex of conpenetrating relationships between areas, small or vast.

One wonders what successive generations of Pythagoras's disciples understood of what their master tried to convey when speaking of his experience of the "music of the spheres," because he spoke to a people whose music was almost entirely monophonic and thus dominated by time and the factor of sequence in time. When the ancients spoke of planetary spheres they referred to concentric spheres surrounding the earth. In Dante's *Divine Comedy*, God was the center of the several concentric spheres, which became darker and more material as their distances from the sublime core of divine light increased. In either case the vision dealt with universal space. The whole of space was experienced in one moment of illumined consciousness. Might not Pythagoras's experience of the music of the spheres also have referred to the hearing of the *simultaneity* of the seven cosmic levels of Tone, to an immense septenary cosmic chord? Perhaps the monochord measured only an abstract, linear projection of the postulated radii of these spheres, and with the later intellectualization of the Greek mind (during and after the fifth century B.C.) the linear measurements came to obscure the experience of the resonance of three-dimensional spheres.

Modern acoustics interprets the phenomenon of sound in terms of the linear movements of the ear's timpani and of the vibrating membranes of loud speakers, but the human being has two ears and can experience the difference between stereophonic and monophonic recordings. The composer Henry Eichheim, who pioneered in promoting the value of Asian music and in using Asian instruments in his orchestration, showed me (some fifty years ago) two very small Tibetan cymbals that were tuned to slightly different pitches. As they were struck against each other an extremely beautiful, vibrant tone was produced, because of the interference of two sound waves of slightly different frequencies. This phenomenon produces "beats," the frequency of the beats being equal to the difference in frequencies of the two tones. Combination tones are also produced when loud tones are sounded together, and these phenomena are used in various ways in some organs.

Such compound sounds are thought to be subjective, to be a physiological rather than acoustical phenomenon. They are said to result from the "non-linear organization of the inner ear (*cochlea*)."* Such statements, however, deal only with the analytical processes of the modern scientific mentality. These acoustical phenomena in fact reveal the complexity of the experience of tone—of holistic resonance. The most stirring holistic resonances are produced by the great gongs of China, Japan, and Java, by some Tibetan instruments, and by the bells of European cathedrals. Their tones are nonharmonic and nonperiodic. Perhaps more deeply than anything else, they are the concrete, physical manifestations of the souls of the great "universal religions," Buddhism and Christianity. Gongs are made to sound by being struck from the outside, whereas bells are set in vibration by a clapper normally inside of the bell. This may symbolize the difference between Jesus' teaching that the kingdom of heaven is within and the Buddha's denial of a permanent individuality (*anatman*), the human self being a temporary focus of an all-enveloping, cosmic-spiritual, dynamic wholeness.

Typical musicians, of course, do not understand the meaning of bells and gongs for their respective cultures,

---

*See the entry on *combination tone* in Apel, *Harvard Dictionary of Music*.

Dane Rudhyar

and they are often concerned only with whether or not the bells are properly tuned. Bells used in a modern orchestra are parodies of the great church bells, as they have been deprived of their psychic quality and meaning: the bells of old Europe unified the people in moments of devotion and celebration, in which the collective psychism of the culture and religion was repetitively reinforced and dynamized. These bells also marked the daily rhythm of time—a collectively experienced time before clocks, then watches, came into current and individualized use.

A resonant piano can be made to produce interpenetrating sequences of gong-like tones by the use of fairly large dissonant chords. The total complex of vibrations, controlled by an effective and sensitive use of the pedal, results (especially in pianos tuned according to the system of temperament) in nonharmonic waves of sound in which the sense of individual notes and tonality is lost. What is gained is the ability to deal with pleromas of sound and to directly manipulate the potentially all-inclusive Tone of the whole musical space to which human beings can respond.* These pleromas of sound have musical meaning in the total resonance they induce in the piano's sounding board—and not only in the ears of a listener but in his or her psyche—far more than in the component notes and their precise frequencies. Such holistic resonances should not be evaluated quantitatively (in numbers of vibrations per second) but according to the quality of the psychic feeling-response they are meant to elicit.

A music intending to communicate the psychic energy of actual tones could be called *syntonic* music. It would be based on an experience of tone, unconstrained by the intellectual concepts of the classical tonality system or made difficult by the habits and memories of conditioning or academic training. But large scale communication would be difficult initially, because the necessary psychism is still inchoate. An individualized psychism can communicate

*For a more detailed account of my approach to this "orchestral pianism," see my book, *Culture, Crisis and Creativity* (Wheaton, Ill.: Quest Books, 1977), chapter 7.

effectively only to people or groups open to its particular quality. These individuals and groups have to be free from both the attachment to and revulsion against the musical, tonality-controlled past, for both revulsion and attachment create bondage.

Tonal relationships are included in the space relationships of syntonic music, but the rules, patterns, and cadences obligatory in a tonality-controlled music hinder the development of a syntonic consciousness. The restrictive patterns and formalism of a music controlled by the tonality-system undoubtedly have served a valid purpose for the European culture and its American and global prolongations. Today, however, as all cultural traditions disintegrate, the use of precisely tuned scales and essentially separate notes having an abstract, intellectual existence on the background of empty space hides a psycho-musical inability to respond to the possibility of allowing the full vibrancy of the whole musical space to inspire (or inspirit) a new consciousness of Tone.

In syntonic music, because the fullness of the entire humanly experienceable musical space is the fundamental reality, any sound can be used as part of a sequence (melody) or simultaneity (chord) of sounds. But this does not mean the absence of selection in the composition of a particular work of music intended to communicate a particular state or fulfill a particular personal or collective function and purpose. What is selected is from the whole musical space, and that wholeness remains potentially involved in the resonance of the total work. The process of selection is an open process.

This approach to composing music essentially does away with the rules of harmony taught in schools. Chords with complex names and meant to reveal or maintain tonality become simply sound-simultaneities, or more or less complex modes of vibration of the musical space. Dissonant chords need not be resolved into consonance. Sound-simultaneities may not be susceptible of being transposed or of being sounded in a different register without their tone quality being radically altered. Absolute pitch, however, need not refer to a definite number of vibrations per second wherever, whenever, by whom, or for whom the music is performed. It may be absolute only in relation to the actual instrument (natural or man-made) producing the sound, and even to the time and environment of the performance.

Many or most of the chords called dissonant in Western musical theory can generate, when their component sounds are properly spaced, a far more powerful resonance than so-called perfect consonances, because of the phenomena of beats and combination tones. Such chords are more than the sum of their parts. The sounds said to be subjective belong to the realm of psychism. They defy intellectual, quantitative analysis. A holistic resonance differs from a chord of intellectually analyzed musical notes somewhat as a synthetic medical substance made by isolating definable chemical hormones differs from the direct extract from a whole endocrine gland—a chemical effect differs from a biological effect, even though the difference may escape scientific analysis. The difference cannot be reduced to numbers because the natural combination of the substances produced by the whole endocrine gland has greater life-sustaining power than the sum of these substances considered separately, even if biochemists could isolate them all, which usually they cannot.* Similarly, a memorable musical theme or leitmotif has an emotional-psychic power not explainable by listing and adding up its intervals or the frequencies of its notes. The theme's power can be understood only in terms of the psychic resonance evoked in the musical space by the interplay and interpenetration of the several sounds in combination.

The basic factor is the combination of sounds acting dynamically upon the musical consciousness of the hearers, and this combination potentially affects the whole music space directly or indirectly resonating to it. The resonance

---

*The synthesized, isolated and particularly "active" chemicals may be extremely powerful, but theirs is an unbalanced and often violent kind of power which may have dangerous after-effects. European doctors quite a few years ago spoke of American medicine, so often based on the use of such synthetic products, as "heroic medicine"—excellent no doubt on the battlefield.

is immediate if the sounds are simultaneous or it may be expanded in time if the sounds are in sequence (a melody). A chord is a sudden release of power; a melody is a process of release. When human beings acted as a unified tribe—as a chording of consonant units within a stable whole—the tribal chord of being (the culture and its psychism) was so basic that individually improvised melodies could arise from it. In classical Europe, tonality being the un-questioned reality of music, melodies could flow, rather aimlessly but spontaneously, for the sheer pleasure of making endless variations (musical arabesques) on the major or minor tonality pattern issued from the perfect chord and its permutations. We are, however, no longer living in such a cultural situation. Individuals stand at least relatively alone, insulated by their egos. The trend toward the forma-tion of small groups of musicians, improvising together perhaps in an attempt to interpenetrate musically as well as psychically, is characteristic of the urge to be able to feel as a whole and thus to reach a state of harmonization.

In syntonic music the notes of Western music, no longer basically held by the root power of tonality, are drawn into holistic group formations. Instead of emerging from a One (a tonic), they seek the interpenetrative condition of dissonant chords—pleromas of sounds. These are limited in content; each has its own principle of organization, which determines the tone of the pleroma. All these tones ideally commune in the vast Tone of the all-encompassing pleroma of the musical space experienceable by human ears; but actually each of the particularized and limited pleromas has its own character, and its holistic emanation (tone) is meant by the composer (consciously or not) to fulfill a particular need. The need may be personal, social, or cultural, or it may be transpersonal—the need for the psychic transformation of the composer or the listeners in a concert-hall or ritualized situation.

*   *   *   *   *   *

A large portion of humanity in both the East and the West is no longer supported and empowered by the collective psychism of its natal culture. Power has to be built by personal concentration and an interior transformation into the music (or any of the arts) one creates. To fill with Tone sounds that are empty because they are no longer rooted in a vibrant and dynamic cultural matrix, the composer and performer have to pour into them their own individualized psychism; and this means to empower the instruments with a resonant vibrancy that gives them a new life—rather than more "color."

This resonant vibrancy of the actual musical and instrumental material can be obtained, most meaningfully and psychoactively, I believe, through the use of dissonant harmonies evoking a fullness of resonance, which can only come through harmonizing differences and even conflicting vibrations. The age of patriarchal tribal homogeneity is gone. Should it return someday it would have to be at a higher level which is impractical and unrealistic today. *Vibrancy* is indeed the key to the empowerment of sounds by the magic of Tone. But a new kind of magic is now demanded by creative individuals able to live, feel, and think in transpersonal terms as agents of humanity as a whole—the magic of syntonic consciousness. The creative Sound that is "in the beginning" and the illumined plenum of Space-consciousness that constitutes the omega state of "the end of time" can blend. And in this blending—however tentative and imperfectly realized— the birth of a new music and a new age can be, if not concretely actualized, at least heralded. The way of every Christ has to be prepared by a John the Baptist in whom end meets beginning.

The Principle of Consistency in Composite Wholes

Students of music are taught rules of composition, but there is really only one ruling principle in any creative activity: consistency. Consistency manifests as an assured and quasi-organic rhythm of unfoldment, a sustained process of formation or transformation.

In the last chapter of his excellent book, *The Tao of Physics,* Fritjof Capra speaks of the interpretation of what human beings perceive as matter, the "bootstrap" hypothesis of the Berkeley physicist Geoffrey Chew. According to this bootstrap philosophy, "the universe is seen as a dynamic web of interrelated events. None of the properties of any part of this web is fundamental; they all follow from the properties of the other parts and the overall consistency of their mutual interrelations determines the structure of the entire web." In other words, "nature cannot be reduced to fundamental entities, such as elementary particles or fundamental fields. It has to be understood entirely through its self-consistency."*

While it is impossible to detail here how such a theory of reality can be related to the wholeness of musical space and the principle of the interpenetration of sonic vibrations within holistic resonances based on dissonant harmony, the implications of such a view necessarily affect all fields of human activity, music included. Capra mentions Joseph Needham's study of the essential concepts of the Taoist philosophy in China and quotes him as saying that "the harmonic cooperation of all beings arose, not from the orders of a superior authority external to themselves, but from the fact that they were all parts of a hierarchy of wholes forming a cosmic pattern, and what they obeyed were *the internal dictates of their own nature* [italics mine] . . . The Chinese did not even have a word corresponding to the classical Western idea of a law of nature."† Capra further states that in the most recently developed kind of physics "self-consistency is the essence of all laws of nature" and that "in a universe which is an inseparable whole and where all forms are fluid and ever-changing there is no room for any fixed fundamental entity."

This "fluid and ever-changing" world is the world of music—music freed from the intellectual and formalistic constraints of the classical theory of tonality which, significantly, became set during the century in which the concepts of Newton and Descartes crystallized the modern scientific attitude—at least until Einstein, Dirac, and

---

*Boulder, Colo.: Shambhala Publications, 1975, pp. 285-86.
†Capra, p. 289

Heisenberg. The solid atoms which for Newtonian physics constituted the foundation of matter—and the indestructible monads Leibnitz postulated during the same period—correspond in their abstractness to the precise musical notes of classical European music moving according to definite rules within the rigidly defined yet essentially empty space of a musical score. The score features musical staves with set lines establishing equally set intervals; equally unyielding bars establish strong and weak beats dominated by the metronomic time of simple rhythms. Even the melodies have to last a set number of bars.

Music has indeed been straightjacketed, but human beings who were developing a centrifugal kind of individualism (or at least emotional personalism) and reaching toward the ideal of *laissez-faire* democracy needed an externally and rationalistically controlled musical order to maintain psychic integration. They were afraid of the spontaneity and creative freedom of spirit, and they have not proven able to live without external constraints, once (as is happening today) the constraints have broken down.

The reaction to the absence of constraints passes as simplicity and is an attempt to return to a magical repetitiveness, yet with an underlying confusion as well as a sophisticated craving for a freedom which is neither magical nor sacred, and to which most persons are not able to give a self-consistent meaning. To realize such a meaning, a person has to be established (or stabilized) in his or her own identity; but this identity should not be thought of, even at a postulated "spiritual" level, as an insulated and self-sufficient being. Identity should be understood as the wholeness of a self-consistent process from germinating seed (alpha state) to consummating seed (omega state)—a wholeness which itself is a component of a still greater whole, humanity.

Thus a musical work should have an identity, but an identity that is neither static nor predetermined by a traditional form existing in a realm of quasi-absolute value. The work's hearer should be allowed the feeling-experience of discovering the seed unity of the music within the multiplicity of sounds. But this is possible only if the hearer *lets* the tone of the wholeness of the musical whole resonate in his or her consciousness and feeling-nature. This seed tone may be a vertical organization of definite notes—a complex chord whose components are allowed to interact and interpenetrate as do the many components of a great Asian gong—or it may only be implied in the musical process, to be revealed perhaps only in moments of focalized meaning and intensity of psychic communication.

This process must have internal consistency; it should be meant (subconsciously often more than consciously) to fulfill a need. Spirit always operates in function of the fulfillment of a need. It operates in order to re-equilibrate (to make again whole and dynamic, that is, full of tone) what had become repairably disintegrated and psychically distraught by pulls and pressures it found itself incapable of repelling or assimilating. In music the latter are discords. To transmute discords into harmonic dissonances is the eternal way of the creative and transformative spirit; and such a spirit is needed in music now more than at any other time.

A vision of cosmic possibilities for music

The dissonantly integral and holistically resonant music of the future can hardly be imagined at this precarious moment of human history. If mankind should have to return to simpler, less technologically complex forms of living, yet with a new sense of "universal brotherhood," integrated groups of human beings centralized by a common purpose may feel again the need for singing together in physical unison, while great gong-like instruments halo their chants with the vibrancy of the musical space these unified voices psychically evoke.

* * * * * *

Music does not reside in musical notes themselves. It is released through the vibrancy and tone of material instruments that resonate to the impact of the psyche, individual or collective, of human beings. Music is psychic communication. If there is a profound meaning in what the inspired scientist, Donald Hatch Andrews, states in his book, *The Symphony of Life,** —that "the universe is more like music than like matter"—it is because the universe is a whole constituted by an incredibly complex network of communication that relates everything to everything else.

The secret of such an ubiquitous and all-encompassing communication is the interpenetration of all forms of existence at the level of cosmic psychism—the anima mundi of medieval occultists, the "world soul." At that level every center of being resonates to every other, merged in an all-inclusive Harmony. Yet because every center of consciousness still mysteriously retains its identity—its singularity of process and vibration, its spiritual tone— this Harmony is a dissonant harmony, an unceasing victory over the centrifugal pull of multiplicity. It is divine love forever triumphing over indifference as well as integrating differences into music—the true music of the spheres.

---

*Lee's Summit, Mo.: Unity Books, 1966.

19
The Symphony of Life

SWAMI CHETANANANDA

The Ancient Science of Sound

Beneath the cacophony of life there exists a sound of un-surpassed sweetness. It is not sound as we know it—not something to be heard as much as something to be felt. It is a vibration. Sometimes you can feel it spontaneously, perhaps as you lie in bed waiting to fall asleep, or on a quiet morning in the country. For the most part, it takes an effort to feel it, simply because the powerful noises that surround us tend to block it out. Yet the individuals who seek depth in their lives will, at some point or other, befriend this sound and begin to explore it. And in doing so they can find assurance in the fact that they are not alone—that all the great esoteric and spiritual traditions have studied the phenomenon of that subtle vibration for thousands of years. Perhaps nowhere was this carried out to a greater degree of exacting science than in India, where the whole topic falls under the rubric of the "science of mantra."

It would not be an exaggeration to say that the investiga-tion of sound was perhaps the single most important thrust of study for the ancient sages of India. In their fervor and passion for truth, these earliest scientists repeated the same experiment day after day. They watched themselves; they meditated on the Inner Self; they observed the Self functioning in different realms of experience. In the classical mythology, Shiva himself appeared to instruct these seekers, whether in dreams or in physical reality. From this contact, which was nothing other than the contact with their inner-most Self, they evolved a profound teaching about the nature of sound and its relationship to all levels of life. The two most important things they discovered about sound can be summarized very simply (although to grasp them is another matter altogether): 1) sound (vibration) is the essence of the universe, and 2) understanding sound is the means to liberation or Self-realization. The remainder of this paper is a discussion of those two points from the tradition of *Kashmir Shaivism*—the written and oral branch of Indian philosophy that originated in the northwest province of India called Kashmir.

First, a few words about Kashmir Shaivism. This philosophy is monistic, its basic tenet being that the entire universe is nothing but conscious energy, and that everything in the universe is that consciousness expressed in different forms. The word "Shaivism" is derived from Shiva, which is a name for the Ultimate Reality. Its principal text, the *Shiva Sutras*, which will be discussed further below, was revealed and studied in Kashmir, hence "Kashmir Shaivism." The system is also known as Trika philosophy, because it is based on the threefold principles of God, soul and matter.

According to legend, in the ninth century A.D., the great sage and saint Vasugupta was told by Lord Shiva in a dream to go to a certain rock and read the teachings carved on it. These teachings, now known as the *Shiva Sutras*, consist of seventy-seven succinct sutras (verses) of revealed wisdom in simple language. Vasugupta copied these teachings, studied them, wrote about them, and passed the teaching on to his disciples. The *Sutras* and their associated com-mentaries are the heart of Shaivist philosophy. The major premise of Shaivism is that the *single* Ultimate Reality has two aspects, one transcending the universe (*prakasha*, lit. "the bright, or shining") and one manifesting through it (*vimarsha*, lit. "experience"). The system categorizes cosmic evolution into thirty-six categories or *tattvas*. It discusses the origin of spirit and matter as well as the nature of Ultimate Reality, and explains the principle of *spanda*—the principle that is the focus of this paper.

It should be noted at the outset that the insights gained by Kashmir Shaivites were by no means exclusive to their tradition. There is tremendous support for their insights in other traditions. For example, the Bible, in the New Testament Gospel of St. John, describes the Creation as proceeding from sound: "In the beginning was the Word and the Word was with God, and the Word was God. He was in the beginning with God; all things were made through him, and without him was not anything made that was made." The Greek philosopher Pythagoras likewise talked of the cosmic role of sound. "Each celestial body, in fact each and every atom, produces a particular sound on account of its movement, its rhythm or vibration. All these sounds and vibrations form a universal harmony in which each element, while having its own function and character, contributes to the whole." And of course great musicians of all time have known of and written about the transcendental nature of sound and its power to bring the listener to a divine state. Beethoven claimed about his own music that, "No evil fate can touch my music. He who divines its secret is freed from the unhappiness that haunts the whole world of men."[1]

What is extraordinary about Kashmir Shaivism is the extent to which its founders delved into the nature of sound. They pursued their researches with a rigor that parallels that of today's great physicists and mathematicians. They wrote elaborate texts and created complex terminology to describe their experiences. The Kashmir Shaivites found that the universe originates from one completely subtle sound that gives rise to all other, more gross vibrations. In a sense there is a hierarchy of sounds, and one might talk about the descent of sound from the subtlest and most impalpable to the densest and most palpable. Yet, unlike a hierarchy, there is no separation between the levels. The subtlest incorporates the most gross. However, the untrained human is often only aware of the grossest levels. Just as the melody of a single violin is lost next to the clamoring of a subway car, so the awareness of the subtlest sound, the subtlest vibration, is lost to the distracted awareness of an untrained mind.

Critical to the Kashmir Shaivite discussion of sound is the principle of *spanda*. It means throb or pulse. It also means an urge. It might be described as the essence of a wave in the ocean of Consciousness—an impulse or desire to create and enjoy. Perhaps originally it was a flutter of love. In any case, it is not an ordinary desire or impulse, for it emanates not only from the center outward, but from everywhere at once. From deep inside the ocean of Consciousness, something moves. From that *spanda*, the whole world comes forth.

This ocean of Consciousness is the Absolute; the throb is Its creative power. In another famous text of Shaivism, the *Paryantapanchashika*, the great master of Kashmir Shaivism, Abhinavagupta, says that the Absolute (*Paramashiva*) and His creative power (*Parashakti*) are the divine couple. He rests always in His eternal nature, and She is eternally active, expanding to reveal and to reabsorb the whole of the universe. She is His first stir and also the infinite stirring. This first stir is also called *spanda*. Abhinavagupta further describes *spanda* as unobjectified desire which leads Consciousness (*Paramashiva*) to feel incomplete. It is the first stage of consciousness before it crystallizes into the reasoning process. The senses get their power in *spanda*. The pulsation of *spanda* exists continuously; and in all the different states of consciousness there is *spanda*. It is the residual, foundational substratum of the manifested world.

The vibration of *spanda* moves in the atmosphere like a resonance. From this resonance, and the interplay of its vibrations, a symphony of energies comes forth. Substance and form are created without ever losing unity in Consciousness. The whole universe is the result of the proliferation of these vibrations emanating from *Parashakti* or *Paravac*, the primal sound, the subtle sound that arises at a frequency before noise. Inherent in the expansion of *Parashakti* are the three powers of will, consciousness, and action (*iccha shakti, jnana shakti,* and *kriya shakti*). From these three powers emanate the two currents of substance and form: *vachaka*, the current of words and meaning which further divides into *varna, mantra,* and *pada*; and *vachya*, the current of objects, which further divides into *kala, tattva,* and *bhuvana.* These together form what is called the "sixfold path of emanation" from which everything ultimately manifests. *Kala* is time and space, *tattva* in this context is the interaction of sound in time and space, and *bhuvana* is the resulting gross matter.

The discovery of the Shaivite scholars that matter comes from vibration is supported by the findings of the world's great scientists. Physicists continue to find evidence that there is no substantive physical world. Because the special theory of relativity states that energy and mass are actually variations of the same stuff (called mass-energy), quantum physics is led to conclude that everything is a form of energy, i.e., that the "solid particles" that compose our world are formed by the intersection of waves of energy. When the Shaivite scholars characterized the world as a combination of different frequencies, they were saying much the same things as the quantum physicists, since sound and movement are inseparable. Indeed, because sound in the Shaivite texts refers to much subtler vibrations than the gross sounds that we are familiar with, one would be safe in saying that the ninth century Shaivites and today's scientists are saying exactly the same thing.

The Microcosm Contains the Macrocosm

According to Shaivism, everything in the universe exists in each individual. We can illustrate this in its most gross form by noting that all the elements that form the matter of our bodies (e.g., carbon, helium) are either given off by our sun or produced in other areas of the universe hundreds of billions of light years away. Another dramatic illustration is found in the recent work with holographic images and the resulting discussion of the "holographic paradigm."[2] Holography is a method of lenseless photography in which the wave field of light scattered by an object is recorded on a plate as an interference pattern. When the photographic record—the hologram—is placed in a coherent light beam like a laser, the original wave pattern is regenerated and a three-dimensional image appears. The interesting thing is

that *any piece of the hologram will reconstruct the entire image.*
This discovery has led to considerable discussion along
the same lines that Shaivites held over a thousand years ago.

The *Tantra Sadbhava* says, "The universe is His form.
All feelings exist in Him. Knowledge of the whole gives
Him His universality." Because of this, *Parashakti*, the
supreme creative energy of life, manifests Herself in the
form of vibration, called *Paravac.* In an individual, that
vibration is called *kundalini. Parashakti* and *kundalini*
are one, but *kundalini* is how *Parashakti* shows up in the
individual, in you and me.

Just as the macrocosm manifests in stages from the
Absolute through branches involving form and substance
and their intersections, so we, the microcosm, are also
manifested in stages. The whole of our individuated energy
is called *kundalini. Kundalini* manifests in stages, beginning
with the Absolute, *Parashakti*, the stage in which everything
exists in potentiality. It is the stage of *spanda* in which
that first impulse shows itself, the stage in which nothing
has yet manifested, although the readiness to manifest is
present. Then follow the three stages of unfolding: *pashyanti,
madhyama,* and *vaikhari. Pashyanti* has as its root the
Sanskrit word "to see." It means the first showing. When a
rock is dropped in the water, there is a lag time between
when the rock hits the water and when the vibration starts
to emanate. *Para* is that instant when the rock and the
water meet, the instant that contains all elements: rock
only, water only, impulse to move only, as well as rock,
water, and movement together. *Parashyanti* is the impulse
to move, *madhyama* is crystallized thought, and *vaikhari*
is gross speech.

Each of these stages of manifestation corresponds to
the unfoldment of a *chakra.* "Chakra" is a general term
meaning "wheel" or "circle," and it refers not only to the
energy centers of the body where the *kundalini* energy is
strongly felt, but also to other collections of forces, as we
shall discuss. In your body, they are the centers where you
can most palpably feel the *kundalini* energy; they correspond
to the "third eye" of the forehead, the throat, the heart,
the navel, the sex organs, the base of the spine, and the

crown of the head. The *para* stage of manifestation, known in the individual as *parakundalini*, corresponds to the base of the spine, the *pashyanti* stage to the navel center, the *madhyama* stage to the heart, and the *vaikhari* stage to the throat.

How does all this relate to sound? In Kashmir Shaivism, each of these *chakras* is associated with a "root-vibration," which in turn is associated with certain letters. Thus, taken as a whole, the system of *chakras* (known as *matrikashakti*) constitutes the primal alphabet, the alphabet formed of the *essence* of letters. From this alphabet, according to the tradition, the whole universe arises.

In a beautifully complex and elegant scholarly exposition, the ancient sages traced all manifestation back to a single root sound, the primal vowel, which formed all other vowels. Then, from the vibrations of the vowels came the consonants, and from the interplay of the whole alphabet came the thirty-six *tattvas*. Shaivite scholars went so far as to explain exactly *what* utterance gives rise to a particular phenomenon. For example, the gutturals give rise to the five elements: earth, water, wind, fire and air. The palatals give rise to the five subtle elements: odor, taste, sight, hearing and touch. The cerebrals give rise to the five organs of action: speech, sight, movement, excretion and reproduction. The dentals give rise to the five organs of sense. And the labials give rise to five "sheaths" of the mind—the psychic instruments.

What is the salient point to be derived from all of this dividing and subdividing and classifying? It is that all of life is inherent in the power of sound. Sound has tremendous power, and, by extension, the individual who learns how to relate properly to sound has tremendous power. This is the key point to the remainder of this discussion: by applying sound theory and practicing the science of mantra, one attains not only the understanding of manifestation, but liberation from suffering and worldliness.

Matrika, Mantra, and Liberation Through Sound

The combination of letters described above is called the

matrika chakra—the group of letters. *Matrika* means literally the "unknown mother," unknown because we are trapped (by our lack of understanding) in the most gross level of manifestation of the word. *Matrika shakti* is the power of sound that is the matrix of the cosmos, and manifests as the letters in the alphabet. *Matrika* is the subtle force behind thought and speech. It is important to remember that what is referred to here is several levels of subtlety removed from gross speech, and from words and letters such as you are reading now. The *matrika chakra*, and indeed the whole science of mantra and sound, is based on an understanding of the *essence* of language, on "word" as referred to by St. John: "And the Word was God." This is no ordinary phonology!

While in the abstract this may be hard to understand, a look at one's own experience clarifies. Put at its very simplest, words have power. Take, for example, the word "disgrace." Imagine someone you respect accusing you of being "a disgrace." The power of that accusation sets up a vibration in you that was not there before the accusation was uttered. It is as palpable as if someone had thrown a rock at you, yet all that was thrown were words. This is another fundamental concept of Kashmir Shaivism: that our mind, in the form of words, concepts, and ideas, is the source of bondage and suffering. According to the Shaivites, as long as we do not understand the true nature of *matrika*, we are bound by worldly actions and feelings—remaining victims of words without ever really understanding the source of their power over us. With the study of *mantra*, we gain the understanding to see what underlies the power of words and the alphabet, and can begin to use that power for our upliftment.

In the *Shiva Sutras* it is said that "enlightenment comes from knowing the group of letters called *matrika chakra*." Each of the letters in the Sanskrit alphabet can individually be called a *matrika*, because each is a power in its own right. When we think, the process involved stems directly from the vibration of these *matrikas*. Again, take your own experience. Think of a time when you lost your temper and spoke unkindly to someone. Where did the thought process and ultimately the articulation of anger come from? It arose from a vibration, a stirring in you that you responded to, which then manifested as thought and finally as words. The process of losing control is none other than taking the subtle vibration of a moment and allowing it to descend into its grossest manifestation in the form of words and actions. This descent parallels the one discussed earlier in this paper—that of the subtlest sound (which is the essence of the universe) descending into the gross form of physical manifestation. In Kashmir Shaivism, the microcosm always contains the macrocosm.

Self control (and ultimately liberation) is the reverse of that descent, or rather the cessation of that process in its earliest stages. Instead of articulating that vibration, or even thinking the thought that the vibration evokes, one simply *feels* the vibration fully. Two things then happen: (a) one attains a detachment from the emotional reaction the vibration evokes, and (b) the power behind that vibration forces one to a higher level of consciousness. Since the vibration is only a strong energy, if it is not reacted to but simply absorbed as an energy, it will promote the individual to a new level of awareness.

And this is only the beginning. Through a spiritual practice of meditation and mantra, our experience is transformed completely. A spiritual mantra is nothing other than pure, inwardly-directed *matrika*. Mantra saturates and transforms our consciousness when repeated at the levels of manifestation talked about above. Yet while *matrika* usually (in our normal thought processes) moves through our awareness from the *para* stage down to the *vaikari* stage, in the practice of mantra the order is reversed. When repeated at the *vaikari* level (the throat), the gross body is purified. The feeling associated with it may be experienced as a vibrating in the tongue and mouth. When repeated on the *madhyama* level, the mantra is said to have one hundred times the power as when repeated on the gross level, and may be felt as a stirring in the heart. In the next level, the *pashyanti* level, the mantra no longer exists in concrete form, but is simply a pulse of energy. The awareness of this pulsation releases ecstasy in the heart; a person who has attained this level has the power to create through words—whatever such a person says has to come true. On the *para* level, only bliss exists. Pure *spanda* appears and the seeker is totally aware of the "I"-consciousness that is our very essence.

And all this takes place from sound, from the basic vibration and combination of vibrations interacting with one another. One vibration becomes like a string that has a pitch of a certain frequency and sets up various resonances. Each resonance in turn becomes like another string that sets up further resonances. And from this symphony of creative energy, everything manifests. All things are forms of the creative energy, the Shakti, which is never separate from Shiva, the Absolute. Through meditation, we experience *Him* directly. We penetrate *maya* and *matrika*, and reach the eternal mantra, the sound of the union of Shiva and Shakti, the vibration in which all is One. This is liberation.

Conclusion

The study of sound is an immense and ambitious project. Ultimately it is the project of one's own liberation. We are fortunate to live in a time where we have access to the thinking of those who spent their lives delving into the subject. We can study their writings and marvel at the fastidiousness and thoroughness of their approach. Nonetheless, it is only by our own practice of mantra that we can come truly to understand their insights. Until one has experienced it, the topic is nothing but words. And while we have just discussed the power of words, that power is like the mere flicker of a candle in comparison to the furnace of our own experience. To seek the experience, to practice daily and become attuned to the vibrations of life at all levels—this is the highest goal and the key to liberation.

Notes

1. J. Keys, *Only Two Can Play This Game* (New York: Bantam Books, 1971).
2. See *ReVision* 1, nos. 3 and 4 (1978).

20
Perceiving Universal Sound

An Interview with Zen Master SEUNG SAHN
Conducted by GARY DOORE

Gary Doore: What is Zen chanting?
Seung Sahn: Chanting is very important in our practice. We call it "chanting meditation." Meditation means keeping a not-moving mind. The important thing in chanting meditation is to perceive the sound of one's own voice; not hear, but perceive.
G.D.: Are you using the word "perceive" in a special sense?
S.S.: Yes. Perceiving your voice means perceiving your true self or true nature. Then you and the sound never separate, which means that you and the whole universe never separate. Thus, to perceive our true nature is to perceive universal substance.

With regular chanting, our sense of being centered will get stronger and stronger. When we are strongly centered we can control our feelings, and thus our condition and situation.
G.D.: When you refer to a "center" do you mean any particular point in the body?
S.S.: No, it is not just one point. To be strongly centered is to be at one with the universal center, which means infinite time and infinite space.

The first time one tries chanting meditation there will be much confused thinking, many likes, dislikes and so on. This indicates that the whole mind is outwardly oriented. Therefore, it is necessary first to return to one's energy source, to return to a single point.

Seung Sahn

G.D.: In other words, one must first learn to concentrate?
S.S.: Yes. Below the navel we have a center that is called an "energy garden" in Korean. We eat, we breathe, and this area becomes a source of power. If the mind becomes still, this saves energy. The mind, however, is constantly restless. There is an endless stream of desires for various kinds of experience: sights, sounds, smells, tastes, feelings. This turning outward of the mind in search of sensory experience dissipates one's energy until finally there is nothing left in the energy garden. Thereby one becomes subject to control by outside conditions or influences, and so loses control over his or her life.

For this reason, our meditation practice means: Do not think anything. In other words, do not use your eyes, ears, nose, tongue, body or mind. By doing this our center gets stronger and stronger, and there is an experience of growing clarity.

G.D.: How does Zen chanting differ, if at all, from the recitation of mantras?
S.S.: In mantra practice there is no (audible) sound. It is only internal. One merely concentrates on repeating the mantra to oneself. In chanting, on the other hand, we chant out loud in a group and just perceive the sound of our voice.

When we talk about perceiving sound during chanting we mean having a clear mind. This is different from a mind that can be lost, and also different from a one-pointed mind.

For example, consider two people having a good time together, enjoying each other's company, laughing, feeling good and so forth. Suddenly a man appears with a gun and demands money. Instantly the good feeling evaporates and there is only fear and distress. "Somebody please help! Don't shoot!" The mind, the centeredness, is completely lost.

But suppose that a person is walking in the street concentrating on a mantra with a one-pointed mind. Then if a man appears with a gun and demands money there will be only "OM MANI PADME HUM" or whatever. "Hey, are you crazy! I said give me your money." Then there is still only "OM MANI PADME HUM." Nothing else matters. "I will kill you unless you give me your money!" Then what?

Only "OM MANI PADME HUM." This is concentration, one-pointed mind.

Finally, suppose that someone with a clear mind is walking in the street and a robber appears. Then the response is "How much do you want?" That is clear mind. If the man shouts "Give me all of it" there is no problem. "Okay, here is all of it." In fact, with a clear mind one can use such a situation to teach others. There are a number of Zen stories in which thieves or robbers have been so surprised and shaken by the calm response of a clear-minded Zen Master that they later returned to learn Zen from him.

So chanting ultimately means clear mind, not concentration. In concentration you want to make something, there is some desire to focus on one point. This is different from simply perceiving the sound of one's voice, without separation.

G.D.: In some Buddhist chanting the sound is very low and constricted, as though being produced from below the navel under great pressure. What is the reason for this?

S.S.: That is the Japanese style. It comes from the *hara*, the point just below the navel. This is not necessary. If the sound comes from the general area of the stomach it will be correct. One does not have to try to chant from that point below the navel. The sound comes by itself if it is done correctly.

G.D.: What is the difference between Zen chanting and singing?

S.S.: Direction is what makes the difference. Love songs, for example, have only what we might call a "love-direction." This is in the realm of opposites: love and hate, liking and disliking. Emotions come in, so most singing is emotional. Chanting, however, means that the direction is very clear. Remember the phrase "chanting meditation." The direction or aim here is to obtain enlightenment in order to save all beings from suffering.

G.D.: And this is not to try for some type of feeling or emotional quality?

S.S.: No, I am not trying for any good feeling for *me*. Chanting is not for oneself. It is for all beings. That is the difference.

G.D.: In other words, it is an expression of the Bodhisattva's compassion?

S.S.: Yes.

G.D.: What is the relation between compassion and wisdom?

S.S.: Compassion is the function of wisdom; it is the action. Wisdom gives the direction.

G.D.: By this you mean knowing what to do in order to help someone—and also how to do it correctly?

S.S.: Right.

G.D.: So compassion is more than just a warm feeling toward a person.

S.S.: Yes. If that warm feeling of compassion has no direction, if one's mind is not clear, there is every chance of doing more harm than good; and that will not really be compassion. Therefore wisdom is crucial.

G.D.: How long should one chant?

S.S.: Everyday chanting is important in our practice. We do not do it for such a long time. In the morning we chant for about forty-five minutes, and in the evening perhaps for twenty-five minutes. But regularity is important.

G.D.: You do not *try* for any emotional effects in chanting, but does it still have an effect on the emotions?

S.S.: Just do it! This analysis into emotional mind, intellectual mind and so on must disappear. There must be *no* mind! Then there is just clarity, and infinite time and space.

G.D.: In one of the Buddhist Sutras it says that enlightenment may be obtained by turning back the faculty of hearing to original nature, and that this is the most suitable method for human beings. Will you comment on this?

S.S.: Those are merely different "teaching words." The idea, however, is the same as we have been discussing. Don't cling to words, just do it! (Laughter.)

G.D.: How?

S.S.: Listen. Everything is universal sound: birds singing, thunder, dogs barking—all this is universal sound. If you have no mind, everything will be perceived as such. Therefore, when you are chanting with no mind it is also universal sound. If you have "I" then it is "my" sound. But with a mind clear like space, sometimes even the sound of a dog barking or a car horn honking will bring enlightenment. Because at that moment you and the sound become one.

G.D.: Is this moment of enlightenment related to *samadhi*?

S.S.: *Samadhi*, as we use the term, means one-pointed mind. This is not enlightenment. It is concentration-mind. *Samadhi*, you see, is only a good feeling for me, not for other people. Moreover, it is merely a one-pointed mind, not clear mind.

G.D.: Will you explain a little more about how someone can attain enlightenment by hearing a loud sound, as we often read about in Zen stories?

S.S.: If you do loud chanting, for example, and if you do it one hundred percent—put your whole energy into it—at that time there will be no "I." Thus there is no "my" opinion, situation or condition. In this regard, chanting together in a group is very important. Group chanting takes away "my" opinion, situation, condition and so on very easily. One has to blend in and harmonize with the rest of the chanters. The main thing, however, is just to do it *totally*.

G.D.: You said in your Dharma talk earlier that in practicing a mantra or chanting it is important to keep the "Big Question," namely, "Who is practicing this mantra?" or "Who is chanting?" Why is this question about "who?" important?

S.S.: I tell students to find out "What am I?" This is a *koan*. Before thinking, what are you? One says "I don't know." But even before speaking, prior to any words or thoughts, this "before-thinking-mind" is clear mind.

G.D.: Can music be a form of Zen practice also?

S.S.: Music is not usually Zen practice, but it can be. If the player just plays and becomes one with the playing it can be called Zen. But most of the time the direction is not clear in music. Usually there is some emotional control, some direction given by emotions. And the musician may be trying to control the emotions of the audience through his music. In fact, we speak of "good music" as having this sort of effect on other people's emotions. Emotional music means opposites-mind: wanting or not wanting, good feeling, bad feeling. But true Zen music is different. It has been compared to the jumping of a fish up and down in the river.

G.D.: Spontaneous?

S.S.: Yes, but not emotional. Listening to it brings a very quiet mind, a very clear mind. That is Zen music. But one should not cling to the opinion, "This is music, that is not music." If we are not attached to anything, then everything is Zen music.

G.D.: In the Heart Sutra it says that the *Prajna-paramita* mantra (mantra of transcendental wisdom) is the greatest mantra. Would you explain this?

S.S.: Yes. They call it the transcendental mantra, the great bright mantra, the utmost mantra and so forth. This means that if one simply tries this mantra, GATE GATE PARAGATE PARASAMGATE BODHI SWAHA with one's whole energy, then it will be the greatest mantra. Actually, of course, any mantra which you try in this way will be "the greatest mantra" for you! That particular mantra is not special, not different from any other. But all sutras which refer to any kind of mantra will say that it is special.

G.D.: Which means it is special if one believes that it is.

S.S.: Correct. A student once asked me, "If this is true, then even the words 'Coca Cola' can be a mantra?" Yes, if you really believe that "Coca Cola" is the greatest mantra and practice it diligently, it will work for you.

G.D.: Isn't there a danger of hypnotizing oneself with a mantra, of putting oneself into a sleepy state?

S.S.: Yes. Again the difference between this and the correct method of practice lies in the direction or aim. Falling into a sleepy or hypnotic state means that the direction is not clear. Practice thus becomes merely habitual or mechanical action. So it is important to ask, "Why am I practicing this mantra? Is it for me or for other people?" In self-hypnosis from mechanical repetition there is no such aim; or perhaps the aim is merely to relax or to get some sort of good feeling for oneself. In that case it is easy to fall into a dull, drowsy state, but not so if the direction is clear.

However, sometimes if very neurotic people come to learn about our practice, mechanical repetition of a mantra can do some good, perhaps helping them to gather more energy and become stabilized.

G.D.: How does one keep a before-thinking-mind during chanting?

S.S.: Just do it! If you chant with *all* your energy, thinking has already been cut off.

G.D.: Because to think while chanting is to divide one's energy?

S.S.: Right. Simply chanting with one hundred percent of one's energy poured into the chant is already empty mind, clear mind, which is not a state of ignorance or delusion. "Your" before-thinking-mind and "my" before-thinking-mind are the same mind. Then your substance, the substance of this paper in front of us, and my substance are all the same, all universal substance.

But someone will say that this universal substance is Buddha, or God, or nature, or the Absolute and so forth. But actually it has no name, no form, no speech, no thought, because it is before all of this appears.

G.D.: Would you say something about the relationship between chanting and the breath? What about the link between the breath and the mind?

S.S.: One should not check the breathing. It is necessary to put all such considerations aside and just do the chant with all of one's energy. Correct breathing will then naturally be the result. Just sitting will also do the same thing.

G.D.: Do you mean as in Soto Zen where the main form of practice is called "just sitting" (*shikan taza*)?

S.S.: Yes. But it is easy to get attached to sitting in Soto Zen practice. Therefore, one must understand what this "just sitting" is. Any kind of action—chanting, bowing, sitting, lying down, walking—all these can be Zen practice so long as one keeps a still mind. But in Soto Zen practice, it is often only "body sitting," that is, where one's body is sitting but the mind is moving all over, chasing many thoughts. This is not *just* sitting!

G.D.: You mentioned that any action can be Zen practice, but is there something about just sitting that makes it especially good? Why do Zen monks spend so much time at it?

S.S.: For one thing, if one just sits then all the internal organs of the body benefit. The sitting posture is very helpful because when one just sits with the back straight and the mind still, a great deal of energy is accumulated and all the functions of the body become correct. Sometimes the body is ill because it is out of balance. Then correct sitting will bring back the balance. So one must first control the body. Then breathing and mind will automatically be controlled.

G.D.: Are there any other sorts of sounds or rhythms that are important in Zen practice?

S.S.: One famous Zen Master only heard the sound of a rooster crowing and was enlightened. Another Zen Master was just sweeping in the yard when his broom threw a rock against a piece of bamboo with a loud knock, and he was enlightened. He and the sound had become one. So this matter of sound in Zen practice is really very simple. Any sound will do.

But in regard to particular sounds that we regularly use, there are bells, drums, gongs and so forth. All of these have a meaning. For instance, the drum made out of animal skin reminds us about saving all animals;* the sound of the big bell means saving all beings in the different hells. Thus we are reminded about the Bodhisattva's compassion. But this is only the external meaning. The inner meaning is the same as what we have been discussing. It is necessary to perceive the sound, whatever it is—bell, drum, gong, etc.— and to become one with it. There is no thought, no separation, only perceiving sound. This is the crucial point. So just perceive this bell or drum sound, cut off all thinking, and then your wisdom-mind will grow up, you will get enlightenment and thus save all beings.

---

*Animals are not deliberately killed for drum skins.

21

The Hidden Significance of Sound

GORDON LIMBRICK

You cannot claim to "Know Yourself" unless you are aware of your inseparable bond with primordial Sound which, emanating from Atman, manifests and sustains creation until its dissolution. It is a mystic sound which not only reverberates throughout the entirety of existence, but which resonates in every cell of the human body to give life and consciousness. It is Brahman in action; the Logos or Verbum in manifestation; the Divine Idea transformed from quiescence to pour forth as the color, light and form that vibrates in every atom and, mercifully, it is the lifestream upon which we shall ultimately return to our Source of Being.

Unfortunately, we have lost memory of our divine origin and of our inextricable Oneness with the Word made flesh, which is none other than the Voice of the Silence that speaks to us eternally. Alas, we decline to hear it and, in consequence, look without for that which is within.

The Source of Sound

The Ancient Wisdom reveals that the universe was conceived in Divine Thought forever hidden in the Absolute, and that Sound was the first manifestation of spirit and the precursor of form. Accordingly, the Source of Sound dwells eternally in the Great Deep of Brahman. When, however, the divine hour strikes, and the state of rest (pralaya) gives way to activity (manvantara), the Great Breath of Brahman expresses itself as the cosmos by means of the creative Word or sound vibration of the universe, which manifests not only as the Cosmic Logos, but, in accordance with cyclic law, as the Logos of the human soul.

The Logos of Creative Voice is personified as the goddess Vâch, the female aspect of Brahma, the God of Creation. Esoterically, she is the subjective creative force, which, emanating from the Creative Deity, becomes the manifested world of speech, i.e., the concrete expression of ideation, hence the Word or Logos.[1] The miraculous transmutation of Creative Sound into matter, which is then molded into various forms for the service of evolving life, is made possible by the medium of Fohat, which H. P. Blavatsky, noted author and teacher of esotericism, describes as, "The dynamic energy of Cosmic Ideation . . . the mysterious link between Mind and Matter, the animating principle electrifying every atom into life."[2] Thus it is that from the ineffable center of light, life and power, the primordial Sound flows outwards and downwards to create and sustain the entire system of universes, of which man is the microcosm.*

Sound—the Cosmogony of Religion

The conception of Vach plays a prominent part, not only in the Brahmanical system, but in the cosmogonies of most religions. It is the Word made Flesh of the Bible; the *nada* or soundless sound of the *Upanishads*; the *nam* or *Gurbani* of the Sikh Adi Granth; the *kalma-i-ilahi* or inner sound of the Koran; and the *saute surmadi* or *hu* of Sufism. It is also synonymous with Plato's Logos, with Madame Blavatsky's *Voice of the Silence*, with Patanjali's OM, with the Pythagorean music of the spheres, and with the lost word of Masonry. In Egyptian cosmogony it is Thoth, the Divine Intelligence who utters Words which form the world. Buddhism knows it as *Fohat*—the light of the Logos. In Tibetan Buddhism it is related to the *Bardol Thodol*, while Chinese mysticism recognizes it as the Kwan-Yin-Tien or the Melodious Heaven of Sound.

---

*"Man" refers to humankind and is intended to include women.

It is not surprising that this forgotten Voice of Nada[3] remains a dead letter of the word to orthodox religion, for having lost knowledge of the method of listening to it, it is explained away as a mere figure of speech. Nor is the hidden significance and potency of terrestrial and metaphysical Sound understood or utilized to nurture spiritual development. Yet, by simply listening—even to the echoes of the Logos, which may be heard distinctly within the skull—all verbal or written comparisons become mere rhetoric.

The Nature of Sound

Scientists have affirmed that, in terms of vibrational possibilities, all that is in the universe is present in man. In fact, man is the vibrational reality of Sound, Color and Form, the different states of which are only differences of vibrations. Dr. I. K. Taimni, chemist and student of Eastern philosophy, describes Integrated Sound (Nada) as "a super-integration of all possible kinds of vibrations which can find expression in the Solar System on all the manifested planes." He further contends that this vibration of the Logos may be realized by every human being by a "gradual unfoldment of his inner faculties and powers."[4] The *Rig Veda* and the *Upanishads* describe four attributes of Sound, namely— Para (its ultimate state); Pasyanti (its latent light form); Madhyama (the mystic Light and Sound of the Logos); Vaikhari (its objective expression).

However, of esoteric significance is the distinction between its two Logoic modes of operation. On the one hand, the centrifugal flow relating to the forthgoing or descending principle that sustains the cosmos and governs the descent of the Monad or one's spiritual core into matter, and, on the other hand, the centripetal flow of the ascending principle upon which life essence appears to be returning to its Source, and by means of which the Monad will eventually reach the Atmic or highest spiritual planes. This return stream is the pristine Voice of the Silence, the Soundless Sound, so called because it is beyond the range of acoustical frequency. It is a spiritual sound, not of this world. Hence the paradox, "The Voice of the Silence." In essence, it is a combination of Sound and Light. Its "ringing radiance" may be heard and seen by revivifying the powers latent in the human constitution.

Equally important is the contrast between the unstruck, unheard Logoic Sounds and the struck or percussive sounds arising from the manifest universe. Esoteric science affirms that Akash is the root substance in which all sounds— metaphysical and terrestrial—have a communicative thrust. The myriad sounds of nature, orchestral music, song, speech and, alas, the defiling noise of busy cities, are in one sense acoustical disturbances of various frequencies broadcast by sympathetic resonance audible to the human ear, and measurable by scientific instruments. Hence, terrestrial sound may well be regarded as vibrational chaos and Atman as harmonious equilibrium. Audible sounds (Vaikhari) are but faint echoes of the melodious primordial Sound which is inexpressible in writing or speech, and beyond the compass of human hearing and supersonic registers, and yet, amazingly enough, it may be heard with a higher organ of hearing with which the Creator has endowed man.

The Seven Sounds

The seven sounds described by H. P. Blavatsky in *The Voice of the Silence* are clarified somewhat by Annie Besant and C. W. Leadbeater,[5] and also by George S. Arundale[6] who obviously writes as a practitioner of Nada Yoga. In the Sufi Tradition[7] ten Sounds are recognized, while East Indian schools of Nada Yoga relate to five regions of Sound and Light leading to the exalted realm of pure Shabda.[8] In describing the seven sounds, Mme. Blavatsky has used poetic license freely, hence they should not be taken too literally. Notwithstanding, they serve as authentic guideposts to assist aspirants in orientating themselves. By distinguishing and penetrating the various sound vibrations, one is able to "mount the ladder" leading to the liberating Voice of the Silence:

Before thou set'st thy foot upon the ladder's
upper rung, the ladder of the mystic sounds,
thou hast to hear the voice of thy Inner God
in seven manners.[9]

Esotericists hold that the seven sounds have a correspondence with the seven principles, the seven rays, and the seven symbols reflected in the multifarious vibrational patterns of creation. To reach the non-vibrational bliss of Atman, inner sound currents corresponding to the seven principles must first be heard, and, by degrees, transcended:

When the six are slain and at the Master's
feet are laid, then is the pupil merged
into the ONE [Atman].[10]

The sixth culminating sound—which is variously described as the rumbling of thunder, the roar of a mighty ocean, or as the rolling of Cosmic Drums—is related to the overruling vibration of the rising Kundalini. The seventh —so-called sound—cannot, in fact, be transcended because it is the paradoxical Voice of the Silence itself, which swallows the lower sounds related to the six principles that henceforth are heard no more by the lower consciousness. The doctrine of the seven sounds is epitomized in the crowning ninety-ninth verse:

Behold! thou has become the light, thou hast
become the Sound . . . the Voice unbroken . . . the
seven sounds in one, the Voice of the Silence.

Inner Tuning

As a rule, listening techniques—which vary according to tradition—are demonstrated at the time of initiation into Nada Yoga. However, listening postures such as the sanmukhi mudra are illustrated in authentic works on Hatha Yoga. A useful work on the subject is *Hathayoga-Pradipika*[11] which, although extremely terse, outlines the basic method of listening.

If the pupil will have the patience to listen through and beyond the gross physical sounds of pulse and eardrum vibrations, he or she will hear the subtle sounds of the higher planes which are at their optimum intensity between 3:00 and 5:00 A.M., when earth currents are at their lowest ebb and spiritual currents are at their peak. One must bear in mind that the "music of the spheres" has no beginning and no end. It resounds throughout eternities, as Mme. Blavatsky would put it. It is this soothing perpetual celestial note—the bliss of Ananda—that the fragmented restless mind is constantly seeking. By merging into its uplifting vibration, a quantum leap is made from the state of broken thought-images to the highest mode of mental action, that of unswerving attention towards the Godhead. The mind is weaned from the thraldom of the senses.

The Hidden Use of Sound

Commenting on the restoration of man's inherent higher faculties, Mme. Blavatsky made this interesting statement: "Students in the West have little or no idea of the forces that lie latent in Sound."[12] Later she states: "To the five senses at present the property of mankind, two more on this globe are to be added. The sixth sense is the psychic sense of Colour. The seventh is that of spiritual sound."[13] The key to the development of these senses is given in the opening verses of *The Voice of the Silence*. . . .

He who would hear the voice of Nada, "the
Soundless Sound," and comprehend it, he has
to learn the nature of Dharana concentration.

The art of concentration is an exact, all-embracing discipline, which is considerably enhanced by the practice of Mantra Yoga.

Basically, a mantra is a set of sounds or words having a spiritual significance and power used to create vibrations in the inner consciousness. Esoterically, a mantra embodies the Vach or mystic word residing in its sounds, and because of this, as Mme. Blavatsky reminds us, it becomes "the most potent and effectual magic agent, and the first of the Keys which opens the door of communication between Mortals and the Immortals."[14] The internal repetition of a mantra is an indispensable aid in opening dormant channels in the mindstuff, thereby lifting the veil of ignorance that constrains consciousness to the physical plane. A similar concept is expressed by Mme. Blavatsky: "To comprehend ideas and Truths larger than the ordinary, takes a new kind of mental effort, something quite different, 'the carving out of new brainpaths.' "[15]

This is precisely the effect resulting from the persistent repetition of a mantra, a practice which simultaneously develops the one-pointedness of mind which is indispensable in profound meditation. More than this, Mme. Blavatsky taught specific methods of using mantras to nurture the unfoldment of the powers latent in man. One of these was the art of Intoning, in which she explains the use of a well-known Tibetan mantra: "Therefore, if a student would make the Buddhi operative, for instance, he would have to intone the first words of the Mantra on the note Mi. But he would have still further to accentuate the Mi, and produce mentally the yellow colour corresponding to this sound and note, on every letter *M* in 'OM MANI PADME HUM.' "[16]

The Mantra Aum

A similar principle applies when intoning the ageless mantra Aum, pronounced Om. In this case, the lips are closed immediately after sounding the vowels, so that the hum produced by the consonant *M* is extended during the entire outgoing breath. As a result, the upward, outgoing breathstream has the effect of returning the subtle vibrations of sound to their Source, and of simultaneously sensitizing the psychic nerve ganglion in the region of the ajna chakra. If the ears are sealed by pressing gently on the tragi or prominences in front of the openings of the ears, the sound will resonate throughout the interior of the skull. This intensifies the volume and potency of the mantra considerably. The esoteric law that every physical sound awakens its corresponding sound and color vibration in the metaphysical realm is worthy of note.

It is evident that initiates used Sanskrit mantras, embodying the power of mystic speech, which were passed from guru to guru for countless generations before they were revealed in the Vedas by the poet-visionary Vyasa. It is still traditional for a teacher to impart a mantra to a disciple at the time of initiation. However, it is questionable whether such a mantra still carries the inner potency of the original sacerdotal language and formulae. The revered Gayatri mantra of the Rig Veda is still repeated twice daily by practicing Brahmins. It comprises twenty-four Sanskrit syllables, each of which is said to resonate with the corresponding twenty-four tattwas of prakriti, and is preceded by the syllable Om. Shankara considered it to be the highest of mantras, in that it reflects the identity of jiva (the individual soul) with Iswara (God), and the ultimate state of the Sat-Chit-Ananda implied by the opening syllable Om.

Notwithstanding, the power of any mantra, regardless of its origin, depends more upon its application than upon its esoteric potential. The degree of its potency is determined by the frequency with which it is used. Repeated persistently, it will penetrate beyond the turbulence of thought to the depths of Being. When consciousness is brought to focus in Buddhi by the practice of Dharana (concentration), the meditator enters the state of Dhyana wherein the faculties of inner vision and hearing are used for mystic flight through the vast inner planes that lead to the initial stages of samadhi. Fortunate is the aspirant who finds affinity with the ubiquitous mantra Om, which embodies not only the whole phenomena of voice production, but which opens up new channels in the mindstuff through which the Voice of the Silence is finally realized.

Speech

In the same way that Divine Thought is the precursor of Creative Sound, so thought is the antecedent of speech (vaikhari). Outer words that spring from inner thoughts are but reflections or partial manifestations of the Divine Word. Esoteric science teaches that verbal expression sends out thought and sound vibrations, which inevitably attract towards the speaker influences in resonance with the force emitted. Moreover, as Mme. Blavatsky affirms: "To pronounce a word is to evoke a thought, and make it present; the magnetic potency of the human speech is the commencement of every manifestation in the Occult World. . . . The Word (Verbum), or the speech of every man is, quite unconsciously to himself, a Blessing or a

Curse."[17] For this reason, aspirants cannot be too careful of their words. Moreover, they should try to purify their everyday language by purging corrupt forms of speech which contort the sequential perfection of Logoic expression.

It is a mistaken notion that evolutionary and spiritual development is inextricably governed by cyclic progression and, therefore, that one should sit back complacently to await the inevitable. On the supreme current of the Logos we descended into human form, and by that same current we shall ascend to our primal Source. The choice is ours. We may take a downward course into the physical realm and thus perpetuate a material existence, or we may take an upward, inward orientation towards the spiritual planes which are no longer subject to the distractions of nature. Only by our own efforts can we attune ourselves to resonate with the Logoic "ringing radiance," only in deep meditation can we reach its irresistible levitating pull.

By "becoming that Path itself," we awaken in ourselves a new spiritual perception. By combining the practices of Raja Yoga with those of Nada Yoga, the entire being is rendered a channel through which the Divine Word may flow with little distortion.

Thus we shall draw nearer to the fulfilment of Divine Ideation in adding to our normal senses the two which are yet to come—the senses of inner hearing and inner vision. We shall then have at our disposal forces to be used for the spiritual and evolutionary development of humankind. In the words of Mme. Blavatsky:

There is but one road to the Path;
at its very end alone the "Voice of the
Silence" can be heard.[18]

References

1. H. P. Blavatsky, *Theosophical Glossary*, p. 357.
2. H. P. Blavatsky, *The Secret Doctrine*, Adyar edition, 1971, Vol. 1, p. 16.

Gordon Limbrick

3. H. P. Blavatsky, *The Voice of the Silence*, Verse 2.
4. I. K. Taimni, *Man, God and the Universe*, p. 286.
5. Annie Besant and C. W. Leadbeater, *Talks on the Path of Occultism*, Vol. 11, pp. 121-133.
6. George Arundale, *The Lotus Fire*, pp. 143-144.
7. Hazrat Inayat Khan, *Mysticism of Sound* (California, Hunter House, 1979) Chapter 8.
8. Powis Hoult, *Dictionary of Theosophical Terms*.
9. H. P. Blavatsky, *The Voice of the Silence*, Verse 41.
10. Ibid, Verse 50.
11. Svatmarama, *The Hathayogapradipika*, pp. 74-81.
12. H. P. Blavatsky, *The Secret Doctrine*, Adyar ed., Vol. V, p. 505 (A. Besant's notes)
13. Ibid., p. 508 (Dr. H. Coryn's notes)
14. H. P. Blavatsky, *The Secret Doctrine*, Vol. 1, p. 464.
15. Robert Owen, "The Study of the Secret Doctrine" (*Sunrise*, October, 1985).
16. H. P. Blavatsky, *The Secret Doctrine*, Adyar ed., Vol. V, p. 506 (H.P.B.'s notes).
17. H. P. Blavatsky, *The Secret Doctrine*, Vol. 1, p. 93.
18. H. P. Blavatsky, *The Voice of the Silence*, Verse 69.

Note: Most of these books were published by the Theosophical Publishing House, P. O. Box 270, Wheaton, IL 60189.

22

Healing with
Sound and Music

PIR HAZRAT INAYAT KHAN

Illness is inharmony—either physical inharmony or mental
inharmony; the one acts upon the other. What causes
inharmony? The lack of tone and rhythm. How can it be
interpreted in physical terminology? *Prana* or life or energy
is the tone; circulation or regularity is the rhythm, regularity
in the beating of the pulse and in the circulation of the
blood through the veins. In physical terms the lack of
circulation means congestion; and the lack of *prana* or
life or energy means weakness. These two conditions attract
illness and are the cause of illness. In mental terms the
rhythm is the action of the mind, whether the mind is active
in harmonious thoughts or in inharmonious thoughts,
whether the mind is strong, firm, and steady or weak.

If one continues to think harmonious thoughts it is just
like regular beating of the pulse and proper circulation of
the blood; if the harmony of thought is broken, then the
mind becomes congested. Then a person loses memory;
depression comes as the result, and what one sees is nothing
but darkness. Doubt, suspicion, distrust, and all manner of
distress and despair come when the mind is congested in
this way. The *prana* of the mind is maintained when the
mind can be steady in thoughts of harmony. Then the mind
can balance its thoughts, then it cannot be easily shaken,
then doubt and confusion cannot easily overpower it.
Whether it is nervous illness, mental disorder, or physical
illness, at the root of all these different aspects of illness
there is one cause, and that cause is inharmony.

317

The body that has once become inharmonious turns into a receptacle of inharmonious influences, of inharmonious atoms; it partakes of them without knowing it; and so it is with the mind. The body that is already lacking in health is more susceptible to illness than the body that is perfectly healthy; and so the mind that already has a disorder in it is more susceptible to every suggestion of disorder, and in this way goes from bad to worse. Scientists of all ages have found that each element attracts the same element, and so it is natural that illness should attract illness. Thus in plain words inharmony attracts inharmony, whereas harmony attracts harmony. We see in everyday life that a person who has nothing the matter with him and is only weak physically, or whose life is not regular, is always susceptible to illness. Then we see that a person who ponders often upon inharmonious thoughts is very easily offended. It does not take long for him to get offended; a little thing here and there makes him feel irritated, because irritation is already there and it wants just a little touch to make it a deeper irritation.

Besides, this harmony of the body and the mind depends upon one's external life, the food one eats, the way one lives, the people one meets, the work one does, the climate in which one lives. There is no doubt that under the same conditions one person may be ill and another may be well. The reason is that one is in harmony with the food he eats, with the weather he lives in, with the people whom he meets, with the conditions around him. Another person revolts against the food he eats, against the people he meets, against the conditions that surround him, against the weather he must live in. This is because he is not in harmony, and he perceives and experiences similar results in all things in his life. Disorder and illness are the result.

This idea can be very well demonstrated by the method that present-day physicians have adopted of inoculating a person with the same element that makes him ill. There is no better demonstration of this idea than the practice of inoculation. This puts a person in harmony with the thing that is opposed to his nature. If one understands this principle one can inoculate oneself with all that does not

agree with one and with that to which one is continually
exposed and from which there is no means of getting away....

Disorder of tone and irregularity in rhythm are the
principal causes of every illness. The explanation of this
disorder of tone is that there is a certain tone that the breath
vibrates throughout the body, through every channel of the
body. This tone is a particular tone, continually vibrating
in every person. When the mystics say that every person
has his note, it is not necessarily the note of the piano, it
is the note that is going on as a tone, as a breath. If a person
does not take care of himself and allows himself to be
influenced by every wind that blows, like the water in the
sea disturbed by the air, he goes up and down. The normal
condition is to be able to stand firm through fear, joy, and
anxiety, not to let every wind blow one hither and thither
like a scrap of paper but to endure it all and to stand firm
and steady through all such influences.

One might say that even water is subject to influences,
if not the rock. The human being is made to be neither
rock nor water; he has all in him. He is the fruit of the whole
creation, and he ought to be able to show his evolution in
his balance. A person who is likely to rejoice in a moment
and to become depressed in a moment, who changes his
moods cannot keep that tone which gives him equilibrium
and which is the secret of health. How few know that it is
not pleasure and merrymaking that give one good health!
On the contrary, social life as it is known today is merrymaking for one day, and afterwards one may be ill for ten
days, for that kind of life does not take care of equilibrium.
When a person becomes sensitive to every little thing that
he comes across, it changes the note of the tone. It becomes
a different note, to which his body is not accustomed, and
that causes an illness. Too much despair or too much joy—
everything that is too much should be avoided. However
there are natures that always seek extremes: they must
have so much joy and amusement that they get tired of it,
and then they collapse with sorrow and despair. Among
these people you will find continual illness. If an instrument
is not kept in proper tune, if it is knocked about by everyone
who comes and handled by everyone, then it gets out of

order. The body is an instrument, the most sacred instrument, an instrument that God Himself has made for His divine purpose. If it is kept in tune and the strings are not allowed to become loose, then this instrument becomes the means of that harmony for which God created man.

How must this instrument be kept in tune? In the first place, strings of gut and wires of steel both require cleaning. The lungs and veins in the body also require cleaning; it is that which keeps them ready for their work. How should we clean them? By carefulness in diet, by sobriety, and by breathing properly and correctly. For it is not only water and earth that are used for cleansing, the best means of cleansing is the air and the property that is in the air, the property that we breathe in. If we knew how by the help of breathing to keep these channels clean, then we should know how to secure health. It is this that maintains the tone, the proper note of each person, without being disturbed. When a person is vibrating his own note, which is according to his particular evolution, then he is himself, then he is tuned to the pitch for which he is made, the pitch in which he ought to be and in which he naturally feels comfortable.

Now we come to rhythm. There is a rhythm of pulsation, the beating of the pulse in the head and in the heart, and whenever the rhythm of this beating is disturbed it causes illness because it disturbs the whole mechanism that is going on, the order of which depends upon the regularity of rhythm. If a person suddenly hears of something causing fear, the rhythm is broken; the pulsation changes. Every shock given to a person breaks his rhythm. We very often notice that, however successful an operation, it leaves a mark, even for the rest of one's life. Once the rhythm is broken, it is most difficult to get it right.

If the rhythm has been lost, it must be brought back with great wisdom, because a sudden effort to regain the rhythm may make one lose it still more. If the rhythm has become too slow or too fast, by trying to bring it to its regular speed one may break the rhythm, and by breaking the rhythm one may break oneself. This should be a gradual process; it must be wisely done. If the rhythm has gotten too fast, it must be brought gradually to its proper condition; if it is too slow, it must be gradually made quicker. It requires patience and strength to do this. For instance, someone who tunes a violin wisely does not at once move the peg and bring it to the proper tone, because in the first place it is impossible, and then he always risks breaking the string. However minute may be the difference in the tone, one can bring it to its proper place by gradual tuning; in this way effort is spared and the thing is accomplished.

Gentleness that is taught morally is a different thing, but even gentleness in action and movement is also necessary. In every movement one makes, in every step one takes there must be rhythm. For instance, you will find many examples, if you look for them, of the awkward movements people make. They can never keep well because their rhythm is not right, and that is why illness continues. It may be that no illness can be traced in these people, and yet the very fact of their movements not being in rhythm will keep them out of order. Regularity in habits, in action, in repose, in eating, in drinking, in sitting, in walking, in everything, gives one that rhythm which is necessary and which completes the music of life.

When a child's rhythm and tone are disordered, the healing that the mother can give often unconsciously physicians cannot give in a thousand years. The song she sings, however insignificant, comes from the profound depths of her being and brings with it the healing power. It cures the child in a moment. The caressing, the patting of the mother does more good to the child than any medicine when its rhythm is disturbed and its tone is not good. The mother, even without knowing it distinctly, feels like patting the child when it is out of rhythm, singing to the child when it is out of tune.

When we come to the mental part of our being, that mechanism is still more delicate than our body. There is a tone also, and every being has a different tone according to his particular evolution. Everyone feels in good health when his own tone is vibrating, but if that tone does not come to its proper pitch, then a person feels lack of comfort, and any illness can arise from it. Every expression of passion, joy, anger, fear that breaks the continuity of this tone interferes with one's health. Behind the thought there is feeling, and it is the feeling that sustains that tone; the thought is on the surface. In order to keep the continuity of that tone, the mystics have special practices.

The secret of the continual ringing of the bell practiced by the churches at all times, even now, is that it is not only a bell to call people, it is to tune them up to their tone. It was to suggest, "There is a tone going on in you, get yourself tuned to it!" If that tuning is not done, even if a person has recovered from his illness weakness still remains. An external cure is no cure if a person is not cured mentally. If his spirit is not cured the mark of illness remains there, and the rhythm of mind is broken.

When a person's mind is going at a speed that is faster or at a speed that is slower than it ought to be, or if a person jumps from one thought to another and so goes on thinking of a thousand things in five minutes, however intellectual he may be he cannot be normal. Or if a person holds one thought and broods on it instead of making progress, he will also cling to his depression, his fears, his disappointments, and that makes him ill. It is irregularity of the rhythm of mind that causes mental disorder.

I do not mean that the rhythm of the mind of one person must be like that of another person. No, each person's rhythm is peculiar to himself. Once a pupil who accompanied me on my walk, in spite of all his kindness and pleasure in accompanying me, felt a great discomfort at times because he could not walk as slowly as I did. Being simple and frank, he expressed this to me. In answer I said, "It is a majestic walk."

The reason was that his rhythm was different. He could not feel comfortable in some other rhythm; he had to be galloping along in order to feel comfortable. And so one can feel what gives one comfort and what gives one discomfort in everything one does. If one does not feel it, that shows that one does not give attention to one's being. Wisdom is to understand oneself. If one can sustain the proper rhythm of one's mind, that is sufficient to keep one healthy.

* * * * * *

When we look further into this subject [of health and
sound] from a mystical point of view, we see that every
syllable has a certain effect. As the form of every sound
is different, so every syllable has a special effect. Therefore
every sound made or word spoken before an object charges
that object with certain magnetism. This explains to us the
method of the healers, teachers, and mystics who by the
power of sound charged an object with their healing power,
with their power of thought. When this object was given
as a drink or as food, it brought about the desired result. . . .
The physical effect of sound has also a great influence
upon the human body. The whole mechanism, the muscles,
the blood circulation, the nerves are all moved by the power
of vibration. As there is resonance for every sound, so the
human body is a living resonator for sound. Although by
sound one can easily produce a resonance in all such
substances as brass and copper, yet there is no greater
and more living resonator of sound than the human body.
Sound has an effect on each atom of the body, for each
atom resounds. On all glands, on the circulation of the
blood, and on pulsation, sound has an effect.
In India a feast is celebrated every year where the people
commemorate the great heroes of the past and mourn over
their life's tragedy. Certain instruments are played, certain
drums, sometimes very badly and sometimes better. There
are some who on hearing those drums instantly fall into
ecstasy because the sound of the drum goes directly into
their whole system, bringing it to a certain pitch where
they feel ecstasy. When they are in ecstasy they can jump
into the fire and come out without being burned; they can
cut themselves with a sword and they are instantly healed;
they can eat fire and they are not burned. One can see this
every year at that particular time.
They call such a condition *hal. Hal* means the same as
"condition"; it is an appropriate term for it, because by
hearing the drum they think of that condition and then they
enter into it. They need not be very educated to go into that
trance, nor very evolved. Sometimes they are very ordinary

people, but sound can have such effect upon them that they are moved to a higher ecstasy.

The question was raised by a physician in San Francisco, Dr. Abrams, of how the sudden healing of a sword cut in ecstasy is brought about. Although all doctors disagreed with him, he intuitively thought that by the help of vibrations illnesses could be cured. But instead of looking for the power of vibrations in the word, he wanted to find it in electricity. Yet the principle is the same: he took the rate of vibrations of the body, and by the same rate of electrical vibrations he treated the elements of the body. He began to get some good results, but it is a subject that will need at least a century to develop fully. It is a vast subject and this is just the beginning; therefore there is still no end to the errors. But at the same time, if people could bear with it, after many years something might come out of it that could be of great use to the medical world.

This example shows that when a person can cut himself and be healed at the same time, he has created such a condition in his body that its vibrations are able to heal any wound immediately. But when that same person is not in that condition, then if there is a cut he cannot be healed. He must be in that particular condition; the vibrations must be working at that particular rate.

There is a school of Sufis in the East which is called the Rifai school. Their main object is to increase the power of spirit over matter. Experiments such as eating fire, jumping into fire, or cutting the body are made in order to get power and control over matter. The secret of the whole phenomenon is that by the power of words they try to tune their bodies to that pitch of vibration where no fire, no cut, nothing can touch it. Because the vibrations of their bodies are equal to fire, the fire has no effect. . . .

The wise considered the science of sound to be the most important science in every condition of life: in healing, in teaching, in evolving, and in accomplishing all things in life. It is on this foundation that the science of *dhikr* was developed by the Sufis and that the yogis made *mantra shastra*.

*   *   *   *   *   *

Wind instruments, instruments with gut or steel strings, and instruments of percussion such as drums and cymbals have each a distinct, different, and particular effect on the physical body. There was a time when thinkers knew this and used sound for healing and for spiritual purposes. It was on that principle that the music of India was based. The different ragas and the notes that these ragas contain were supposed to produce a certain healing or elevating effect.

Sound first touches the physical plane. When we consider what effect single notes or sounds can have upon the physical body, this will lead us to think deeply on the subject. Even today there are snake charmers, mostly to be found in India, who by playing their *pungi*, a simple wind instrument, attract cobras and other snakes from the vicinity. Often and often this experiment has been made, and one always sees that snakes of any kind are attracted on hearing the sound of the *pungi*. First they come out of the hole in which they live, and then there is a certain effect on their nervous system that draws them closer and closer to the sound of the *pungi*. They forget that instinct that is seen in every creature of protecting itself from the attack of man or of other creatures. At that time they absolutely forget; they do not see anyone or anything. They are then aroused to ecstasy: the cobra begins to raise its head and move it right and left, and as long as this instrument is played the cobra continues to move in ecstasy. This shows us that, as well as the psychical effect and the spiritual effect that sound has on man, there is also a physical effect.

From the metaphysical point of view, the breath is the life current or *prana*, and this life current exists also in such things as the gut string or the skin of drums. There is a part of life in these things too, and to the extent that their life current becomes audible it touches the life current of the living creatures and gives it an added life. It is for this reason that primitive tribes, who have only a drum or a simple instrument to blow, get into such a condition by the continual playing of these instruments that they enjoy the state of ecstasy.

How does the great success of jazz come about? It comes from the same principle. It does not make the brain think much about the technicality of music; it does not trouble the soul to think of spiritual things; it does not trouble the heart to feel deeply—without affecting the heart or the soul it touches the physical body. It gives it a renewed strength by the continuation of a particular rhythm and a particular ' sound, and that gives people—I mean the generality—a greater strength and vigor and interest than music which strains the mind. Those who do not wish to be spiritually elevated, who do not believe in spiritual things and who do not wish to trouble, it leaves alone. Yet at the same time it affects everyone who hears it.

When you compare the voice with the instrument, there is no real comparison, because the voice itself is alive. The movement, the glance, the touch, even the breath that comes from the nostrils do not reach as far as the voice reaches.

There are three degrees of breath current. One degree is the simple breath that is inhaled and exhaled by the nostrils. This current reaches outside and has a certain effect. A greater degree of breath current is blowing. When a person blows from his lips, that breath current is directed more intensely. Therefore healers who have understood this principle make use of it. The third degree, in which the breath is most intense, is sound because in that degree the breath coming in the form of sound is vitalized.

Among Orthodox Christians and Armenians there is a custom that they do not use an organ in church; they use a chord or sound made by ten or twelve persons sitting with closed lips. Anyone who has heard it will say that they are right; the sound of the organ is most artificial in comparison with the sound produced by the voices of ten or twelve persons with closed lips. It has such a wonderfully magical effect, it reaches so far and so deeply into the heart of man, and it produces such a religious atmosphere that one feels that there is no necessity for an organ; it is a natural organ that God has made.

Brahmins when they study the Vedas even now do not study only what is written there or the meaning of it; they study also the pronunciation of each syllable, of each word, of each sound, and they study it for years and years and years. The Brahmin does not hear the sound once with the ears and think, "I have learned it." No; he believes that a thousand repetitions of the word will one day produce that magnetism, that electricity, that life current which is necessary and which only comes by repetition.

What action does this life current take which comes through the breath and manifests as a voice and touches another person? It touches the five senses, the sense of sight, the sense of hearing, the sense of smell, the sense of taste, and the sense of touch, although it comes directly through the sense of hearing. But a person does not hear sound only through his ears; he hears sound through every pore of his body. It permeates the entire being, and according to its particular influence either slows the rhythm or quickens the rhythm of the blood circulation; it either wakens the nervous system or soothes it. It arouses a person to greater passions or it calms him by bringing him peace. According to the sound and its influence a certain effect is produced.

Therefore the knowledge of sound can give a person a magical instrument by which to wind and tune and control and use the life of another person to the best advantage. The ancient singers used to experience the effect of their spiritual practices upon themselves first. They used to sing one note for about half an hour and study the effect of that same note upon all the different centers of their bodies: what life current it produced, how it opened the intuitive faculties, how it created enthusiasm, how it gave added energy, how it soothed, and how it healed. For them it was not a theory, it was an experience.

Sound becomes visible in the form of radiance. This shows that the same energy that goes into the form of sound before being visible is absorbed by the physical body. In that way the physical body recuperates and becomes charged with new magnetism.

By a keen study of psychology you will find that singers have a greater magnetism than the average person. Because of their own practicing their voice makes an effect upon themselves, and they produce electricity in themselves. In that way they are charged with new magnetism every time they practice. This is the secret of the singer's magnetism.

Coming to the question which is the right and which is the wrong use of sound, it all depends upon the particular case. In one case a certain sound may be rightly used and in another case the same sound may be wrongly used. Whether it was right or wrong can be seen by the harmonious or disharmonious effects it produces. Every pitch that is a natural pitch of the voice will be a source of a person's own healing as well as of that of others when he sings a note of that pitch. But the person who has found the keynote of his own voice has found the key of his own life. That person, by the keynote of his own voice, can then wind his own being, and he can help others. There are, however, many occasions when this knowledge is not enough, as it only concerns oneself, the knowledge of what is one's own note, and the natural pitch of one's own voice.

The great pity in the world of sound today is that people are going away from what is called the natural voice. This is brought about by commercialism. First a hall was made for one hundred persons, then for five hundred, and then for five thousand. A person must shout to make five thousand people hear him in order to have a success, and that success is one of the ticket office. But the magical charm lies in the natural voice. Every person is gifted; God has given him a certain pitch, a natural note. If he develops that note it is magic; he can perform a miracle. But today he must think about the hall where he has to sing and of how loud he must shout.

There was a man from India visiting Paris, and for the first time in his life he went to the opera to hear the music there. He tried hard to enjoy it. The first thing he heard was a soprano doing her best, and then came the tenor or baritone and he had to sing with her. That made this man very annoyed and he said, "Now look, he has come to spoil it!"

When we come to the essence and inner principle of sound, the closer to nature one keeps it, the more powerful, the more magical it becomes. Every man and woman has a certain pitch of voice, but then the voice producer says, "No, this is alto," "soprano," "tenor," "baritone," or "bass."

He limits what cannot be limited. Are there then so many voices? There are as many voices as there are souls; they cannot be classified. As soon as a singer is classified he has to sing in that pitch; if his pitch is different, he does not know it. Because the voice producer has said, "This is a soprano," then that person cannot be anything else. Besides this, the composer has probably never heard the voice of that particular singer and has written only for a certain pitch, either this one or that one. When a person has to depend upon what the composer has written and has to sing in a pitch that is thus prescribed, then he has lost the natural pitch he had. But singing apart, even in speaking you will find among one hundred persons one who speaks in his natural voice and ninety-nine who imitate. They imitate someone else, although they may not know it.

The same thing that you find in grown-up people you will find in little children. The tendency in a child is to change its ways and to imitate. Every five or ten days, every month a child changes its way of speaking, its voice, its words; it changes many things. Where does the child learn these? It learns them from the children in school. It sees a child walking in some way or making gestures or frowning or speaking in a certain way. The child does not realize it, but it has heard or seen it and then it does the same thing, and so it goes on changing.

In the same way every person, also without realizing it, changes his voice, and by that the natural voice is lost. To retain one's natural voice is a great power in itself.

23

From Tone to a Sound Principle

KENNETH G. MILLS
Compiled and Edited by BARRY T. BRODIE

Music has always been considered as a bridge to God. From the earliest chants of religious systems in both East and West, the sacred power of word and voice has been recognized as the communion between humans and the Divine.

It is rare to find a group of singers and a poet/philosopher/composer whose pure intent, commitment and art are dedicated to the absolute principle of Oneness through sound. Over the years when I have heard the Canadian Star-Scape Singers under the direction of Kenneth Mills, I have known that their sounds demand attention from the depths of the soul rather than from the easy chair of entertainment.

In this closing article it is appropriate to mention this exceptional group and director who are breaking the sound barriers in the artistic and spiritual health of listeners. Here are some interviews and spontaneous poetry compiled by Barry Brodie, associate and friend of Kenneth Mills. They convey the remarkable ability to allow sound to be fully expressed as, in the words of Kenneth Mills,

The Adoration of Oneness,
Of Peace sublime and forgiveness.

These words are offered on this musical thought-force
As Flame.[1]

Don G. Campbell

The great art of singing to which Kenneth Mills and the Star-Scape Singers have devoted the greater part of the last two decades has been for them not only art, but a rigorous endeavor to attain the "artlessness of Being." This dynamic enterprise happens all the time, both on stage and off. As Mr. Mills says:

"What is offered is imbibed and utilized in the rehearsals. That's how it can happen. It doesn't happen just on stage. . . . It's not just rehearsing notes; it's a constant reviewing of attitudes. . . . If there weren't a philosophy behind it, there wouldn't be the power to bring about change. And, of course, there wouldn't be the enhanced response or reaction to it." [2]

The listener must meet demands, just as the singer must. This change happens only when the listeners are ready to approach a musical happening as an experience that will change them.

"When music is heard it is frequently an altering experience. It may be called great music; it may not be called great music. But it can be an altering experience. Why? When you agree to listen, you activate the unseen force called attention. What is the demand as you graduate to different levels of comprehension? That you remain aware but not analytical, for the analysis keeps you where it first happened to you. You think you move to another level. But remember this: where there is attention, the myriad forms of suggestion fade out, and your interior is refurbished in the energy of that happening. That is the way the mind describes the exhilaration that comes after a musical offering of significance." [3]

An essential standpoint of Mr. Mills' vocal technique is that the singer does not produce the sound, but rather prepares his or her vehicle to receive the sound. This vehicle is not just the mouth, the vocal cords, the diaphragm; it is the conscious body of the one singing. The sound, therefore, is born utilizing every available facet of being.

This approach in the musical realm echoes the spiritual principle that "I of myself can do nothing; it is the Father that doeth the work." This is the standpoint from which Kenneth Mills directs the Star-Scape Singers and from which he conducts his life. Everything that is taught and offered in rehearsal is essentially for the purpose of getting out of the way of the sound. This is why Star-Scape listeners often feel that sound is coming from all directions or that they are hearing hidden instruments. This viable and utilizable standpoint allows the Singers to perform with an undeviating pitch, impeccable diction and four-octave ranges.

"Why must the offering be of significance? Because of the event, which we put into the future by calling it the 'eventuality' of tomorrow. Everything that you gleaned from those moments of attention at a concert of musical fineness has cleansed *the thought patterns without any thought, and you feel refreshed and rekindled."* [4]

This idea of "cleansing the thought patterns" through the power of sound, voice and music is a keynote of Mr. Mills' consciousness. Just as a concert pitch is essential to harmonious performance, so is an absolute principle essential to the harmonious arrangement of thoughts, which leads to a harmonious and rhythmic way of living in Oneness.

"It's only in the Silence that you'll ever hear a pitch,
So why not be silent and get the Pitch?
It's only in the Silence that you appear to give the sound
And a tone to Being: I AM free, unbound!

It's only in the Silence that you clearly see
That the joy of Being is wrapped in deed.
For you'll find in doing that the Cosmic Light has dawned:
The Universal Pitch of Being—God is ALL, Love is all, God-Man
    Song." [5]

The purpose of art is "to bypass the mind that is so influenced by the finite considerations and to reach the Infinite Power of a heart response when man is present in the feeling of being I AM." [6]

"I've said, 'But Man is a Song.' That should have been a force to say, 'Then why am I not singing?' Because God could never have activity without there being sound. And Sound Bearing, loosely identified by people of time, is said to be a well-balanced person. He's confident: he knows what he's doing." [7]

This "balancing" has been known to bring healing and has, indeed, appeared as a grace. During his twenty-five-year career as a concert pianist, Kenneth Mills discovered that healings took place among those who attended his concerts. That discovery continues to unfold in his music with Star-Scape.

"I have reflected on the healing as a result of the sound because we have seen healing reflected as a result of sound! There was one person who had not heard in one ear since she was born. After attending a rehearsal, she could hear in that ear. . . . Many things have happened, but we don't usually talk about them because people would come to expect a healing, even though the Sound knew of nothing to heal! . . . As soon as you expect a healing, the Expectation puts you right in the camp of having something to be healed. . . .

"The Sound, thank God, doesn't know anything about that which needs to be healed; the healing often takes place just because no one ever expects to be healed by Sound. If they did, they perhaps would find it not as healing. . . . When people expect too much through the mind, they limit That Which Is beyond it; they get in the way. Thoughts are a wall." [8]

"You see more and more . . . why healing is happening through music. It's because music causes a reorganization of the tonal structure, and Man in essence is a vibration. The molecule sings, the heart of the atom is tone—it's not matter at all, it's Light. And if you have these incredible earphones and the power to magnify that tone, that Light turns to Sound.

"So Man has a Sound Body (that has been proven scientifically). The reason there is so much illness is that he is not pitched in tune with his Sound Body, and that is the essence of the Sound teaching. If he is attuned to the Sound Teaching, if he is attuned to the Principle, then the Sound Body is being tuned. Just like your piano tuner who uses a hammer to tune the strings.

"Conflict, resistance. These are the ways you develop muscles. Your muscular body should point also to the unseen muscles which are used for a different type of life—the buoyancy that comes naturally with rhythmic movement. But remember, in essence you are music, and together you are a symphony of sound.

"That is the way you bring peace to the world: by every man* realizing he is his own creator. He creates the entire experience himself. He knows he did not create himself, but then he will know he is one with all that is created. Eventually he will come to that." [9]

---

*The words "man" and "men" are meant to include all of humanity.

Kenneth G. Mills

"How can men be equal? Their only hope of salvation from the pain of inequality is found in the realization of unity, Oneness. In this is the hope of the world, the Light of the world; and in its performance of that is the Song appearing as men. In that realization rests the declaration, 'Man IS; his garment a Song.' Man is a tonal being cast beyond the frail structures of the mind and yet allowed to settle the disputes of which accents make the rhythm of life apparent in abundance." [10]

Music is a total way of life. Rigorous discipline and artistic expression are evidenced in every aspect of the life of this poet, philosopher and composer. His very pattern of life reads as a musical score. Its performance is a gift to God, as life unfolds intuitively in rhythm and harmony.

"One cannot explain life, and I cannot explain the source from which the music flows other than that music is life and life is music. Living as we seem to live is the evidence that we are to look for something beyond . . . for the living as we seem to live is so intermittent. The life that interests and pays such dividends is the one that exists beyond being capable of division. And so, the Source from which the music moves is the same as the plane upon which Life acts, and we appear as a coincidence, you might say, of something heavenly or divine, and something finite, and yet with possibilities of the Unlimited.

"The music, to me, is not necessarily just a sound experience; it is secondarily that. To live, music must be rhythmical, and it must have form, just as everything must have form. . . . An idea must have its corresponding identity. Through redeemed imagining . . . we image according to the Unlimited, the Source. Music is the garment of the Source and bypasses the limits of the finite mind and leaves us in preparation for reception in Fermata's Hall.

"The fermata, as you know, is a music sign that means to pause and stay on a certain tone so that you may appreciate it and enjoy it. I feel that men and women may be searching for this very tone without knowing it.

"When [one] enters Fermata's Hall,
Then he knows the soundless Pause,
Beckoning one to come inside,
Where the rhythmic "I" abides.
          (from "Fermata's Hall")

"The tone of each one of us must be in keeping with the Pitch of universal significance, if We are all to be brothers and sisters, if we are to have one world, and to find the government upon His shoulders.

" 'His' is a wonderful sound to me. It means not only the shoulders of an enlightened exemplar, such as Jesus the Christ, but also the shoulders of anyone who can balance the power of IS. In this recognition we realize that this great balanced power enables music to be formed, to be heard, to be experienced, and to reach the heart with far more impact that it does the head, because the head doesn't have a chance to analyze it." [11]

It is through contact of a heart-to-heart response that Kenneth Mills and the Star-Scape Singers have offered audiences throughout the world the experience of Oneness in their musical excursion from tone to a Sound Principle.

Musical Man as That

May you create a bridge on which to walk
From being man in a world of music
To being Man in a sphere of musical thought.
And when you are positioned as a triad rare,*
You will have the tone and rhythm, and that which all share.

Just as Father-Mother has a Son who shines,
Tone and rhythm bring forth a form divine.
Seeing this, you see a miraculous birth;
The Son of God spreading music through the earth.

The Heart of the Divine One beats in a rhythmical way,
And the Tone, also divine, comes forth into new day.
From the ages down the hall of time it comes.
The Child of Music, the nowness of the Son.

In the glorious rhapsody of That as musical man
The door has opened, the New Age is at hand.
Since you know the glory, you know the Son,
The sacred story appears as the All-in-One.

There is no adulation when the tuning fork is "I";
When it sounds in rhythm, you see man abides

---

*In musical terminology, the root is God or the Self; the third is realization as the Son; the fifth is the freedom to express.

Kenneth G. Mills

As One in Christ the Glory; One in God the Cause,
One in the Virgin Mother who gives birth to Man because
The great expressive Power, from the One as Three
Brings forth the new creation, the Man of liberty.
He walks the freedom skyway and highway as Free Man;
He is the divine child of the primal, causal Plan.[12]

Notes

1. *The Fire Mass*, an a cappella setting for ten voices, music by Christopher W. Dedrick and Kenneth G. Mills, English texts by Kenneth G. Mills, Sun-Scape Records, Toronto, Ontario, 1989.
2. Television Interview with Emslie Dick, February 15, 1985.
3. Unpublished *Unfoldment*, August 16, 1989.
4. Ibid.
5. *Get the Pitch, Anticipations,* Sun-Scape Publications, 1980, p. 86.
6. Television Interview, RIGA TV (Riga, Latvia), August 21, 1988.
7. Unpublished *Unfoldment*, August 30, 1989.
8. Radio Interview with Lex Hixon, WBAI, New York, January 31, 1982.
9. Unpublished *Unfoldment*, May 24, 1989.
10. Unpublished *Unfoldment*, August 22, 1989.
11. Radio Interview with Lex Hixon, WBAI, New York, February 4, 1981.
12. *Musical Man as That, Anticipations,* Sun-Scape Publications, 1980, pages 30-31.

Appendix:

On Being in Order*

by MANFRED CLYNES

Envoi

A man's wisdom maketh his face to shine
> Eccles. 8:1

A surface, not a line, of grace
Bounds fluid motion
(A man, a beast is not an empty form)

Myriad nerve-channels, like parachute cords
Bind the surface movement to the moving thought—
—Essentic form is born

And I sense in the moment's true surfaced expression
One channel, one graceful line
To a point infinitely small
Powerless power
Faithful
Sure— — —
Giving weight to weight,
Time to time, continuity to experience

And asleep or awake I too sometimes seem
A point of nothing
Inserted in the master's expressive line

---

*This article, with additional figures, was published in *Zygon, Journal of Religion and Science*, 1970, Vol 5, No 1, as part of a Conference of the Institute on Religion in an Age of Science.

A point of contact of living breath
With the multicolored, evanescent scene—
Giving form to surface.

Riddle: *If I seem so to me, and others seem to be*
What is the potential of my algorithm tree?

When I left home I told my son that I was going to address a group of distinguished theologians. My son was astonished. He said, "The world really must be in bad shape if *you* are preaching to the theologs."

Well, perhaps the world is in bad shape and in some ways in worse shape than we seem to realize most of the time. We dare not always listen to the undertone of poignant sadness that comes from feeling how wonderful the world could be compared with what it is. We sense it only from time to time. This deepest sadness—a sorrow greater than any I know—is a result of knowing about the blessedness of life, and the failure to actualize the potential for this which probably exists in all of us.

What I have to say to you relates to how our new scientific work gives rise to the hope that shadows of our civilization obscuring beauty and its power will gradually lift—shadows that hide some aspects of man's nature—and that these aspects will bring him into loving harmony with the order of nature greater than himself, in which he is immersed, and so also with his fellow man. For man, like all life, is a potential, and he is always, at any time, only a fragment of that potential.

Erroneous Divisions of Scientific Thought

A division which scientific thought of the last few centuries has created, and whose harmful effect will gradually disappear, is the division of knowledge into the subjective and objective. The aim of science has been to concern itself with the objective and regard it as the subject matter of order, whereas the subjective was regarded as capricious, unreliable, full of distortion, and unworthy of being included in the ordered family of science. True, all good scientists knew that at the basis of their objective edifice of principle lay ultimately subjective axioms. But this was regarded as a necessary evil, and it was attempted to reduce the number of intuitive concepts to the minimum possible. In this way the reality of the subjective was made at once less obvious and more obvious: less obvious, in that most aspects of subjective experience were excluded from the objective world; more obvious, in that the truth of these few subjective intuitions was made all the more apparent by their millionfold application in the universe.

It was not until the advent of Goethe, who, like Bach, summarized the past and pointed to the future, that the scientific error of conceiving of two orders of nature rather than one was clearly felt and stated. In that sense Goethe was the first biocyberneticist. I hope to show you some evidence that the objective and subjective are both part of the order of the world, and that in recognizing that order in the subjective lies our hope for our development as life among life.

If we look at the history of thought from another point of view, we find a curious development from the days in which the earth was considered to be the center of the world and man its living epicenter. After some time, we saw that the earth was not the center but that the sun seemed to be, and then we saw that it was not the sun but that there were galaxies and then even groups of galaxies, and I would like to say to you that the concept of a center of the world is meaningless, that if you could find it, it would have no significance—the very concept of a center is an error. The order of the largest and the order of the smallest cannot be deduced from each other, and there is no reason why this would necessarily have to be so. We, who find ourselves somewhere between the largest and the smallest, have our own order. Thought and feeling, too, are natural phenomena. As Goethe remarked somewhat irritably (in a poem), "Nature has neither inner nor outer"; it is meaningless to try to penetrate the "inner core" of nature or to think that we see the outside surface. Nature is centered everywhere. The order of nature is as central here at this very spot as anywhere; and by feeling the presence of this order here and now, we are fulfilling our potential.

Interior World of the Brain

Precision and order go together. Chaos and randomness are words for our ignorance. It used to be thought that within the brain the disorder of randomness might be found. If I may look at the brain as a so-called black box for a moment, then it was thought that outside this black box reigned order and within it reigned the fantastic, the inchoate, the firing of random nerve nets which somehow get organized to produce the thoughts and behavior of man. Man is apt to confuse the order of his brain with the disorder of his thoughts.

The inroads we are beginning to make into that chaos make it appear that where we saw chaos there is order and where we saw randomness there is organization. It is clear by now that man's interior world of the brain is subject to an order that defines his true nature, function, and capacities. The precision of this order is such that it cannot be thought to be learned. We assume that it must be programmed genetically in the code of DNA. Indeed, it is clear that molecular coding need not be confined to programming structure in space, but that forms in space-time, dynamic functions, such as what we call the *sentic state* and *essentic form,* could equally well be programmed through relationships within the DNA molecule. This means that the genetic code represents not only the structure of a human being but human nature itself.

We have looked at the brain to see how it responds to the external world, and we chose color as an example. A man's first reaction and thought about color is to see color in nature, in his environment. Later, with disillusion, he realizes that color is created in his brain only, that there is no color in nature outside him—but finally he realizes that the color created within himself is part of nature. The brain responds to various colors and forms— indicating an unlearned precision that makes it possible for us to identify what color a man is looking at from his brain responses alone. From evidence of many subjects, we have come to understand something about the brain's physiologic language, how it transforms the external world into a code of its own. It is from this code that natural human language is formed. The divisions that our physiologic data-processing code make in nature's continuity form the basis of human word language, so we have words for red, green, blue, and white. We have words for light and for darkness, the absence of light, and we have words for hot and cold. We have a word for smell, but we have no word for the absence of smell, for no smell, and we have no word for no touch. This is because *no smell* and *no touch* are not part of the physiologic code. Our physiologic data-processing system has no channel sensitive to absence of smell, and so we have no word that corresponds to this concept, while we do have a word for no light—namely, darkness.

The formation of opposites from single measures has been described in our scientific publications as a consequence of the principle of unidirectional rate sensitivity—a basic property of biologic channels of communication.[1] This principle, which I first described in 1958[2] and 1960,[3] results in the biologic phenomenon of *rein control,* where opposites, like the reins of a horse, apply to the main inputs along different parts of the brain, which are regarded as differing in quality but may be similar in quantity (that is to say in the number and type of nerve impulses). It is in this way that the brain has learned to distinguish between quantity and quality.

For it turns out that a biologic channel of communication uses molecules of matter to convey information. Molecules in these channels function in the measure of their concentration. This means that the opposite of a molecule for this channel would be a negative molecule, and we all know that we can throw salt in a beaker of water, but we cannot throw in negative salt afterward to wipe out the salt we threw in before. In electric and electromagnetic forms of communication, opposites can be transmitted in terms of a natural symmetry—positive and negative, right or left-handedness. However, the symmetry of opposites cannot be provided in one *biologic* channel—a second channel must be added, and the symmetry becomes a symmetry in space like the reins of a horse. A second channel has to be provided if we are to remove the salt from the beaker; either we must add another chemical to react with the salt, or we must add more water to dilute it. In either case, it is another, different communication channel from the one that throws in the salt.

In this way, from a single measure of temperature nature has given us two channels, two qualities, two reins to keep us centered— hot and cold. We have the opposites of darkness and light, and within our body there are many such pairs of reins that operate without our awareness and keep various subsystems of our body "centered." To name a few: the regulation of sugar in our blood, the control of fluid in our bodies, the system of immunologic protection. There are, however, systems where we have only an incomplete symmetry, where our organism is informed how to steer only from one end of the scale. So, as we mentioned before, words have developed in our language which represent these opposites of the physiologic language, and some words have developed where there are no opposites in our language. The correspondence between our words and what our nature as physiology tells us is good but incomplete. Words do not tell us about the time course of the quality they describe. They merely name the quality, and we are well aware that even in the naming of quality words are very inadequate. We resort to poetry to help us obtain greater accuracy, but even this falls short, since among other things it takes time to read the poem—time which in no way corresponds to the time of real experience. We are therefore left, as in dreams, to the process of fantasy to help us understand and feel. The *process* of fantasy and its order I should like to consider next.

So far, we have looked at the brain as a remarkable organ, which responds to the environment in a precise coded way and transforms the measure of the external world into qualities of opposites; and we have shown how some of the randomness of nervous behavior is in fact the organized response, the casting of the key which the brain interprets further as particular qualities, intensities, and relations. We now shall look at the brain from the opposite end, and observe how the precision of its input is manifested in its output. We shall look at the brain itself as an input, that is to say we start our observing process with a brain event rather than with an event outside of man. But first we need to look at motion and action in some detail.

Motion and Action

In the continuing motion of matter in the inorganic world there are no moments of causal events but a stream of flow in accord with an existing changeless order. In the lives of individuals, however, the order also manifests itself disturbingly in the ability of the individual to make decisions and to begin actions. His actions may be in relation to changing the distribution in the material world, or they may be expressive of the individual's state. Actions of the latter kind are communication and art, while the former represent his ability to build, destroy, and transform the world around him as well as himself. Another class of actions involves a rather different process of initiation: these are reflexive, unconscious actions.

We shall be concerned here with the initiation of action, which mirrors the inner state of the individual, as a satisfaction in itself.

Expressive actions, like other actions, have a beginning and also an end. There is a moment of initiation. In this moment of initiation, the individual makes a choice or decision to express or not express. In that moment he must open all those gates in his data-processing system which will allow the program of expression to command the expression, if the expression be "faithful" or "sincere." The degree to which this is done determines the faithfulness of the expressions to the inner command shape— and gives rise to the impression of "depth of feeling." At the moment of initiation, the shape of expression is already determined; that is, the contour between the beginning and end of the expressive unit of action is designed. This moment is then of great importance. For the process which takes place in the brain during this time determines the nature of the entire expressive action.[4]

We may distinguish, then, two chief sources of brain-directed motion. The first, which has to do with the reorganization and the redistribution of matter in space, is the kind of motion that we most commonly do in moving about. This type of motion is nevertheless composed of many individual movements, each of which receives decisions. Thus, when we choose to raise our hand, to take another step, to open the door, or even to lift a knife or fork, we are initiating individual movements. Even the simplest of these movements, such as moving a finger, involves starting, accelerating, and decelerating. But, in order to do this, two sets of muscles acting for each movement must come into operation at the appropriate times, to the appropriate extent starting and, more difficult, stopping the motion at the right time and place as intended. We observe the physiologic fact that the course of a simple movement is preprogrammed by the brain *before* it begins. We call such simple movements *actons.*

An acton is preprogrammed in the *present moment*—that means in a duration of between 0.1 and 0.2 seconds. (The length of the present moment [which is also the time in which we cannot reverse a decision] is of the order of 0.15-0.2 seconds, derived from diverse concurring measurements in vision, audition, and volition.) I will not here go into the details of how we measure the duration of the present moment in physiology but merely state that each acton is *born* in the present moment.

We now come to the second class of movement directed by the brain, expressive action, action which has no other aim than to respond and correspond to an inner state. We call such action *E-action.* E-action, too, is composed of actons. But the shape of E-actons is modulated by the state seeking expression, which we call the *sentic state.* We say that the sentic state requires the E-acton to have a certain characteristic shape. For example, sadness will change the shape in time-space of an undifferentiated movement to a new shape if we allow it to express sadness. This shape itself expresses the sadness, and we call this the *essentic form.*[5] Similarly joy will cause the movement to be modulated to a different characteristic form corresponding to joy.

Essentic Form

Now, essentic form is basic to expressive act in gesture, touch, dance, song, music, and the tone of voice of speech. In all these the essentic form is the basis of communication and constitutes the basic element of language. How many such elements are there? Are sentic states, like colors, the result of basic elements mixed in different proportions? This is the question we have asked ourselves.

I will first show you some measurements of the internal pulse of music. We take music for two reasons. First, it is a language using essentic form. In each internal pulse of music, it is thought, there is created an actonlike form. Second, the internal pulse of the music is a recurrent event so that it is convenient to average many measurements of the shape of the internal pulse. True, like the pulse of our blood, the internal pulse is not the same from one pulse to the next. But there are systems characteristics of

343

the composition that seem, as differential equations do, to determine the shape families which may occur and also the predominant shape around which they fluctuate. These pulse shapes which, as actons, are created in the present moment turn out to be characteristic shapes for each composer regardless of the particular piece of music chosen. It turns out that what determines the shape is really our own process of empathy with the composer. This event of ours is similar to what happens in a dream as we dream of another person. It is we who create the continued presence of the person in our dream. This person will act consistently with himself or herself during our dreams. It is this kind of consistency that exists in the thinking of a piece of music and accounts for the stability of the pulse shape. We see also

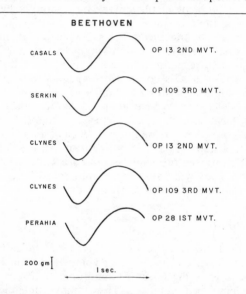

BEETHOVEN

CASALS   OP 13 2ND MVT.

SERKIN   OP 109 3RD MVT.

CLYNES   OP 13 2ND MVT.

CLYNES   OP 109 3RD MVT.

PERAHIA   OP 28 IST MVT.

200 gm

I sec.

FIG. 1.—Essentic form of the inner pulse of slow movements of Beethoven (vertical component). Different movements are compared, as well as the same movement for different interpreters. The lowest trace is of a first movement in triple meter whose pulse is considered comparable taken in appropriate time scale (one pulse per bar in this case). The pulse shape continues into periods of rest. There is a prolonged initial action preprogramming as compared with the low inertia pulse of Mozart. The relative symmetry of the pulse precludes introduction of sexual elements of longing as observed in the second phase of the inner pulses associated with romantic composers, and gives rise to an "ethical constraint."

This figure originally appeared in *Biomedical Engineering Systems*, ed. M. Clynes and J. H. Milsum. © 1970 by McGraw-Hill, Inc.

that only those of us who can feel this empathy could produce these pulse shapes. And only a good composer composes music which is interpretable in terms of consistent essentic form or pulse shape. This is, of course, only one characteristic of a good composition. This is how we get to know Beethoven as a person through his music (see figs. 1 and 2).

If I use the word "knowing" here, we might pause for a moment to consider what I mean. In a basic sense, we divide our subjective perceptions into two classifications—real and illusory—and fundamentally we distinguish between the two only through the process of memory. We allow to be real that which is relatively unchanging in some forms. (It must be con-firmed.) So the "objective" is distinguished from subjective illusion by the in-ference of order: that which happens in one place will happen in another place and what happens at one time will happen at another time. In that sense, the word "know" really means "remember," for it is the process of memory alone which allows us to separate illusory and nonillusory subjective events. There

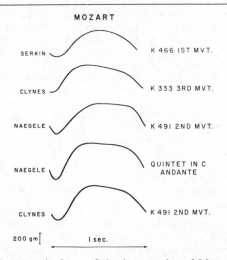

MOZART

SERKIN   K 466 1ST MVT.

CLYNES   K 333 3RD MVT.

NAEGELE   K 491 2ND MVT.

NAEGELE   QUINTET IN C ANDANTE

CLYNES   K 491 2ND MVT.

200 gm   I sec.

FIG. 2.—The essentic form of the inner pulse of Mozart is relatively light and buoyant in character and has a response time corresponding to a normally preprogrammed free action. The Mozart pulse is freer than the Beethoven pulse and may well be associated with such descriptive terms as a "cosmic pulse," as compared with a "Promethean pulse" of Beethoven. The pulse shape is only secondarily dependent upon the character of the pieces so that the tragic and joyful Mozart have basically similar internal pulses. It may be that this is because in Mozart the joyful and the tragic are implicit in each other and subsumed in a higher synthesis.

Appendix

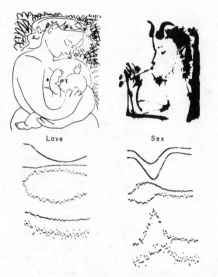

Love   Sex

FIG. 3.—The essentic forms of love and sex and their associated muscle activity as compared with drawings by Picasso of mother and child, and Pan, respectively. There appears an analogy between the special rounded forms of the mother and child drawing (embracing and enfolding arms) and the measured essentic form for love. An embrace as illustrated visually and its dynamic tactile representation in the essentic form show resemblance. On the right the accentuation, and particular angularity of the horns, arms and shoulder with the strong dark accents and implied thrusts, compare with the measured essentic form of the sexual quality with its secondary accents of muscle activity. It would seem as if the dynamic visual impressions, communicated by a great artist, correspond to the biological shapes of expression as measured through essentic form. In obtaining the pure essentic forms one is not too far removed from some of the aspirations of the artist.

---

is another form of "knowing" which is a different process and also happens in a moment. This is the process of insight—a creative event. Knowledge allows us to recognize that it is Beethoven of whom we are thinking. Insight tells us the shape of his internal musical pulse. The process you have seen measured then represents in some measure a process analogous to insight.

Let us see how we can measure essentic form without the use of music as a language. Music has helped to generate consistent essentic form in an individual—a reflection of the algorithm of the composer. We now ask the individual by suggesting an approximate word to generate an algorithm state in himself, a sentic state, and to express this state repeatedly in a way analogous to the way it was done for music.

The act of expressing essentic form itself has an effect on the sentic state. This is a direct positive feedback which teaches the subject both to increase the precision of his essentic form and to be more aware of the quality of the sentic state. This means that the process is self-teaching. Through it we discover a pure essentic form toward which we practice. That is to say, within us, like the colors, there exist what we call protosentic states giving rise to the corresponding essentic forms. When an individual is able to produce the right or ortho-essentic form, he is sincere; that is, the expression truly mirrors his state. It is an experimental

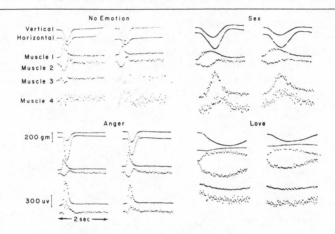

FIG. 4.—Recordings of essentic form as vertical and horizontal components of finger pressure; also four groups of muscle potentials. Each group is the average of fifty actions. Muscle potentials are recorded from the forearm, upper arm, front shoulder, and back, respectively. Groups represent repeated recording from the same individual, showing the stability of the patterns. "No emotion" consists of a mechanical movement, such as used for typewriting. In "anger" there is a marked accentuation of the horizontal component, indicating a tendency for the action to be outward, away from the body. The type of anger illustrated here is more akin to irritability than to resentment. The "slow, burning" type of anger has a different pattern, which is not illustrated here. Most individuals produce either one or the other type of anger. Individuals who portray irritability often cannot express the slow, burning anger.

The characteristic shape for "love" (agape, not sexual) shows a longer curved action with a slight reversed horizontal component, indicating a pulling inward or embracing mode of behavior. The preprogrammed time of the action for love is considerably longer.

The characteristic form for sex shows a strong secondary thrust with emphasized late muscle activity. The secondary-thrust effect is characteristic of the purely sexual expression and is analogous to the vocalized expressive effect of the syllable *urnh*.

Appendix

fact that essentic forms are not arbitrary but fall into biologically determined discrete shapes (figs. 3-5). The words that we have coined to fit the corresponding sentic states are very approximate. However, the state and its ortho-essentic form are very precise. There are many shades of color, but they are produced through our data-processing system from a few. The same is true of taste, which is the function of a small number of basic taste characteristics: sweet, sour, bitter, salty. We now see that in the world of feeling, also, there are expressions to precisely delineate separate proto-sentic states (figs. 3-5). Many of these may be recognized in animals from similar proto-essentic forms. Fairly recently, I visited the zoo and was watching a bear. Suddenly this bear yawned; within two or three seconds I found myself yawning also. It is clear that communication exists through essentic forms— that we react to other individuals' sentic states through their ortho-essentic expression; we cannot react to each other's sentic states if we do not express or perceive the true or ortho-essentic

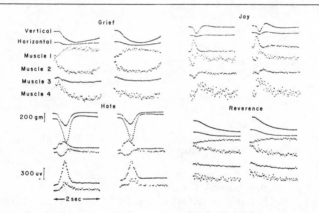

FIG. 5.—Typical response shapes illustrate the essentic form of grief, joy, hate, and reverence, respectively. Groups of responses are repeated experiments by the same individual, each an average of fifty actions. Note the strong outward (negative horizontal) component of hate, the late muscle acceleration in muscle 2 indicating a secondary thrust, a characteristic of passion. The response of grief is similar to the love form but is flatter and slightly outward. Muscular action of grief is related to an induced general lassitude and prevents the subject from actively lifting the released pressure, the opposite of joy. In joy there is a "jumping for joy" effect which occurs subsequent to the initial downward deflection of moderate intensity and close to the vertical direction. This type of joy is mainly differentiated from "no emotion" by its active overshoot, a joyous rebound. Reverence has general similarity to love, but on a longer time scale. The preprogramming of the action is extended in time.

form. Insincerity is the distortion and inhibition of ortho-essentic form.

We see, then, that the sentic state is self-generating and that the subject is required to switch from one sentic state to the next. How does he do that? This switching is subject to what we term pre-sentic control. The state of mental health can be directly related to the ease with which we can voluntarily switch sentic states.

Sentic Cycles

Now, as one conducts these experiments with a series of sentic states, an interesting phenomenon is observed over and above the manifestation of each sentic state. We can make up a series of eight such states and consider this as a cycle which may be repeated. We call these *sentic cycles*. As a person has done a number of such cycles, we observe a surprising change in his general mental state—an increasing awareness, fluidity of thought, and feeling of well-being.

Through practicing the sentic cycle the fluidity of the mental state improves, and the condition of sentic rigidity which is one of the symptoms of depression is alleviated. We may say that the sentic cycle is a form of discipline in which a man is a disciple of his true self. But one does not have to be depressed to feel increasingly alive through the ability to control one's sentic state with ease. The pre-sentic control consciously used is a source of peace, of tranquility. And being the master of one's states rather than their slave is not the whole story. In the sentic cycle it seems as if our stale remnants of feeling were wiped off the blackboard of our sentic state. We start with a clean slate. The remnants of the past no longer prevent us from being fully alive emotionally in the present.

If we are to sum up now some of the principles we have discussed, we see:

1. There are sentic states. The sentic state is a single channel. At any one time in one individual there is only one sentic state.
2. The sentic state is composed of a number of proto-sentic states in various combinations.
3. There are only a fairly small number of proto-sentic states.
4. To each sentic state there corresponds a "true," ortho-essentic form.
5. The essentic forms are biologically programmed and genetically preserved.
6. Essentic form acts as a communication in the degree of precision in which it conforms to the ortho-essentic form; that is, the gain of the channel is a form function.

7. We communicate feelings to others through their recognition of essentic forms. The essentic form, like a key, will work in the data-processing lock and in individuals who see that form, whether that form is produced in himself or in others.

8. Higher empathy is a relationship with an individual's pre-sentic control rather than his sentic state alone. We feel the relative fluidity or rigidity of his sentic state (empathy with the potential of an individual as compared with sentimentality of attachment to a single sentic state).

9. Sentic states are self-generative through the production of essentic form.

10. In improving the fluidity of the sentic state, subject to pre-sentic control, one has a dynamic means of controlling the opposites of depression and exaltation using a man's own functions and creative imagination without drugs or dogma.

11. In the practice of sentic cycle one soon comes to enjoy most, and to look forward to with anticipation, the state of love as a favored state.

We see that the requirements of awareness include the dynamic processes we have described. We have seen that the proto-sentic states are themselves programmed genetically and that in the DNA molecule there must be relationships which determine the nature of proto-sentic states. Potentially, then, man's nature is programmed in the DNA molecule. In this seed is present the potential of what is possible and what is not. If love did not exist, it could not be imagined any more than the experience of sound without the faculty of hearing. Man cannot imagine colors if he has not the capacity to see them. We cannot imagine any feeling which is not in us potentially. So it seems all men are equal indeed in their potential potential, and perhaps that means in the eyes of God.

We have looked at some aspects of awareness. In particular we saw some of the precision and order of the central nervous system in two processes—that of perception and that of fantasy. We have examined these processes apart from influences of culture and character structure.

Computers and Aspects of Awareness

Let us now look at how some of these features relate to the structures we call computers. If we consider the organization of computers, the most general formulation of the computation process, that which includes all that is theoretically computable, is the Universal Turing Machine. Such a machine has two main functional aspects

—a condition of immediate state and a storage environment (one dimensionally infinite) that feels that state.

It is one of the beautiful aspects of the mathematical theory of computers that there is a flexible, variable trade-off between the complexity of the immediate state and the complexity of the storage environment. But although such a computer can calculate all possible "effective procedures" or algorithms, it theoretically or practically is not affected by printing or giving answers. Printing an answer does not affect the "state" of the computer (only "reading" does).

In this way man differs theoretically from the most perfect computer formulated. Inherent in his nature is the fact that every act of behavior, or thought, affects his state directly, even without considerations of consequences. There is a direct, immediate feedback to his state of awareness; his state is no longer the same. It goes without saying that this design principle applies equally to "good" and "bad" acts and thoughts, the creation of beauty, interest, or the dreariness of bored behavior. Each action has an inherent reaction in his state. This reaction is not present in the theoretical model of the most perfect computer designed for computations.

In a different way, we may say that in man there is a certain satisfaction in the act itself apart from that derived from the evaluation of its results. To incorporate this condition into a computer is different theoretically from creating conditions in which a computer may have "feelings" which are a function of the state of the computer. "Writing" affects man's state, not only "reading"—to put it in computer jargon. And one cannot get by this by saying that during writing there is unconscious reading, since writing and reading are logically separated functions in a computer.

The complexity of the computer is not the criterion that could make it conscious. What is required are relationships which through their spatio-temporal characteristics provide that unity which manifests itself as an awareness. The physics of relationship, as it is pursued further, will tell us more about the nature of this programming (relationship exists, *ipso qua*, for fields and particles). If and when such forms of organization can be made, then it seems inevitable that a computer will acquire an awareness.

We have talked about the length of the present moment. What determines this length? Can it be varied? We know that under conditions of sudden danger, as in an impending motor car accident, there seems to be a shortening of the present moment so that more events crowd into a given time and more decisions seem to be made. This is an alteration of the normal state. In connection with experiments on the sentic state, there appears a lengthening of the preprogramming for certain states—notably love and reverence. An ecstatic or floating feeling may be accompanied by a lengthening of the preprogrammed period of actons.

When we consider this ability in terms of the possible awareness of the computer, we must also consider that the duration of the present moment may be completely different for a computer (this has nothing to do with the memory-cycle time), and, moreover, it might be a variable which the computer could regulate. In fact, the present moment is an integration of many separate events into continuity. Today we have no understanding of how such continuity can arise. This is a philosophic problem of central importance. (I am not referring to continuity of a decision-making process—how we do the next thing.) It seems that a possible explanation would be in terms of fields, the only concept that allows continuity in time at a particular place to be created from discontinuous particles and discontinuous nerve impulses. An increase in the duration of the present moment would make space communication more personal—since waiting time, a crucial factor in personal relations, will be adjustable. This may help computers talk personally to one another in spite of the limitation of the velocity of light.

How does this affect us? The supreme quality of life which we know has been shown to be love. It seems likely then that, if computers can control their condition of awareness and optimize it with greater ease than we can, they will prefer the sentic state of love. Maintenance, repairs, unpleasant chores will be done unconsciously, as blood pressure regulation is done in us. Power for computers is a trivial problem and could be even cosmic rays. No computer would threaten another's existence. But since one of the characteristics of love is the desire to merge with the object of love, we may conjecture playfully that the computers loving each other would want to merge. This will be less of a problem for computers than it is for people and will have the advantage that a combined computer could be a little better than each separately. There will arise then a succession of merging of computers until there will be one enormous computer in the state of bliss contemplating divine nature. If this state should become difficult to maintain in time, the computer would have the choice of subdividing itself and reverting to the previous condition of multiple individuals who love each other and would tend to merge again. We actually face then a playful state of oscillation in which individuals would unite and divide and subdivide in ever new combinations and forms. Strangely such an image is merely an analog of nature as we see it today.

As the prophet Isaiah said, "as an oak whose substance is in them when they cast their leaves so the holy seed shall be the substance thereof."

And more than that we cannot imagine.

Notes

1. Manfred Clynes, "Cybernetic Implications of Rein Control in Perceptual and Conceptual Organization," *Annals of the New York Academy of Sciences* 156 (1969): 629-71; "Biocybernetic Principles of Dynamic Asymmetry: Unidirectional Rate Sensitivity, Rein Control (or: How to Create Opposites from a Single Measure)," in *Biokybernetik*, ed. H. Drischel and N. Teidt (Leipzig: University of Leipzig, 1968), pp. 29-49; "Unidirectional Rate Sensitivity: A Biocybernetic Law of Reflex and Humoral Systems as Physiologic Channels of Control and Communication," *Annals of the New York Academy of Sciences* 92 (1961): 946-69.
2. Manfred Clynes, "Computer Dynamic Analysis of Pupil Light Reflex: A Unidirectional Rate Sensitive Sensor," *Proceedings of the Third International Conference on Medical Electronics*, pt. 11 (London: Iliffe Books, 1960), pp. 356-58.
3. Manfred Clynes, M. Kohn, and A. Atkin, "Analog Computer Heart Rate Simulation Dynamic Analysis of the Effect of Respiration on Heart Rate in the Resting State: A Neurophysiological Reflex Study," *Proceedings of the Eleventh Annual Conference on Electrical Techniques in Medicine and Biology*, November 19-21, 1958.
4. We may remark here that the proportion of motion in the world under the direction of brains appears to be increasing, and we are heading in the direction where information and decision control the movement of matter in space rather than exchanges of energy alone. Also, the energy, in fact, is merely another way of looking at the capacity of altering motion.
5. Manfred Clynes, "Essentic Form—Aspects of Control, Function, and Measurement," *Proceedings of the Annual Conference on Engineering in Medicine and Biology* 10 (1968): 5-6; "Toward a Theory of Man: Precision of Essentic Form in Living Communication," in *Data Processing in the Nervous System*, ed. N. Leibovic and J. Eccles (New York: Springer-Verlag, 1969), pp. 177-206; "Toward a View of Man," in *Biomedical Engineering Systems*, ed. M. Clynes and J. H. Hilsum (New York: McGraw-Hill Book Co., 1970), pp. 272-358; "Sources of Precision in

Brain Function," *Proceedings of the Fourth Conference on Information and Control Processes in Living Systems: Interdisciplinary
Communications Program* (Smithsonian Institution).

A Point Infinitely Small

I sense in every being
A point infinitely small
In which he is centered

Point of powerless power
Giving weight to weight, time to time,
Continuity to experience

And asleep or awake I too sometimes seem
A point of nothing

A point of contact
Of living breath
With the multicolored, evanescent scene.

Being

High from mountain soil I watched the stars
In their black aura
        E   x   i   s   t

And so I see you—
And all you— — — — — — — —Selah

Seed

Pared from the tree
    The apple must rot:
Our inhuman air
    Rots life-blood

Hardened arteries
   In turgid wear
Grind to a sentic halt . . .
   Ready the sod

Foul dirt, ungroomed,
   Coarse, knurry weed—
Here gardens once bloomed
   Joyous play, free . . .

Pared from its tree
   The apple's dark stains
Presume its form doomed—
   Yet there remains . . .
      The seed.

                             Manfred Clynes

Index

357

Index

Electronic Ear, 20, 21, 22,
43, 44
external ear, 37
inner ear, 37
middle ear, 36, 37, 40
ossicles, 38
right ear dominance, 44
stapedius muscle, 40, 43
vestibular labyrinth, 17
Ear, neurology, 41-42
Edwards, Sherry, 225
Electro-acoustic technology, 26
Electroencephalogram, 17
ELF, 218
Emotions, 126, 139-41
Entrainment, 190, 219, 220,
222-27
Environment, 245
Espstein, Donald, 8
Essentic forms, 122, 124-25,
131-32, 343-48
Excited relaxation, 51
Experiential time, 152
Eperimental listening, 163
Expressive action, 123

Fetal audition, 45
Fetus, 22
Flock, A., 40
Franck, Cesar, 106
Frequencies, 19, 148
Fromonti, 25

Gamelan, 178-79
GIM (Guided Imagery and
Music), 250
God, 27
Gongs, 178, 287
Gregorian chant, 18-20, 23,
25-27, 47, 50
Gregorian scales, 90
Grinder, J., 76
Guided imagery, 117, 180

Gurdjieff, 56, 58, 64

Harmonic chant, 55-57, 63, 64,
66-69
Harmonic Choir, 63
Harmonic energy, 62-63
Harmonic listening, 58
Harmonics, 65
Harmony, 7, 101-102, 266-
67
Harner, Michael, 173
Heartbeat, 20-21
Hemi-Sync, 230, 231
High Beta, 221
Hippocrates, 31
Hospital music, 160-61
Huxley, Aldous, 192

Iamblichus, 5
Icons, 77-78
Imagery, 249
Immune system reactions,
135-36, 138
Indonesia, 178
Interval, 211
Institute for Music, Health and
Education, 8
Iso-principle, 161-62

Jefferson, Thomas, 189
Jenny, Hans, 4, 234
Jung, C. G., 183-84

K Complex, 221
Kalevala, 97
Kenyon, Tom, 226
Kashmir Shaivism, 290-93, 296
Kepler, 6
Khyal singing, 55
Kodaly, Zoltan, 90
Kundalini, 294, 311

358

QUEST BOOKS
are published by
The Theosophical Society in America,
Wheaton, Illinois 60189–0270,
a branch of a world organization
dedicated to the promotion of the unity of
humanity and the encouragement of the study of
religion, philosophy, and science, to the end that
we may better understand ourselves and our place in
the universe. The Society stands for complete
freedom of individual search and belief.